Our knowledge of Debussy's life and music has increased considerably during the last decade or so, largely through the efforts of those working on the long-overdue complete edition of his music. Many of the contributors to the current volume have worked on various pieces in the complete edition and the significance of their research is apparent here. Topics include an examination of Debussy's working methods, his visual tastes and his response to literature, his reception in England, as well as aspects of performance practice. It also includes a close study of Debussy's relationship to the poet Stéphane Mallarmé. An appendix reproduces a discarded scene from Maeterlinck's 'Pelléas' for the first time, and the book is particularly rich in previously unpublished facsimiles and other little-known illustrative material.

DEBUSSY STUDIES

Debussy Studies

edited by RICHARD LANGHAM SMITH

Reader in Music, University of Exeter

CAMBRIDGE
UNIVERSITY PRESS

Published by the Press Syndicate of the University of Cambridge
The Pitt Building, Trumpington Street, Cambridge CB2 1RP
40 West 20th Street, New York, NY 10011–4211, USA
10 Stamford Road, Oakleigh, Melbourne 3166, Australia

First published 1997

Printed in the United Kingdom at the University Press, Cambridge

A catalogue record for this book is available from the British Library

Library of Congress cataloguing in publication data

Debussy studies / edited by Richard Langham Smith.
    p. cm.
    Includes bibliographical references and index.
    Contents: The definition of timbre in the process of composition
of *Jeux* / Myriam Chimènes – Waiting for Golaud: the concept of
time in *Pelléas* / David Grayson – Sirens in the labyrinth: amendments
in Debussy's *Nocturnes* / Denis Herlin – Debussy's piano music: sources
and performance / Roy Howat – Portrait of the artist as Roderick Usher /
Jean-Michel Nectoux – The reception of Debussy's music in Britain up
to 1914 / Roger Nichols – Debussy and Satie / Robert Orledge – Semantic
and structural issues in Debussy's Mallarmé songs / Marie Rolf – La
jeunesse du Cid: a mislaid act in *Rodrigue et Chimène*? / Richard Langham
Smith.
    ISBN 0 521 46090 5 (hardback).
    1. Debussy, Claude, 1862–1918 – Criticism and interpretation.
I. Smith, Richard Langham.
ML410.D28D39   1996
780'.92–dc 20   95–49838 CIP

ISBN 0 521 46090 5 hardback

SE

Contents

Preface

A book entitled 'Debussy Studies' inevitably causes reflection on the state of the art: where are Debussy studies compared, say, to where they were thirty years ago? Thinking back to the mid 1960s is instructive, a useful marker, for in 1962, the centenary of the composer's birth, a spate of publications both advanced the cause and revealed the weaknesses of our understanding of the composer who has unarguably influenced twentieth century music more than any of his fellow countrymen.

Among the strengths of the centenary year was its spawning, in particular, of two major biographies: Dietschy's *La passion de Claude Debussy* and Lockspeiser's two-volume *Debussy, his Life and Mind*. While Dietschy's unearthing of source materials and Lockspeiser's broad cross-cultural sweep have indelibly enhanced our comprehension of the composer, in another way both books revealed the lack of material on the music itself, either in analysis or what might be called informed commentary. Both analysts and commentators seemed lost, lacking a language with which to penetrate the mysteries of Debussy's music. Beside this, another gaping gap also stared scholars and performers in the face, namely, the lack of a complete edition of his music.

Meanwhile musicological armies regrouped. Analysis moved forward on several fronts, with distinct methodologies all of which have by now been proved to enhance penetration of the music itself. Jean-Jacques Nattiez's work on segmentation; Richard S. Parks's work combining Schenkerian analysis and set theory; as well as the work on numerological proportion by Roy Howat who among Debussy analysts is one of the most informed by the study of original texts – each of these has pushed forward the type of study which centred on the notes themselves, where the earlier part of the century had largely produced books which ignored them.

Source studies *per se* have also deepened their roots, and in Debussy's case, the most unquestionably important advance in scholarship has been the inauguration of the Debussy *Oeuvres Complètes* originally from the combined publishers Durand and Costallat, and under the overall guardianship of François Lesure. Several of the contributors to the present volume have edited, or are editing, volumes for this edition. Its importance cannot be overestimated, not only because it will reveal seminal areas of Debussy's output which even now remain unperformed, but also because it has revealed to us some of the kitchen secrets of the composer's working methods.

Into the veiled category of Debussy's output fall the early songs, better known than they were, but for the most part still not yet published or only available in dribs and drabs. Among the major works unavailable in scholarly editions may be cited the 'other' opera *Rodrigue et Chimène*, performed and recorded (after a fashion) but unavailable in score; the (very beautiful) unpublished cantata *Diane au bois*, many early songs and *La chute de la maison Usher*, not to mention *Pelléas*.

Those working on the complete edition have added to our knowledge of the composer's work in more senses than one. How did he 'work'? The assembling and comparison of the sources necessary to arrive at a text for the new edition have thrown up all kinds of fascinating processes too broad for the critical apparatus of the *Oeuvres Complètes* editions themselves. The present collection is fortunate in being able to capture the working methods of the various editors while their *grands travaux* are still fresh in their minds.

It is hoped, though, that this volume is more than a collection – to use a well-worn phrase, more than the sum of its parts. How could it be otherwise? The team of scholars working together on the edition have, of course, revealed common practices, sometimes to their annoyance, with this composer so meticulous in some ways, and so frustrating in others. Corrections; notations at once fastidious and careless; confusions and incompatibilities have already affected the way we perform his music, performance in this respect meaning not only how we play the notes but which notes we play, for one of the most tangible fruits of the *Oeuvres Complètes* has been to reveal that Debussy's constant changes of mind were not always for the best. Or were they? The dispute rolls on – even on to the opera stage, as various permutations of interludes and post-production changes in *Pelléas* are used by this or that conductor. At the same time, *La mer* can now be heard to sing without its fanfares, and there can be little doubt that alternative versions of other pieces will be put before us as the edition progresses.

Meanwhile literary source materials have been trickling out in a steady stream, quite a lot of them in articles in the *Cahiers Debussy*, originally the organ of the *Centre de documentation Claude Debussy* which cannot be allowed to pass by without mention of its role, and particularly that of its first *animatrice*, Margaret Cobb, in focusing Debussy scholarship, bringing scholars together, and in short, providing it with a warm and international welcome. Meanwhile the *Cahiers Debussy* performed the valuable service of maintaining an updated bibliography (by Claude Abravanel) while François Lesure's 'Catalogue de l'oeuvre de Claude Debussy' has charted sources, editions and first performances. In the way of a critical biography, James Briscoe's Garland Press 'Guide to Research' has also put down a marker.

As far as biography is concerned, since Dietschy and Lockspeiser, only François Lesure's two recent biographical volumes are dense in their presentation of new source material while the same author's continuing publication of Debussy's correspondence has also enriched our documentation on the composer. Those who have dealt with biographical aspects – and hardly any of the present contributors have resisted the occasional aside in this respect – show how Debussy's personality, wide ranging interests, and working methods all continue to fascinate scholars primarily concerned with other approaches, just as they fascinated both Dietschy and Lockspeiser in the 1950s and 60s.

A few other crucial studies deserve signalling, not that they exclude others but because they have initiated new angles of approach. Among these, Robert Orledge's *Debussy and the Theatre* deepened our understanding of the composer partly by illuminating his unfinished projects, while Jean Barraqué was perhaps unique in his perspective as a composer at the forefront of French music in the post-war period, and able to relate Debussy's music to current trends. For the English reader, Roger Nichols's edition of Debussy's letters, and his *Debussy Remembered* have been invaluable in their presentation not only of the best known sources, but also of many not easily available in French.

So much for context. The way in which the present collection came about is worth a mention. Firstly, it was animated by a desire to hold a colloquium of international Debussy specialists in Britain, a country which, after all, impinged on the composer's imagination in a number of ways, and which has (as Roger Nichols shows in his contribution) been particularly favourable as regards the reception of his works. Secondly, it was spurred on by a recognition that those working on the complete edition had uncovered wide areas of knowledge of a new kind, of infinite variety, not through biographical delving or the application of particular analytical methods, but simply by close and prolonged contact with Debussy's own manuscripts.

Thirdly, and most importantly, it was catalysed by the willingness of the Institut Français du Royaume-uni in London, and in particular of its *musicomane* director M. Michel Oriano, to host a series of *Journées Claude Debussy* in September 1993, centred on an academic conference and public concerts of Debussy's music. These concerts, which included a couple of unknown pieces, were given by both French and English artists while at the same time an exhibition of photographs pertinent to the composer's life was brought over by Myriam Chimènes especially for the occasion from the Centre de documentation Claude Debussy. Then came the agreement of Cambridge University Press that the series of papers given at the Institut Français *colloque* might fit well into a 'studies' volume and thanks to Penny Souster, Cambridge University Press chipped in with an exhibition from their unparalleled list of English-language books on French music, including many Debussy volumes, while Rosemary Dooley presented those of Minkoff. In the evening concerts, Alain Planès played, Véronique Diétschy sang and Robin Bowman accompanied – all thanks to the support of *Action Artistique*.

Meanwhile interest from both North and South America had mushroomed and while the contributors to the present volume were commissioned at the outset – although there were withdrawals and changes of topic – the conference expanded to include further contributions, several of which have appeared in the *Cahiers Debussy*. Although the initial plan was more balanced in its inclusion of more analytical contributions, the final volume has ended up with only one analytical contribution, that of Marie Rolf, which in any case leans equally towards literary analysis. Finally, no order seemed either better or worse than the alphabetical.

From the interest shown in what was by no means a large-scale conference, it was clear that there will be room for a second *Debussy Studies*, centred on purely analytical papers, while the present volume may even be strengthened by their absence, in that it may show a diversity of angles broad enough to convince the reader that biographical and inter-disciplinary approaches, as well as those of source-studies and source-study-informed performance practice, have enough to recommend them in themselves, and more than adequate to fill a volume.

Richard Langham Smith

Acknowledgements

Thanks are due to many people who have helped in the process of this book coming to fruition. First and foremost, gratitude is due to all the contributors for agreeing to the formula of a conference 'try-out' followed by publication, and particular thanks go to the contributors from France and the USA in this respect. Secondly, thanks go to the staff incumbent at the Institut Français at the time of the *Journées Claude Debussy*: firstly, to Michel Oriano whose support for the venture was sustained and unfailingly warm and secondly, to Charles Giry-Deloison who smoothed the path throughout the conference and provided all the conference peripherals in an exemplary way.

Many of the contributors deserve thanks for services far beyond the mere provision of copy: virtually every contributor has given a second opinion on something or other but in particular many of the contributors have expressed, in an editorially deleted footnote, their gratitude to Roger Nichols whose translations they have drawn upon. A collated vote of thanks is therefore due in this respect. Thanks also to Sidney Buckland for signalling several points which might otherwise never have been noticed.

Detailed acknowledgements, contributor by contributor, are as follows. For Myriam Chimènes: to the Pierpont Morgan Library, New York, for a copy of the *Préparation orchestrale*, from the Robert O. Lehman foundation, formerly on deposit at the Pierpont Morgan Library, and to the Rychenberg Foundation, Stadtbibliothek, Winterthur, Switzerland for the *particelle*. For David Grayson: to James Hepokoski and to the Pierpont Morgan Library, New York, for permission to publish the discarded scene from *Pélléas* (sic), from the Dannie and Hettie Heineman collection. For Denis Herlin: to Madame Daudy and Madame de Lastic at the Collection Musicale François Lang at Royaumont, and to Davitt Moroney, to whom the article is dedicated. For Jean-Michel Nectoux: to Rémy Copin at the Maison Claude Debussy at Saint-Germain-en-Laye, Rodolphe Rapetti,

ACKNOWLEDGEMENTS

Vidar Poulsson, Denis Herlin, François Lesure, Pierre Guien, Patrice Schmidt and Myriam Chimènes. For Robert Orledge: to Ornella Volta of the Fondation Erik Satie. Other more specific acknowledgements appear in the footnotes.

A note on the references

Each article in the current volume has been footnoted as a separate unit and no overall key has been provided since the first time a citation is given in a particular article it is given in full. Subsequent references to the same work, within a particular article only, are designated by author followed by a short title and a page number where relevant.

References to Debussy letters have been given to the most recent accessible volume at the time of going to press, i.e. François Lesure's second collection *Correspondance 1884–1918* published in paperback by Hermann, Paris, in 1993. Readers wishing for the complete letters from which the present volume gives quotations are recommended to this volume where appropriate but may also find the complete letters in Lesure's earlier collection *Lettres* published in an illustrated hardback edition in 1980 by the same publisher. The 1993 volume contains all those found in the 1980 volume with the addition of 75 letters. The same letters may also be found in one of the earlier collections of letters, variously listed, for example, in the bibliography to Debussy in *The New Grove Dictionary of Music and Musicians*, 6th edition; in Claude Abravanel's *Claude Debussy: A Bibliography*, Detroit, 1974 and in James R. Briscoe's *Claude Debussy: A Guide to Research*. Readers are also referred to Roger Nichols's translation of *Debussy Letters*, Faber and Faber, London, and Harvard University Press, Cambridge, Massachusetts, 1987. This volume contains letters not in either Lesure volume, in which cases the reader will be referred to a source for the original French in a footnote. Translations from Nichols are marked † in the footnote, those unmarked are by the chapter author, or in chapters 1, 3 and 5, by the translator.

As the book goes to press, publication of volumes for the Debussy *Oeuvres Complètes* has unexpectedly slowed down, indeed seized up. Volume and part numbers for published editions have been given, but although a complete projected list of volumes for the edition exists in the publicity material for the *Oeuvres Complètes*, these details have not been given for volumes not yet published.

1 The definition of timbre in the process of composition of *Jeux*

MYRIAM CHIMÈNES

The music of *Jeux* made relatively little impact at the time of its first performance by the *Ballets Russes* on 15 May 1913. It was somewhat over-shadowed two weeks later by *The Rite of Spring*, which provoked an unfor-gettable scandal in the history of music. Some forty years on, a number of young, avant-garde composers, in the forefront of whom were Jean Barraqué and Pierre Boulez, drew attention to the innovations apparent in Debussy's score, which they rightly saw as a determining influence on the development of twentieth-century music. Without re-examining their analyses and conclusions, the intention of this study is to bring a further historical perspective to bear on this work, to describe its genesis with a view to understanding the process of its composition, and to compare this process to that of the earlier works. The objective is not to contrast the com-poser's viewpoint with that of the historian, but rather to investigate to what extent historical research can further an analytical approach.

Present musicological research, in particular for the *Edition critique des Oeuvres Complètes de Claude Debussy*,[1] has led to the discovery of musical and historical sources hitherto unknown. Progress in this field has brought a greater understanding of the composer's working methods and has highlighted the possibility of a thorough investigation of the process of composition in Debussy's works: indeed this must surely be one of the functions of a critical edition. Those responsible for such an edition must assess to what extent this 'autopsy' of the manuscript is instructive. The *Fantaisie* and the *Nocturnes* are among the most complicated pieces – but also the most fascinating – to be unveiled by such editorial methods. There,

---

[1] *Edition critique des Oeuvres Complètes de Claude Debussy* (Paris, Durand et Costallat, in progress).

1

the discovery of copious sources, and editions strewn with corrections, reveal the composer's constant quest for perfection. Each work has its own identity, each runs its own course, but the gestation of each is different. It is therefore hoped that an eventual comparison of all these findings will one day yield the key to a greater understanding of Debussy's creative processes.

To borrow a term from Pierre Boulez, for whom the phenomenon of composing is 'expressed by a series of gestures' (*gestes*), one of the aims of such collective research is to try to define the sequence (or the simultaneity) of the composer's 'gestures'.[2] To penetrate the mystery of the passage from the conception of an idea to its realisation, and to explain when and how the various parameters which constitute the material of the composition are used, should surely be a primary aim of a project combining the efforts of all those working on the critical edition of Debussy's orchestral works.

With regard to these, previously unsuspected chronologies are often revealed by reviewing existing musical sources in conjunction with historical documents which range from correspondence to contracts; press articles; programmes; reviews; printers' plate numbers; publishers' copyright listings; registers of deposits at the *Bibliothèque Nationale de France*; memoirs and testimonies. In this respect, the orchestral works yield particularly rich rewards concerning their gestation. Rough drafts; *particelles*; the fair copy of the manuscript; the piano reduction; corrected proofs of both the orchestration and the piano reduction; certain scores belonging to conductors who were Debussy's contemporaries – all these sources, when carefully analysed and cross-checked with historical documents, particularly correspondence, can prove extremely enlightening. Ultimately, an understanding of this entire body of material is a prerequisite for any real editorial work to begin.

Some ten years ago, Marie Rolf devoted an article to the early orchestral manuscripts of Debussy, basing her study on the *particelles* of *Prélude à l'après-midi d'un faune*, the *Nocturnes* and *La mer*.[3] By way of introduction to a further projected study, the present article takes a similar line of approach to *Jeux*, Debussy's last orchestral work and a supreme example of

---

[2]   Pierre Boulez, *Jalons (pour une décennie) dix ans d'enseignement au 'Collège de France' (1978–1988)*, ed. Jean-Jacques Nattiez (Paris, 1989), p. 110.

[3]   Marie Rolf, 'Orchestral Manuscripts of Claude Debussy: 1892–1905', *The Musical Quarterly*, 4 (1984), 538–66.

the subject. I propose to focus this examination on timbre, an essential element in the composition of an orchestral work. Pertinent to such a study is the availability of a particularly impressive number of sources, enabling us to determine with a certain degree of precision the genesis of the composition of this score.[4]

It therefore seems of interest to take *Jeux* as a starting point for examining the process of composition; tracing the sequence of 'gestures'; estimating the rate of composition; and attempting to evaluate the ease or difficulty of creativity, without, however, raising the problem of regrets or second thoughts such as those found most extremely in 'Sirènes'.[5] To pose the central question: at what stage of composition did Debussy introduce timbre? An investigation of this point seems fundamental in determining whether or not, for Debussy, timbre is inherent in the germ of the musical idea. To use Boulez's terms once again, the question can be formulated as follows: in Debussy's case, does 'orchestral-invention' (*orchestration-invention*) replace 'orchestral-dressing' (*orchestration-vêtement*)?[6]

In the first place, it is essential to retrace in detail the genesis of the composition of *Jeux*. Due to the abundance of musical sources, combined with documents of an historic nature, a relatively precise chronology can be established.

On 18 June 1912 a contract was drawn up between Claude Debussy and Serge de Diaghilev.[7] The subject of this contract was a commission for ballet music for the following season of the *Ballets Russes*, namely June 1913. According to the terms of this contract, Debussy undertook to deliver the piano score by the end of August 1912 and the full orchestral score by the end of March 1913. It is appropriate to note that in the case of ballet music the piano reduction was the first requirement, both for the choreographer to create the ballet and for the dancers to rehearse. In accepting the terms

---

[4] See Debussy, *Jeux*, ed. Myriam Chimènes and Pierre Boulez, *Edition critique des Oeuvres Complètes de Claude Debussy*, series 5, vol. VIII (Paris, 1988).

[5] See Denis Herlin, 'Sirens in the Labyrinth: amendments in Debussy's *Nocturnes*, in this volume, pp. 51–77.

[6] Pierre Boulez, 'Debussy', in Paule Thévenin (ed.), *Relevés d'apprenti* (Paris, 1966), p. 344.

[7] A copy signed by Diaghilev and retained by Debussy is in the Bibliothèque Nationale de France, Paris, (Musique). Rés. Vm dos 13 (7).

of this contract the composer thereby implied that he felt capable of composing the piano reduction (the music) in less than three months and completing the orchestration some nine months later. The time scale was thus extremely brief.

From Debussy's correspondence we learn that by 2 July 1912, he had not yet received the scenario and so had not yet begun to compose the music.[8] However, on 9 August, a further letter to his publisher Jacques Durand confirms that the composition of *Jeux* was already underway. Debussy writes that he has received a visit from Diaghilev, enabling him to 'sort out one or two details that were still rather vague. They are in a hurry for the music of *Jeux* because Nijinsky wants to work on it during his stay in Venice!' Debussy adds, however, that he refused, despite Diaghilev's impatience, to play him what he had done because he did not want those 'Barbarians sticking their noses into [his] experiments in personal chemistry!'[9] Less than three weeks later, on 25 August 1912, Debussy wrote to André Caplet: 'I've finished the piece called *Jeux* I spoke to you about. How was I able to forget the troubles of this world and write music which is almost cheerful, and alive with quaint gestures?' And he continues: 'I'll have to invent for it an orchestra "without feet". Not that I'm thinking of a band composed exclusively of legless cripples! No! I'm thinking of that orchestral colour which seems to be lit from behind, of which there are such wonderful examples in *Parsifal*.'[10]

The date and contents of this letter are particularly significant. What exactly comprises the *music* of *Jeux*? The above text, when examined in

---

[8] See letter of Debussy to Jacques Durand, 2 July 1912, in Claude Debussy, *Correspondance 1884–1918*, ed. François Lesure (Paris, 1993), p. 307.†

[9] 'réglé utilement quelques détails restés dans l'ombre. Ils sont pressés d'avoir la musique de *Jeux*, sur laquelle Nijinsky voudrait travailler pendant son séjour à Venise!' Debussy continues, 'à lui jouer ce qu'il y a de fait, n'aimant pas que les Barbares mettent leur nez dans [ses] expériences de chimie personnelle!' Debussy, *Correspondance*, p. 309.†

[10] 'J'ai terminé la composition de *Jeux* dont je vous ai parlé. Où ai-je trouvé l'oubli des ennuis de ce monde pour écrire une musique à peu près joyeuse, rythme de gestes falots?' He continues, 'Il faudrait un orchestre "sans pieds" pour cette musique. Ne croyez pas que je pense à un orchestre exclusivement composé de culs-de-jatte! Non! Je pense à cette couleur orchestrale qui me semble éclairée par derrière et dont il y a de si merveilleux effets dans *Parsifal*!' Debussy, *Correspondance*, pp. 310–11.†

conjunction with the musical sources, confirms that the first draft of the work (no preliminary drafts are known) is in fact the *particelle*, dated '23rd, 28th, 29th August 1912, 1st, 2nd September'.[11] Written on four staves, this *particelle* contains practically no indications of tempo, dynamics or articulation, and no more than a dozen indications of instrumentation. Therefore, in Debussy's terms ('I've finished *Jeux*'), the completed work would seem to be this embryo of his final score, in other words the original *particelle*, the earliest materialisation of the musical idea. The composer had no hesitation in declaring the work finished when in fact he had not yet begun the orchestration.

Once this *particelle* was completed, Debussy very quickly produced what is usually considered to be a piano reduction, although in this case the term 'reduction' is somewhat inappropriate. Logically, a piano reduction is a piano score reduced from an original orchestral score, yet in Debussy's case, the reality often seems to be quite different. Debussy's piano reduction was no doubt almost completed when he received another visit from Diaghilev, as he related in a letter to Jacques Durand the following day: 'Diaghilev seemed satisfied, requesting only that I extend the ending a little, which I have been busy doing all day.'[12] What was Diaghilev satisfied with? What had Debussy played to him that day? Had he been reading from the *particelle*, as he had done with *Pelléas* whenever friends asked him to play fragments of his opera still in gestation?[13] Or had he already made some headway with the piano reduction? The *particelle* in fact shows no trace of either alteration or extension.

This manuscript of 678 bars (the final score would comprise 709 bars) is completely free of any such amendments. On the other hand, the changes requested by Diaghilev appear very clearly on the manuscript of the piano reduction,[14] as well as on a page written in Debussy's hand and attached to

[11] Manuscript on deposit in Winterthur, Stadtbibliothek, Rychenberg-Stiftung, Dep. RS 11/3.

[12] 'Diaghilev a semblé satisfait, il m'a demandé seulement d'allonger un peu la fin, ce à quoi je me suis employé tout ce jour.' See Jacques Durand (ed.), *Lettres de Claude Debussy à son éditeur* (Paris, 1927), p. 111. Letter incorrectly dated 1 November 1912 instead of 1 September 1912. Regarding this error, see the preface to the edition of *Jeux* in Debusssy, *Oeuvres Complètes*, p. xiii, note 21.

[13] See David Grayson, *The Genesis of Debussy's 'Pelléas et Mélisande'* (Ann Arbor, 1986).

[14] Bibliothèque Nationale de France, Paris, (Musique). Ms. 1008.

the copy[15] made at this time for Nijinsky by the publishers Durand from the manuscript of the piano reduction. This proves that the reduction was therefore already completed in its first version. The changes required also explain why Debussy was slightly late in meeting his deadline. On 5 September 1912 he wrote to his publisher: 'Diaghilev's request for a few more bars has meant a change – for the better – in the ending of *Jeux*... It feels more balanced now, and is brimful of passion.'[16] Finally, Debussy must have delivered the manuscript of the piano reduction to Durand on 12 September, as shown by a letter to his publisher dated that same day: 'You'll find considerable changes at the end of *Jeux*. I've been working on it up to the last moment.'[17]

Having honoured the first part of his contract, Debussy appears to have put aside *Jeux* for several months. He began work again on the orchestration of 'Gigues', completed the second book of *Préludes* and returned to some 'old projects' (*La chute de la maison Usher* and *Le diable dans le beffroi*). Once this preliminary stage of composition was over, all that remained was the routine side of the orchestration, according to the classical procedure of 'orchestral-dressing' (*orchestration-vêtement*). This surprising fact may also reveal that Debussy had by then a fairly good idea of his own capacities. The composition of the *particelle* and the piano reduction of *Jeux* had taken little more than a month. The composer then waited until the last moment before proceeding with the orchestration, which he also completed within a month. There is no documentary evidence of his having begun any earlier this final stage of the composition of *Jeux*.

The following stage in the creative process of *Jeux* consists of a draft orchestration, entitled by Debussy himself: *Préparation orchestrale* and dated very precisely at the end '28 March 13 Midday – 24 April 13 6.15'.[18] This manuscript is a source of major importance, particularly since there exists no equivalent for any of the other orchestral works. Indeed, for the

---

[15] In the Frederick R. Koch Foundation Collection on deposit at the Pierpont Morgan Library, New York.

[16] 'Les quelques mesures demandées par Diaghilev m'ont obligé à modifier – assez heureusement – la fin de *Jeux*... C'est mieux en place et la volupté coule à pleins bords.' Letter to Jacques Durand, in Durand (ed.), *Lettres*, p. 110.

[17] 'Vous trouverez de grands changements dans la fin de *Jeux*. J'y ai travaillé jusqu'à la dernière minute.' In Debussy, *Correspondance*, p. 312.†

[18] Collection of the Robert O. Lehman Foundation, New York.

earlier works, there are no known intermediate sketches between the *particelle* and the final, definitive manuscript. The *préparation orchestrale* of *Jeux* includes an as yet incomplete nomenclature of instruments: the string parts, for example, are written on four staves, already showing many indications of the division of the parts. This manuscript, however, contains no indications whatsoever of dynamics, nuances or tempi. The latter, it should be noted, were indicated with great precision – greater even than in the final orchestral manuscript – on the manuscript of the piano reduction dated September 1912.[19] To orchestrate *Jeux*, Debussy therefore wrote a *préparation orchestrale* which he developed straight into the fair copy of his final manuscript,[20] and which would be used in the first place by the copyist for the orchestral parts, and subsequently by the engraver for the edition.

Although the final manuscript is not dated, it seems permissible to put forward this hypothesis. We know that the publisher Durand extracted the manuscript from Debussy page by page, so that the orchestral parts could be produced in time for the rehearsals preceding the first performance by the *Ballets Russes* on 15 May 1913.[21] The *préparation orchestrale* therefore cannot have been written very long before the definitive manuscript and is more likely to have constituted a type of rough draft on which Debussy worked simultaneously with the definitive manuscript. The final date of 24 April is therefore probably the date on which the definitive manuscript was also completed.

This detailed chronology speaks volumes. Not only does it enlighten us as regards the process of composition, it also reveals Debussy's conception of the meaning of 'completion' in terms of an orchestral work. In August 1912 Debussy informed Caplet that he had completed *Jeux* when in fact only the *particelle* had been composed. In November 1912, while waiting for a new proof of the piano reduction of *Jeux*, Debussy wrote to Stravinsky: 'As soon as I have a reasonable proof of *Jeux* I'll send it to you ...

---

[19] These indications have been taken into account in the edition of *Jeux* in Debussy, *Oeuvres Complètes*. Obviously pressed for time, Debussy did not take the trouble to record them in his final manuscript and they were omitted in the 1914 edition.

[20] Bibliothèque Nationale de France, (Musique). Ms 966.

[21] See autograph letter from Debussy to Emile Vuillermoz, 6 April 1913, in the collection of the Humanities Research Center, University of Texas at Austin.

I'd like to have your opinion on this 'trifle'... for three people!'[22] These two documents lead one to believe that for Debussy the essence of his work was contained in his initial draft or in his piano reduction. Consequently, it would seem that he viewed timbre as no more than a supplementary element, of decorative function, added at a later stage. This discovery is particularly surprising when one considers the final result: a work in which timbre is integrated in an unprecedented way into the musical fabric, of which it is a major component.

A similar examination of an earlier work, the *Nocturnes*, confirms that Debussy had this very particular conception of the notion of completion. On 25 June 1898, Debussy wrote to his publisher Georges Hartmann: 'the *Nocturnes* are finished'.[23] His subsequent letters, however, tell us that right up until the end of the following year he was still hard at work on their orchestration. Once again, Debussy is no doubt referring to the *particelle* on which appears, as in the case of *La mer*, the date of completion of the final manuscript. It is therefore advisable to treat only with the greatest caution the dates inscribed by Debussy on his manuscripts – as, moreover, is the case with his letters.[24] Further examples could be cited, notably concerning the composition of *Pelléas et Mélisande*.

One important question, however, remains: can one consider Debussy's indications of timbre in the *particelle* as inherent in the germ of the musical idea? By deduction, would the corollary then be that whatever does not appear in the *particelle* cannot be considered germinal? An answer may possibly be found by examining the sources of *Jeux*, and in particular comparing the *particelle*, the *préparation orchestrale* and the final manuscript. Examples drawn from the *particelle* and from the *préparation orchestrale* are given below. For comparison with the final stage of the work, readers should refer to the edition of *Jeux* in the *Oeuvres Complètes*.

At bars 74–5, where the scenario indicates 'Une balle de tennis tombe sur la scène' (a tennis ball falls on to the stage), Debussy very clearly notes in

---

[22] 'Aussitôt que j'aurai une épreuve convenable de *Jeux*, je vous l'enverrai... j'aimerais avoir votre opinion sur ce badinage... à trois.' See letter dated [5 November 1912] in Debussy, *Correspondance*, p. 35.†

[23] 'les *Nocturnes* sont finis'. See Debussy: *Correspondance* p. 133.

[24] Note, as an example, the title page of the *particelle* of *Jeux*, where the following incomprehensible dates appear in Debussy's hand: '1913–1915'.

Example 1.1a. *Jeux: Particelle* bars 74–5

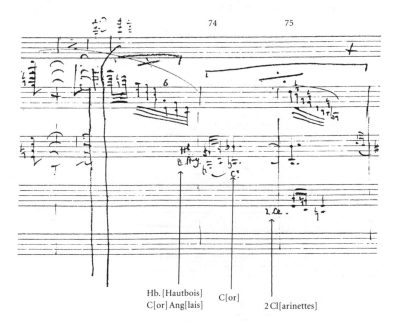

the *particelle* oboes, cor anglais and horns (bar 74) as well as two clarinets (bar 75). The descending passage in bar 75, however, appears without reference to timbre (ex. 1.1a). The piano reduction remains faithful to the *particelle*, with similar motives and in particular the descending passage of bar 75. In the *préparation orchestrale* (bar 74), Debussy retains the motif destined for oboe but assigns to the bassoon the part initially intended for the cor anglais. He maintains the horns, however, without indicating this in full in the nomenclature. At bar 75 he gives the strings the motif intended for the clarinets and, in return, assigns to the latter the descending passage. He adds, on the same beat, an ascending passage in the harps (ex. 1.1b). In his final manuscript, Debussy retains the oboes, bassoons and horns at bar 74 but does away with the descending passage in bar 75 which had appeared in all previous sources. He keeps the ascending passage in the harps, added at the time of the *préparation orchestrale*; as well as the motif in the second violins and the *pizzicato* in the violas. Debussy therefore retains in his definitive version only part of what he had conceived in his initial draft, developing his score at each new stage of the process of composition (ex. 1.1c).

Example 1.1b. *Jeux:*
Préparation orchestrale bars 74–5

[Hautbois]

[Cor Anglais]

[Bassons]

Example 1.1c. *Jeux:* Final version bars 71–5

At bar 157, while the two girls are dancing, at the point where the scenario states: 'l'autre jeune fille danse à son tour' (the other girl dances in turn), Debussy's clear intention in the *particelle* is to assign the dominant motif to the flute and the bassoon (ex. 1.2a). In the *préparation orchestrale* he gives this motif to the cor anglais, doubled by the bassoon in bars 158 to 159 and taken over by the oboe at the end of bar 159 and in bar 160 (ex. 1.2b.) The final manuscript conforms strictly to the *préparation orchestrale*. All that remains of Debussy's initial intentions in the *particelle* is therefore the timbre of the bassoon (ex. 1.2c).

At bar 378, while the three dancers are at their game and where the scenario states: 'la jeune fille s'échappe et va se cacher derrière un bouquet d'arbres' (the girl runs off and hides behind a clump of trees), Debussy gives an ascending chromatic *glissando* to six first violins (ex. 1.3a). This glissando is omitted in the *préparation orchestrale* in favour of a tremolo in the violins and violas (ex. 1.3b). The final manuscript is identical to the *préparation orchestrale*. The initial idea has therefore been abandoned (ex. 1.3c).

At bars 107–8, a few bars after the two girls make their entrance on stage, Debussy introduces a motif in the *préparation orchestrale* which did not appear in the *particelle* and which he assigns to the clarinets (ex. 1.4a and ex. 1.4b). He retains this motif in his final manuscript, but replaces the clarinets with flutes (ex. 1.4c).

One last example, however, contradicts all the preceding ones by showing that the initial idea can sometimes contain the germ of the final timbre. At bars 435–7, during the passage where the first young girl expresses her resentment, Debussy very clearly indicates two clarinets at bar 435 and the oboe and the flute at bar 437. It should be observed that the oboe part is written in a register above the flute, thus indicating that the oboe motif must predominate, while the flute has a secondary function (in the piano reduction the order of the tessitura is reinstated) (ex. 1.5a). Debussy makes no changes here, nor in the *préparation orchestrale* (ex. 1.5b). The final manuscript is consistent both with the *particelle* and with the orchestral preparation, thereby retaining the original concept of the timbre (ex. 1.5c).

From these five examples, one may conclude that it is impossible to assume that Debussy employed a consistent method, principle or process of composition. Several different instances have been observed. Debussy may

Example 1.2a. *Jeux: Particelle* bars 157–61

Example 1.2b. *Jeux: Préparation orchestrale* bars 157–61

Example 1.2c. *Jeux*: Final version bars 157–60

Example 1.3a. *Jeux: Particelle* bar 378

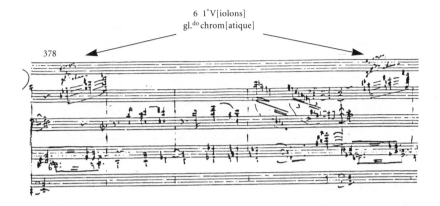

partially retain his initial intention but evolve and invent elements at each new stage: none of the three stages is identical (see ex. 1.1). On the other hand, he may retain a single element from the *particelle*, and invent and modify elements in the orchestral preparation but make no changes in the final manuscript (see ex. 1.2). In other cases Debussy abandons the initial idea; but on the other hand the final manuscript is consistent with the orchestral preparation (see ex. 1.3). He may also add to the orchestral preparation a motif that did not exist in the *particelle*, resulting in double invention – both of motif and timbre – since he retains the motif in the final manuscript but introduces a new timbre (see ex. 1.4). Finally, Debussy can be extremely precise from the moment he writes the *particelle*, making no changes whatsoever in any of the subsequent sources (see ex. 1.5).

The *préparation orchestrale* of *Jeux* should in fact be considered as a second germ of the work, in the sense that it contains the major part of the creativity regarding timbre. It is at this stage of the process that Debussy's inventiveness in marrying motif to timbre becomes evident. As Jean Barraqué remarked, 'This orchestral technique enables him to break up the melody, scattering short motifs throughout the different parts of the orchestra, in this way creating a whole "gamut of tone colour"'.[25]

---

[25] 'Cette technique orchestrale lui permet de briser la mélodie, éparpillant de courts motifs aux différents étages de l'orchestre; il crée ainsi une sorte de "gamme de timbres".' Jean Barraqué, *Debussy* (Paris, 1962), p. 171. New edition revised François Lesure (Paris, 1994), p. 216.

Example 1.3b. *Jeux: Préparation orchestrale* bars 377–80

C[or] Ang[lais]

Cl[arinette]

Example 1.3c. *Jeux*: Final version bars 377–80

Example 1.4a. *Jeux: Particelle* bars 106–9

Comparison with earlier works seems relevant here. The *particelle* of *Prélude à l'après-midi d'un faune*, luminous in its clarity, provides indications of instrumentation, most often written in red ink.[26] In the *Nocturnes*, instrumental indications on the *particelle* are written in black or coloured pencil.[27] In both instances, it would appear that these indications were added at a later stage. This hypothesis seems highly plausible as in the case of both these works no intermediate sketch exists between the *particelle* and the final manuscript, equivalent to the *préparation orchestrale* of *Jeux*. The additional layer of indications replaces, in brief, the *préparation orchestrale*. In other words, it is highly likely that Debussy added these indications to the *particelle* as he was orchestrating, instead of formulating an elaborate draft orchestration, as in the *préparation orchestrale* of *Jeux*. This would seem to explain the often deceptive similarity between the *particelle* and the final manuscript of these two works.

While taking the preceding remark into account, it is nevertheless possible to choose an example from the *Nocturnes* in which the intentions expressed in the *particelle* are seen to be identical with the final version. In the *particelle* of 'Fêtes', the second of the three *Nocturnes*, at bar 124, Debussy already has in mind the trumpets so characteristic of this piece: he

---

[26] Collection of the Robert O. Lehman Foundation, New York. Published in colour facsimile (Washington, 1963).

[27] Library of Congress, Washington.

Example 1.4b. *Jeux*: *Préparation orchestrale* bars 106–10

notes in the margin, in thick pencil (probably a subsequent addition) '*3 tromp*[ettes] *sourd*[ines]'. He retains this timbre in the final manuscript: (ex. 1.6).

An example taken from a later work, *Images,* is equally significant. In the *particelle* of 'Rondes de printemps', the third of the *Images* for orchestra, Debussy has already fixed on an instrument of very particular timbre, the tambourine.[28] That he notes this in ink leads one to believe that this was an

28 Winterthur, Stadtbibliothek, Rychenberg-Stiftung.

Example 1.4c. *Jeux*: Final version bars 105–9

Example 1.5a. *Jeux: Particelle* bars 435–9

Example 1.5b. *Jeux: Préparation orchestrale* bars 434–8

Example 1.5c. *Jeux*: Final version bars 435–8

original choice and not a subsequent addition, as was probably the case in the preceding example from 'Fêtes'. Debussy retains the tambourine in the final manuscript: (ex. 1.7).

This very brief survey, giving precise examples as illustrations, calls for some observations. As Marie Rolf has pointed out in her article, the *particelle* of *Prélude à l'après-midi d'un faune* is far more precise than that of *La*

Example 1.6. *Fêtes*: bar 124 ff.

Example 1.7. *Rondes de Printemps*: bar 134 ff.

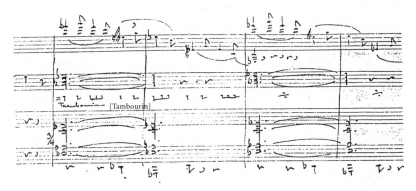

mer.[29] The more Debussy 'progresses', the less detailed his *particelles* become. Extending this line of investigation as far as *Jeux*, and concentrating on the question of timbre, interesting statistical information can be gleaned by looking at the number of instrumental indications that figure in each of the *particelles*. Calculating the percentage of bars containing instrumental indications in relation to the total number of bars in each *particelle* yields the following results:

Prélude à l'après-midi *d'un faune*	35.0%	(38 indications for 109 bars)
Nocturnes	13.0%	(60 indications for 523 bars)

[29] See Marie Rolf, 'Orchestral Manuscripts'.

La mer	9.0%	(64 indications for 681 bars)
'Rondes de printemps'	9.5%	(21 indications for 235 bars)
'Gigues'[30]	15.0%	(35 indications for 221 bars)
Jeux	1.6%	(12 indications for 678 bars)

With the exception of 'Gigues', the result is significant: Debussy feels less and less the need to note down his intentions. Marie Rolf, taking into account all the parameters of composition, attributes the development between *Prélude à l'après-midi d'un faune* and *La mer* to Debussy's evolution as a composer. This would signify that with experience, he no longer needed to note everything down, thus complying with Boileau's now proverbial observation: 'Ce que l'on conçoit bien s'énonce clairement' (What is well conceived is expressed with ease). Is it therefore possible that the *particelle* of *Jeux* contained in some mysterious way the germ of the instrumentation which later materialised in the *préparation orchestrale*? This would imply that what was clear to Debussy would undoubtedly appear elliptical and enigmatic to others. We recall that Debussy did not want anyone 'sticking their noses into [his] experiments in personal chemistry!'

A further question should be considered: when Debussy undertook the composition of *Jeux*, had he already decided that he would have a second, intermediate draft before the final orchestration, in other words the *préparation orchestrale*? If so, this would then justify the very minor number of indications of timbre in the *particelle*. It should be noted, however, that these indications seem to have been marked initially, rather than added at a later stage, as in the case of the *particelles* of the previous works.

Two other compositions come to mind at this point, *Khamma* and *La Boîte à joujoux*. Both are of particular interest here as they, too, are works for ballet, the one written before, and the other after *Jeux*. In both cases Debussy composed so-called piano 'reductions' but did not complete the orchestration. Unfortunately, no *particelle* for either of these works is known to us. Nevertheless, a comparison between the first pages of the orchestration and the piano reduction of *Khamma* is sufficient to show

---

[30] As the complete short score of 'Ibéria' has not been located to date, I have had to examine separately 'Gigues' and 'Rondes de printemps'.

Debussy's inventiveness at the stage of orchestration. It is also known that Debussy passionately defended the score of *Khamma*, as if it were a completed work.

Examination of the sources of *Jeux* reveals that this inventiveness in relation to timbre is apparently lacking in the original *particelle*. At a time when he was familiar neither with the genesis of the composition nor with the manuscript sources, Pierre Boulez was able to say of *Jeux*: 'Orchestral-dressing, that primary notion, disappears in favour of orchestral-invention; the composer's imagination is not limited to composing first the basic musical text and then embellishing it with instrumental ornamentation; the very act of orchestrating releases not only musical ideas but a way of writing that will best express them: original alchemy rather than subsequent chemistry.'[31] Boulez wrote those lines a good many years before studying the sources while collaborating on the critical edition of *Jeux*. The facts have proved that the situation is far more complex.

The conclusion, however, does not imply that timbre represents for Debussy a mere colour accessory, a minor embellishment. He certainly integrates timbre into the music, but this fusion takes place only at the intermediate stage of the *préparation orchestrale*. In other words the entire sound phenomenon is therefore not completely inherent in what we call the germ of the musical idea.

(*Translated by Sidney Buckland*)

---

[31] Boulez, *Debussy*, p. 344.

2   Waiting for Golaud: the concept of time in *Pelléas*

DAVID GRAYSON

In 1892, the same year that Maurice Maeterlinck published his play *Pelléas et Mélisande*, Belgium, his homeland, adopted World Standard Time – our current system of twenty-four worldwide time zones measured from Greenwich, England – as had been established in 1884 at the Prime Meridian Conference in Washington.[1] Intended to co-ordinate and thereby facilitate and promote international transportation and communication, World Standard Time collaterally drew attention precisely to that which it sought to eliminate from the world of commerce: the plurality and relativity of time(s) as well as the actuality of private or psychological time.[2]

These important cultural and artistic themes may profitably be explored in the works of Maeterlinck. For example, in *L'Intruse*, his one-act *drame d'attente* of 1890,[3] the passage of time is an unremitting preoccupation of the characters on stage. As a ubiquitous reminder, a large clock is continually in view, successively striking ten, eleven, and finally twelve o'clock, but as measured in 'real' time these chimes sound at irregular intervals, of far less than sixty minutes each. The disparity between 'real' time and 'stage' (or psychological) time is thus made explicit. Time is so important that one character even identifies as a precondition for the will to live the ability to perceive the visible changes by which the passage of time is made manifest: 'No longer to distinguish midday from midnight, nor

---

[1] Stephen Kern, *The Culture of Time and Space 1880–1918* (Cambridge, Massachusetts, 1983), p. 12.

[2] Ibid. p. 8.

[3] Written in 1889, *L'Intruse* (*The Intruder*) was published in 1890 and had its première the following year. It was dated 1891 when it was reprinted in volume I of Maeterlinck's collected plays, *Théâtre* (Brussels, 1901). For details of its somewhat complicated publication history see Georges Hermans, *Les premières armes de Maurice Maeterlinck* (Ledeberg-Ghent, 1967), pp. 105–9.

summer from winter. . . I would rather live no longer. . .'[4] The acute awareness of time that accompanies their constant waiting causes the characters
increasing anxiety, illustrating another contemporary theme: that the
period's heightened concern for punctuality had an injurious effect on the
human psyche and was a major source of neurosis.[5] 'What time is it?' asks
the blind Grandfather, who alone cannot see the clock. That key question
worried Maeterlinck as well – and from the outset, using this very phrase for
the opening line of his very first play, *La Princesse Maleine* of 1889.

In *Pelléas*, too, characters are often waiting, and they, too, sometimes
seem to have an excessive, even unnatural, preoccupation with time. In one
passage in act III, which Debussy excised in fashioning his libretto, Pelléas
and Golaud disagree over how much time they have just spent in the previous scene, in the underground vaults of the castle. It is noon (Pelléas has just
heard the chimes of midday) and Golaud remarks that they had entered the
vaults at around eleven o'clock. Pelléas, however, is sure they went down
somewhat earlier because he recalls having heard the clock strike half-past
ten. Golaud is willing to compromise but insists on the validity of his 'personal' sense of time despite the scientific evidence to the contrary: 'Half-
past ten', he says, 'or quarter to eleven. . .'[6] As in *L'Intruse*, Maeterlinck here
uses explicit references to the clock in order to legitimise the priority of
'stage' over 'real' time, both of which are distinct from Golaud's psychological perception. The scene itself may have taken less than five minutes to play,
but we are urged to remember it as having endured for well over an hour.
The few moments of marked tension that we witnessed in the underground
vaults, we are told, were not merely oppressive, but protracted – and worse
(i.e. longer) for Pelléas than for Golaud. The clear implication is that the
'intuition' of duration takes precedence over the scientific measurement of
time in determining one's sense of reality, an idea advanced during this
period by Henri Bergson.[7] From another perspective, the characters' discussion of time accords the underground scene a characteristic of dreams

---

[4] 'Ne plus distinguer midi de minuit, ni l'été de l'hiver . . . j'aimerais mieux ne
plus vivre . . .'
[5] George M. Beard, *American Nervousness* (New York, 1881), p. 103, quoted in
Kern, *The Culture of Time and Space*, p. 15.
[6] 'Dix heures et demie ou onze heures moins le quart . . .'
[7] Donald M. Lowe, *History of Bourgeois Perception* (Chicago, 1982), p. 110.

identified by French psychiatrist Victor Egger three years after the publication of the play: that of condensing lengthy sequences of events into short episodes.[8]

Another illustration of Maeterlinck's handling of time in *Pelléas* may be derived from examining a scene contained in a manuscript draft of the play but eliminated prior to publication.[9] In this manuscript it is the fourth scene of act I. To place it in context, it is necessary to summarise briefly the three preceding scenes. The first, not set by Debussy, takes place at dawn before the closed castle door. Maidservants are heard inside, calling upon the sleeping porter to open the door. There is going to be a celebration, they explain, and they must therefore wash the threshold, the door, and the steps. As the door opens the sun rises. In the second scene Golaud meets Mélisande in the forest. In the third, which takes place more than six months later, Geneviève reads Golaud's letter recounting his meeting of and subsequent marriage to Mélisande. He wishes to return home and plans to arrive three days later. As a signal that he and his bride will be welcome he asks that a lantern be placed on the top of the tower overlooking the sea. Geneviève instructs Pelléas to do so.

In the unpublished, and originally the fourth and concluding scene of the act,[10] Arkël, Geneviève, and Pelléas stand beneath the watchtower awaiting a signal from Claudius, the unseen watchman, to indicate that he has spotted the ship carrying Golaud and Mélisande. It is dark and windy, long after midnight, and Arkël falls asleep. Dawn is approaching when

[8]   Egger, 'La durée apparente des rêves', *Revue philosophique* (July 1895), 41–59, quoted in Kern, *The Culture of Time and Space*, p. 82.

[9]   Heineman MS 279, The Pierpont Morgan Library, New York. See appendix p. 46. The scene is described in Charles Van Lerberghe's analysis of the play, published as *Pelléas et Mélisande: Notes Critiques* (Liège, 1962). This analysis was written in two stages: the first, on the basis of a manuscript copy of the play, on 30 March 1892, and the second, on 13 May, by which time the play had been published. Van Lerberghe compared this scene to the tower scene (act I, scene 4) of Maeterlinck's earlier play *La Princesse Maleine* and commented that it 'perhaps made the mistake of reminding one a little of *Tristan*'. The latter parallel in particular may have contributed to Maeterlinck's decision to cut the scene.

[10]   The scene which is act I, scene 4 in the published version of Maeterlinck's play (and act I, scene 3 in Debussy's opera) was, in the manuscript draft, originally designated act II, scene 1, then act I, scene 5; only when the unpublished act I, scene 4 was removed did it definitively become act I, scene 4.

Claudius sounds the signal, awakening Arkël. The watchman announces that the ship is entering the port, and they go off to meet it. (The scene is reproduced in the appendix, pp. 46–50.)

In this pre-publication form the act takes on a circular structure: indeed, the times of day depicted in the first and last scenes suggest that the pre-dawn setting of scene 4 leads directly to the sunrise of scene 1. The unspecified festivities alluded to in scene 1 may now be understood to have been to celebrate Golaud's return home with his bride; and we may in retrospect reinterpret scenes 2, 3, and 4 as flashbacks serving to provide the background necessary for understanding the opening scene – the past explaining the present, but following it, as a collective memory ('collective' in that no one character participates in all three scenes), or a dream, or a myth retold. In its unpublished form, act I thus emerges as a prologue which exposes the events that led up to Mélisande's arrival in the castle and, moreover, explicitly characterises them as 'background' by using the flashback technique. The 'past-ness' of these scenes is conveyed by the circularity of the organisation: the ending has led up to the original starting point, which, by this time, is itself already in the past. And since the setting of the play is ostensibly in an indefinite historical past – Maeterlinck described it as the eleventh, twelfth, or possibly the fifteenth century[11] – we encounter in act I a doubly deep past: a past within the distant past.

Circularity, of course, is a prominent theme of the play. The closing lines – when Arkël says of Mélisande's daughter shortly after Mélisande's death, 'She must now live in her [mother's] place... It is the poor little girl's turn now...'[12] – suggest patterns of behaviour that have repeated and are destined to repeat generation after generation in a cycle of 'eternal return'. Yet this cyclical ending, this expression of 'eternal return', produces a feeling less of hope and comfort than of resignation and fatality.[13]

If her daughter is the Mélisande of the future, then Geneviève is in

---

[11] Letter to Lugné-Poe, reproduced in Lugné-Poe: *Le sot du tremplin* (Paris, 1930), p. 237.

[12] 'Il faut qu'il vive, maintenant, à sa place ... C'est au tour de la pauvre petite ...'

[13] This is consistent with the observation of Henry J. Schmidt that 'normally ... the theme of eternal recurrence tends to be cloaked in cynicism or resignation in twentieth-century Continental drama.' See Henry J. Schmidt, *How Dramas End. Essays on the German 'Sturm und Drang'. Büchner, Hauptmann, and Fleisser* (Ann Arbor, 1992), p. 19.

some respects the Mélisande of the past (or perhaps more accurately, Geneviève seems to represent Mélisande's potential but unrealised future). Geneviève, too, was brought to the castle as a bride[14] and loved two men who were brothers (or at least half-brothers: all we can reasonably presume is that they were both sons of Arkël). Only one of the brothers, Pelléas's father, is alive. Was this generation, too, marked by fratricide? Did Geneviève marry Golaud's father, bear him a child, and then fall in love with his brother, provoking a quarrel ending in murder? Fanciful perhaps, but certain vague details in the family tree – and the representation on stage of no fewer than four generations – encourage a consideration of this possibility.

Inevitably, the circularity of the play as a whole suggests another interpretation of the opening scene. Perhaps the castle door was so difficult to open because it had been kept shut for years, superstitiously shunned because it was there that Mélisande and Golaud had been discovered, huddled together, the morning after Pelléas was slain, the blood from their wounds staining the sill.[15] This would explain, for example, the observations of the servant and porter that they will never be able to wash it clean, not even with all of the water of the Flood.[16] Rather than celebrating

[14] Geneviève indirectly discloses this history when she tells Mélisande that she has lived in the castle for nearly forty years: considering the age of her elder son (Golaud) it is clear that she was not born in the castle and therefore must have married into the family.

[15] Martin-Harvey, the Pelléas of the first English stage production in 1898, suggested something along these lines, though he seems to have forgotten that Pelléas's corpse had been dumped into Blind Man's Spring. He described the scene as 'that strange prologue in which the servants in a scared body at last force open the door of the castle, which has remained closed, grown over with tangled briars, since the body of Pelléas had been discovered prone upon the door-step. "Strange", because Maeterlinck has introduced this scene to open the tragedy rather than to close it'. According to Harvey, Mrs Patrick Campbell, the Mélisande of the production, considered the scene 'eccentric', and it was thus omitted, along with the third and fourth scenes of act III (Debussy's act III, scenes 2 and 3). See Martin-Harvey, *The Autobiography of Sir John Martin-Harvey* (London, 1933), p. 388.

[16] Additional layers of interpretation have been proposed by others. Gaston Compère, for example, believes the gesture refers to the washing of original sin; see his *Maurice Maeterlinck* (Paris, 1990), p. 181. A more metaphorical explanation has also been proposed by Maryse Descamps: that the inability to wash the threshold clean represents the impossibility of reversing the force of destiny; see her *Maurice Maeterlinck* (Brussels, 1986), p. 77.

30

Golaud's return home with his bride, the celebration prompting the opening of the door would then become some event far in the future, perhaps even the wedding of Mélisande's daughter, an occasion that might inspire the hope that she would fulfil the destiny Arkël had imagined for her mother: to 'open the door of the new era. . .'[17] In this analysis, the entire action of the play becomes a re-enactment of past events – like the showing of a film, as opposed to a 'live' drama that appears to be happening in the present.[18]

Balancing the circular (and circularising) prologue of act I is the concluding act V, an epilogue in two scenes, the first, like act I, scene 1, involving the women servants. They are gathered in a lower hall of the castle, discussing the recent, tragic events while waiting to be called upstairs. The children, who had been screaming outside, are suddenly silent and huddle together. The old servant takes this as a sign that it is time to go upstairs, and they all exit in silence. The second scene finds Mélisande on her deathbed, three days after having given birth to her daughter. Approximately nine minutes into the scene, immediately after Mélisande utters her final words and lapses into the sleep from which she will never awaken, the servants ominously enter the room and stand silently against the wall. Now, the question arises: how do we explain the time that elapsed between the exit of the servants at the end of scene 1 and their arrival in Mélisande's bedroom, about nine minutes later, in scene 2? Certainly in a large, old castle there may be many steps to climb from the lower hall, and perhaps, too, the servants waited outside the room in order to enter at the 'right' moment. But such 'rational' explanations are hardly satisfactory. A more intriguing possibility is that the two scenes portray in succession events that take place at the same time.[19] Indeed, considering the playing times of the two scenes, it is as if they 'begin' in different physical spaces but at the same moment, and then merge in both time and space. Alternatively, one might say that time moves backwards for the

17 'Et c'est toi, maintenant, qui vas ouvrir la porte à l'ère nouvelle que j'entrevois . . .' (act IV, scene 2).

18 This distinction between film and play is made by J. B. Priestley, *Man and Time* (London and New York, 1964, reprinted New York, 1989), p. 121.

19 Maryse Descamps discusses this aspect of act V in *Maurice Maeterlinck*, pp. 82–5.

beginning of scene 2, or perhaps even that time is suspended at the beginning of scene 2 and only resumes when the servants enter the room – suggesting that Mélisande had been living on borrowed time, that she was somehow not of this world.

Such temporal distortions, particularly in the discrepancy between 'stage time' and 'real time', are not without precedent in the history of the theatre. The most celebrated, perhaps, is Shakespeare's *Othello*, with its so-called 'double-time scheme', described as early as 1850.[20] Maeterlinck acknowledged an indebtedness to Shakespeare, translated *Macbeth*, and even described his play *La Princesse Maleine* as 'a mere Shak[e]spiterie'.[21] Parallels between *Pelléas* and *Othello* are as basic as their plots. Both are 'domestic' tragedies in which a jealous husband's suspicion of his wife's infidelity results in her death.

Quite apart from issues of influence or dramaturgical technique, Maeterlinck's philosophical justification for a repeatable or extended present may perhaps be traced to a comment in his article from later in the decade, entitled 'The Future': that 'time is a mystery which we have arbitrarily divided into a past and a future, in order to try and understand something of it. In itself, it is almost certain that it is but an immense, eternal, motionless Present...'[22]

Acts I and V thus offer different kinds of departures from 'real' time: in the former a series of scenes depict events as being of the past, while in the latter we are shown alternate versions of the present. The associated reversals and distortions of time, together with the fragmentary quality of individual scenes, contribute to the dream-like atmosphere often ascribed to the play. As Sigmund Freud similarly observed in 1897, fantasies and dreams are characterised by temporal distortions and

[20] Norman Sanders (ed.), *Othello*, by William Shakespeare (Cambridge, 1984), pp. 14–16.

[21] W. D. Halls, *Maurice Maeterlinck: A Study of his Life and Thoughts* (Oxford, 1960), p. 26.

[22] Maurice Maeterlinck, *Thoughts from Maeterlinck*, ed. E.S.S. [Esther Stella Sutro] (New York, 1903), p. 185. The article appeared in *Fortnightly Review* (1899–1900) and was reprinted in *Le temple enseveli* (Paris, 1902), p. 287: '... le Temps est un mystère que nous avons arbitrairement divisé en passé et en avenir, pour essayer d'y comprendre quelque chose. En soi, il est à peu près certain qu'il n'est qu'un immense Présent, éternel, immobile'.

'a process of fragmentation in which chronological relations in particular are neglected'.[23]

Of course, Maeterlinck's decision to cut the watchtower scene from act I and the associated rearrangement of scenes eliminated the circularity of the act and obscured the flashback nature of the central scenes. Furthermore, for an 1894 revival of the play by Lugné-Poe's *Théâtre de l'Oeuvre*, the time reversals may have been completely eliminated from the play through the suppression of both servant scenes, which, according to the programme, was the playwright's wish.[24] If so, key factors concerning the perception of time were shrouded in silence and thereby made unknowable. Since Maeterlinck, at a meeting with Debussy in November 1893, advised him to make certain cuts in the opera – cuts which the composer characterised as both very important and very useful[25] – it is surely no coincidence that the two servant scenes were among the four that Debussy omitted. Significantly, however, Maeterlinck never sought to remove the servant scenes from his printed text, even though he twice had the opportunity to do so when he revised the play for publication, first in 1898 and again in 1902.[26] Furthermore, he apparently had second thoughts about eliminating act V, scene 1. For a performance of the play at his home, the Abbaye de Saint-Wandrille, on 28 August 1910, with Georgette Leblanc as Mélisande, the servant scene of act I was omitted, but that of act V was performed.[27]

[23] Notes enclosed in a letter dated 25 May 1897 in *The Standard Edition of the Complete Psychological Works of Sigmund Freud*, trans. and ed. James Strachey (London, 1966), vol. I, p. 252, quoted in Kern, *The Culture of Time and Space*, p. 31.

[24] 'Selon l'indication de l'auteur les scènes des servantes seront supprimées.' The first page of the programme is reproduced as slide 8 in Katharine J. Worth, *Maeterlinck in Performance* (Alexandria, Virginia, 1984). This direction is rather surprising in view of the importance that Maeterlinck previously ascribed to act V, scene 1. For the première production (17 May 1893) he had personally recommended Louise France for the role of the old servant in that scene, explaining in a letter to Lugné-Poe that he considered the role (and by extension, the scene) important for preparing the mood of the final scene. (See Lugné-Poe, *Le sot du tremplin*, p. 237.)

[25] Letter to Ernest Chausson, reproduced in Debussy, *Correspondence*, pp. 92–4.

[26] The second revision appeared in the second volume of Maeterlinck's *Théâtre*, the three-volume collection of his plays, published in 1901–2.

[27] The programme is reproduced in facsimile in Roger Bodart, *Maurice Maeterlinck ou l'absurde dépassé* (Brussels, 1960), p. 37.

33

Without the servant scenes the entire action gives the illusion of unfolding in the 'present'. Debussy's motivation for removing the two other scenes – Maeterlinck's act II, scene 4, and act III, scene 1 – may also have been related to considerations of time. Both are non-contiguous with the adjacent scenes within the same act in that their relationship *in time* to those scenes is not well defined. The first three scenes of act II transpire in a single day, from shortly before noon until night-time, but there is no clue as to how much time elapses before scene 4, in which Arkël persuades Pelléas to delay his departure; presumably this conversation takes place at least a few days later.[28] Similarly, act III, scenes 2–4 (Debussy's scenes 1–3) cover a single twelve-hour period, from shortly before midnight to around noon the next day; scene 1, however, is temporally more clearly defined in relation to act II than it is to the scenes that follow it in act III.[29]

While Debussy's excision of the four scenes eliminated the temporal reversals and some of the dislocations – thus making the text ostensibly more 'realistic' – the orchestral interludes connecting the scenes within each act enhanced the dream-like qualities of Maeterlinck's dramatic fragments by blurring their edges. This was particularly true in the opera's early

---

[28] Maeterlinck evidently had doubts about the placement of this scene. In the Morgan Library draft the scene was initially the first of act III and was then moved to follow act II, scene 1, before it reached its definitive place.

[29] In act III, scene 1 Pelléas and Mélisande discuss Golaud's rapid recovery from the injuries that he sustained in falling from his horse, an event which took place in act II. There are admittedly parallels between the first two scenes of act III – Mélisande sings the same song in both scenes, and in both, Golaud interrupts a nighttime meeting of Pelléas and Mélisande – but their temporal relationship is not specified. Maeterlinck's act III, scene 5 is also noncontiguous with the act's central scenes, but it was retained by Debussy as his act III, scene 4. The four scenes of act IV take place within a single day, and Debussy set them all. See David Grayson, *The Genesis of Debussy's 'Pelléas et Mélisande'* (Ann Arbor, 1986), pp. 118–20, for further discussion and speculation as to Debussy's motivation for excising the four scenes.

Applied to Maeterlinck's play, the test of temporal contiguity within the unit of the act yields a consistent pattern of progressive concentration. Act I, the servant scene apart, has scenes separated by more than six months and more than three days, respectively; no two scenes are contiguous. Both acts II and III, as noted, have three contiguous 'central' scenes which are followed and/or preceded by noncontiguous 'outer' scenes. In act IV all four scenes are contiguous (and in the original production of the opera they were even merged into two tableaux of two scenes each). Finally, act V involves temporal overlap.

form with the original, short interludes, before they were expanded in order to provide sufficient time for the set changes required in the première production. By and large, Debussy's 'strategy' in planning the original interludes was to sustain and dissipate the atmosphere of the scene's ending as 'absolute' music (and thereby elevate it to a higher order of intangibility and mystery), then to ease into the mood of the next scene's opening. As I have discussed elsewhere, one striking feature of some of the interlude expansions was a reliance on 'themes of foreboding' (to use Wagnerian terminology): orchestral themes whose symbolic or even mimetic associations are not defined until their recurrences in the scenes that follow.[30] A telling example is the theme associated with the bolting of Golaud's horse, which is first heard in the interlude connecting the first two scenes of act II.[31] It is not until scene 2, however, that we learn its significance, when it accompanies Golaud's narrative of how his horse inexplicably bolted, throwing him as the clock struck noon. From scene 1 we know that this was precisely the moment when Mélisande's wedding ring fell irretrievably into the well. The telepathic talent of Golaud's horse thus finds musical correspondence in Debussy's thematic handling, but with temporal distance (in the opera) serving as a substitute or metaphor for spatial distance. In this manner, telepathy (or clairvoyance) is linked with prophecy. On a more modest scale musical telepathy (or perhaps more accurately, prophecy) is invoked whenever the *leitmotifs* of the characters are introduced in the orchestra in anticipation of their entrances, as is characteristically found in the music that immediately precedes the opening of each scene. In the play these extrasensory powers belong to animals, like Golaud's horse, and to children (who are suddenly silent when they sense that Mélisande is about to die), in other words, beings who are instinctive or intuitive rather than rational, who are preconscious or naive.[32] The ability to prophesy is similarly associated with the subconscious when Pelléas's father, who is emerging from a near-fatal illness, accurately predicts that his son does not have long to live (act IV,

---

[30] David Grayson, 'The Interludes of *Pelléas et Mélisande*', *Cahiers Debussy*, 12–13 (1988–9), 100-22.

[31] Ibid., 117.

[32] Maeterlinck's interest in telepathy led him in April 1892 to conduct a series of (unsuccessful) experiments in telepathic communication with Charles Van Lerberghe, who was living in Brussels while Maeterlinck was in Ghent. See Halls, *Maurice Maeterlinck*, p. 34.

scene 1). In Pelléas's words, his father is still partly in 'the other world', but we might profitably reformulate this phrase to read, 'the world of the "other"' – a world of 'alterity' whose inhabitants share the extrasensory powers just described. This world would also include the women servants, who are the first to sense that Mélisande has died, and who belong by virtue of their gender and class. It would also include Pelléas and Mélisande, the latter because she is a woman and a foreigner in the kingdom of Allemonde, and the former because he is young, naive, and, it has been suggested, sexually ambiguous.[33] Both foretell their own tragic ends.[34]

[33] Pelléas was labelled a homosexual even before the opera's première through a malicious play on words when some individuals intent on denigrating the work scurrilously dubbed it *Pédéraste et Médisante* (Pederast and Scandal-monger). See Pierre Lalo, *De Rameau à Ravel*, (Paris, 1947), p. 368. Similar insinuations were made relative to male enthusiasts of the opera in Jean Lorrain's infamous article, 'Les Pelléastres', printed in *Le Journal* of 22 January 1904 and reproduced in the posthumously published volume *Pelléastres. Le poison de la littérature* (Paris, 1910).

More recently, Ned Rorem has suggested that Pelléas and Marcellus might have been lovers, arguing that this would provide a compelling motivation for the former's strong desire to leave his father's sickbed to visit his dying friend and also explain his resentment of those who prevent his departure. Rorem commented further: 'If only one baritone could determine that, for himself, Pelléas was or was not homophilic (at least so far as Marcellus is involved), the role, and by extension the music for the role, would shed its habitual sappiness and don a carnal dimension, a fullness, a reasonableness that only Martial Singher has thus far lent to it.' 'The Mélisande Notebook' in Rorem, *Setting the tone. Essays and a Diary* (New York, 1983), p. 256; the essay is reprinted from *Opera News* (4 March 1978).

Maeterlinck merely emphasised the character's youth and revealed that Pelléas represented himself at age eighteen (Martin-Harvey, *The Autobiography*, p. 201). For the stage première the part had been assigned to a woman, as it was in a subsequent production (1904–5) in which the sixty-year-old Sarah Bernhardt played the role *en travesti* opposite Mrs Patrick Campbell. Debussy, however, was determined to defend the masculinity (and heterosexuality) of the character. With evident distaste he considered a female Pelléas for the second season of performances of his opera (1902–3). He wrote to conductor André Messager that producer Albert Carré had suggested that the role be entrusted to soprano Jeanne Raunay, who had 'confessed an irregular love for Pelléas, which, in the present case, curiously smacks of lyrical onanism or, to be less clinical, narcissism. On the whole, Pelléas has none of the amorous ways of a Hussar, and his belated manly resolve is so abruptly cut short by Golaud's sword that perhaps there would be no drawback to this substitution? In other respects, I admit, I would need to see . . . Without even speaking of the sexual shift, there

In Debussy's view, music is gendered female (he wrote, 'Those devoted to Art are irretrievably in love with her, and, besides, it is impossible to know how feminine music is. . .'),[35] and in his opera it, too, aligns with alterity. It, too, exhibits a capacity for telepathy and prophecy and, by extension, associates with the pre- or subconscious. Operating in a realm transcending reason, it, too, offers insight. Correspondingly, the musical style eschews 'rational' tonality in favour of 'ambiguous' modal and whole-tone constructions, and it avoids linear, goal-oriented progressions in favour of static or circular patterns.[36]

While the *leitmotifs* of reminiscence and presentiment restore to the opera a temporal freedom whose explicitness was effaced through Debussy's elimination of the time-reversing scenes, one motive achieved even greater independence, freedom from all referential function (thus anticipating the modern concept of the 'free play of signifiers'), as a result of an 'accident' of the compositional process. Debussy's setting of act III, scene 3 (the scene at the exit of the vaults) originally included the scene's closing lines: Golaud observes something on the road toward the forest, which Pelléas identifies as flocks being led to town. 'They are crying like lost children,' says Golaud. 'It seems they already smell the butcher. It will be time to go back. What a fine day! What a wonderful day for the harvest!. . .'[37] The

is a sonic shift that worries me a little; consequently I have more curiosity than real liking for this idea.' Debussy, *L'Enfance de 'Pelléas'. Lettres de Claude Debussy à André Messager*, ed. Jean André-Messager (Paris, 1938), pp. 31–2.

34 Pelléas, in act IV, scene 1, accurately predicts that the day will end badly, and Mélisande, in act II, scene 1, warns Golaud that she will die if she remains in Allemonde.

35 'Je n'ose le croire, les passionnés d'art étant d'irréductibles amoureux, et, d'autre part, on ne saura jamais combien la musique est femme. . . .' 'Le bilan musical en 1903', *Gil Blas* (28 June 1903); English version in *Debussy on Music*, trans. and ed. Richard Langham Smith (New York, 1977), p. 215.

36 These aspects of Debussy's style are discussed in Arthur Wenk, *Claude Debussy and Twentieth-Century Music* (Boston, 1983), pp. 56–61.

37 'Ils pleurent comme des enfants perdus; on dirait qu'ils sentent déjà le boucher. – Il sera temps de rentrer. – Quelle belle journée! Quelle admirable journée pour la moisson! . . .' 'Il sera temps de rentrer' was Debussy's replacement for 'Il sera temps d'aller dîner', which appeared in the 1892 edition of the play. Debussy's musical setting is contained in the *particelle*, act III, ff. 19 recto – 19 verso (Koch 15; Frederick R. Koch Foundation Collection, on deposit in the Pierpont Morgan Library, New York).

DAVID GRAYSON

Example 2.1. Debussy, *Pelléas et Mélisande,* act III, scene 3 (*particelle,* act III, fols. 19 recto – 19 verso; Frederick R. Koch Foundation Collection, on deposit in the Pierpont Morgan Library, New York). The transcription reproduces the final version, except in the case of the vocal line in bars 6–7, where the revision is somewhat ambiguous and is thus offered on a separate stave. Bars 14–15 constitute a revision in the manuscript, the instrumental

portion notated on separate staves, and, as the transcription shows, seem
to have been conceived without key signature. Irregularities in Debussy's
rhythmic notation have been rationalised. (The first and last bars of the
example correspond to bars 406 and 407 of the definitive version of act III,
i.e. bars 3 and 4 on p. 157 of the Durand vocal score.)

music accompanying this passage contains three principal motives (see ex. 2.1): one representing the flocks (bars 5–10), a second heard during Goulaud's exclamation, 'What a fine day!' (bars 14–15)[38] and a third for his closing line, 'What a wonderful day for the harvest!' (bars 16–19).[39] The

[38] The ascending four-note scalic pattern resembles the cor anglais figure in bar 5 of 'Nuages', from the *Nocturnes* for orchestra.

[39] This motive is a reharmonisation and transformation of one heard earlier in the scene.

40

Ditto

second of these motives also appears in the interlude following the scene,[40] remaining there even after the episode was eliminated. As a result, the motive appears in the opera without its dramatic *raison d'être*: the reverberation of a sentiment that has been left unexpressed. Once again, the key to unlocking the mystery has been shrouded in silence. The two other motives

[40] This motive was not part of the original draft but was added, both within the scene and in the interlude, as a revision.

41

Example 2.2a. Debussy, *Estampes*: 'Pagodes' bars 15–18

Example 2.2b. Debussy, *Pour le piano*: 'Prélude' bars 43–7

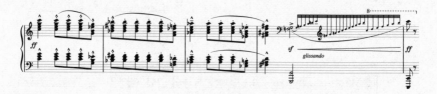

did not go to waste either: at least it could be argued that Debussy transformed and 'recycled' them in two piano pieces composed around the time of the première of *Pelléas*: the former in 'Pagodes' from the *Estampes* of 1903, and the latter in the 'Prélude' from *Pour le piano* of 1901.[41] (Compare ex. 2.2a with ex. 2.1, bars 7–8, and ex. 2.2b with ex. 2.1, bars 16–17.)

One of the more curious documents pertaining to the opera's early history is the *livret* published for the première – 'curious' because its numerous, and serious, defects rendered it virtually useless for its intended purpose.[42] Probably as a consequence of the estrangement of composer and playwright that followed the assignment of the role of Mélisande to Mary Garden in preference to Maeterlinck's mistress Georgette Leblanc, the editor who prepared this volume apparently had no access to Debussy's

[41] Roy Howat has shown, similarly, that some material originally conceived for 'Ibéria' found its way into 'La cathédrale engloutie'. See his introduction to Claude Debussy, *Préludes*, book I. *The autograph score* (New York, 1987), p. ix.

[42] '*Pelléas et Mélisande*', *drame lyrique en cinq actes, tiré du théâtre de Maurice Maeterlinck, musique de Claude Debussy*, Edition spéciale pour la France (Brussels, 1902). A copy is in the Bibliothèque de l'Arsenal, Paris, Fonds Rondel, Re 16.673. Another, in the collection of James J. Fuld, is listed in his *The Book of World-Famous Libretti: The Musical Theater from 1598 to Today* (New York, 1984), pp. 246–7.

score and was given only rudimentary information about the textual relationship between play and opera. While Debussy's text was based on the original 1892 edition of the play,[43] the *livret* relied exclusively on the 1902 edition.[44] Furthermore, Debussy's modifications of the text were not incorporated, and the only 'editing' that was done was to omit entire scenes – unfortunately, not always the right ones. Some scenes that Debussy had set were inadvertently omitted,[45] and one that he had left out was erroneously included.[46] The cast list also includes one character from the play – the porter – who appears neither in the opera nor elsewhere in the *livret*.

Two passages in act V of the *livret*, however, include text that is found in no other published source. In the doctor's opening speech the *livret* includes the phrase 'that you have caused her' in the sentence, 'It cannot be from that little wound *that you have caused her* that she is dying.'[47] This rather indiscreet accusation appears in none of the published editions of the play, nor is it found in any draft of the opera, which quotes the line according to the original edition of the play: 'It cannot be from that little wound that she might die.'[48] In a similar vein, Golaud's first speech contains a blunt and anguished confession which is likewise unique to the *livret*: 'I have killed Pelléas without having meant to, in my blind rage! ... I was a mad fiend, and with the same heinousness I wanted to kill her whom I loved too

---

[43] He made numerous cuts and also some modifications, drawn in part from Maeterlinck's own revised texts, published in 1898 and 1902. For a discussion of Debussy's editing of the libretto see Grayson *The Genesis*, pp. 113–32

[44] Thus, for example, Mélisande's song in act III is not 'Mes longs cheveux', published in the 1892 edition and set by Debussy, but 'Les trois soeurs aveugles', which replaced it in subsequent editions.

[45] Debussy's act III, scene 3 and act IV, scene 1. The libretto also omitted act IV, scene 3, which Debussy composed but which was omitted from performances at the Opéra-Comique during the première season. The erroneous omission of the two scenes in act IV might have resulted from a miscommunication from the Opéra-Comique. Producer Albert Carré originally planned to stage the act in two tableaux of two scenes each and only during rehearsals decided to cut scene 3. If told that the scene included only two tableaux, the editor of the libretto might reasonably have concluded that this meant two scenes and thus chose the two that corresponded to the settings used for the two tableaux: 'un appartement dans le château' and 'une fontaine dans le parc'.

[46] Maeterlinck's act III, scene 1.

[47] 'Ce n'est pas de cette petite blessure que vous lui avez faite qu'elle se meurt.'

[48] 'Ce n'est pas de cette petite blessure qu'elle peut mourir.'

much . . .'[49] A likely explanation for the appearance of these lines is that the editor of the *livret* was working, not from the final state of the 1902 edition, but from a corrected draft or a set of proofs that were not in definitive form. Indeed certain other of Maeterlinck's revisions to the play also tended to make descriptions more explicit, while elsewhere he curtailed the characteristic repetitiousness of the dialogue to produce conversation that sounded more 'natural'.[50] The cumulative effect of such changes was to abridge some of the very features that define symbolist drama. In the playwright's *oeuvre*, after all, examples of bourgeois naturalism and fairy-tale symbolism stand side by side, and in *Pelléas* those elements commingle – as we have seen, even in Allemonde they keep one eye on the clock.[51] In the case of the revisions to the *livret*, however, Maeterlinck evidently had second thoughts about such blunt, even violent, descriptive additions and removed them prior to publication.

The operatic world that Debussy's *Pelléas* entered at its first performance was quite different from the one in which it was first conceived, nearly a decade earlier. If the earliest drafts were haunted (to use his own characterisation) by 'the ghost of old Klingsor, alias R. Wagner',[52] by the time of the première he evidently considered the newer realist and naturalist operas to be his principal 'competition'. That he sought to beat them at their own game is evident from a note entitled 'Why I wrote *Pelléas*', in which he stated: 'The drama of *Pelléas* . . . despite its atmosphere of dreams contains much more humanity than those so-called documents of real life. . . The characters in this opera try to sing like real people.'[53] Indeed, as I have demonstrated elsewhere, one aspect of Debussy's revisions of the vocal parts was to make the melodic contours and dramatic pacing more vivid, varied, and flexible, in short, more realistic than they had been in some early

---

[49] 'J'ai tué Pelléas sans l'avoir entendu dans ma fureur aveugle!... J'étais un démon fou, et dans la même horreur j'ai voulu tuer celle que j'avais trop aimée...' These lines are inserted after 'Est-ce que ce n'est pas à faire pleurer les pierres!...'

[50] See Grayson *The Genesis*, pp. 114–17.

[51] The classic account of *Pelléas* as bourgeois naturalism is Virgil Thomson's tongue-in-cheek essay-review for the *New York Herald Tribune* (30 January 1944), reprinted in Thomson: *The Musical Scene* (New York, 1945), pp. 165–7.

[52] Debussy's letter to Chausson, dated 2 October 1893; in Claude Debussy, *Correspondence*, pp. 87–9.

[53] Langham Smith (trans. and ed.), *Debussy on Music*, pp. 75.

drafts, which relied on a style of disembodied, formulaic, and sometimes near-monotone chanting,[54] ostensibly more attuned to symbolist drama and likely imitative of the special, stylised manner of intoning lines used by Lugné-Poe's troupe for the stage première of *Pelléas*.[55] These progressive tendencies – towards certain features more closely associated with realism – are hardly surprising in view of the changing cultural landscape during the decade throughout which Debussy composed and revised his opera. But if he felt a desire to embrace aspects of realism, he obviously did so without losing sight of his opera's symbolist roots. Indeed, as I hope to have shown here, certain of his revisions (as well as Maeterlinck's own) may be interpreted precisely in those terms, as preserving a tension and balance between the sometimes opposing values of realism and symbolism.[56]

It has been said of symbolist art that its quest for a rarefied atmosphere of vague mystery carried with it the risk of sacrificing both plausibility and humanity.[57] Debussy's avoidance of these pitfalls, in part by reinforcing certain of the play's realist aspects, has resulted in a work capable of accommodating a range of performance styles and adaptable to changing aesthetic fashions. This, along with its sheer beauty, has doubtless contributed to its continued theatrical viability and longevity.

---

[54] This tendency is illustrated in Grayson, 'The opera: genesis and sources' in Roger Nichols and Richard Langham Smith, *Claude Debussy, 'Pelléas et Mélisande'* (Cambridge, 1989), pp. 42–7.

[55] Gertrude Rathbone Jasper, *Adventure in the Theatre. Lugné-Poe and the Théâtre de l'Oeuvre to 1899* (New Brunswick, New Jersey, 1947), pp. 249–50.

[56] This aspect of the opera and play is discussed by Pierre Boulez in an essay that accompanied his 1970 recording of the opera and was reprinted in *Orientations. Collected Writings of Pierre Boulez*, ed. Jean-Jacques Nattiez, trans. Martin Cooper (Cambridge, Massachusetts, 1986), pp. 306–17.

[57] Cecil M. Bowra, *The Heritage of Symbolism* (London and New York, 1943), pp. 12–14.

Appendix: A discarded scene from *Pelléas et Mélisande*

The scene which follows derives from an autograph manuscript draft of Maeterlinck's *Pelléas et Mélisande* in the Dannie and Hettie Heineman Collection of the Pierpont Morgan Library, New York. This scene, which Maeterlinck eliminated prior to publication, originally came between the current scenes 3 and 4 of Act I of the play (i.e. Act I, scenes 1 and 2 of the opera which omits the first scene of the play). Previously unpublished, the scene portrays the final moments of the vigil held by Arkël, Geneviève and Pelléas as they await Golaud's return home with his bride, Mélisande. The scene was still part of the drama as late as 30 March 1892, just a few weeks before the publication of the play in May. The scene is reproduced with the unfamiliar spellings of Pélléas and Arkël found in the autograph and the first edition of the play.

Pélléas et Mélisande

ACTE I SCÈNE 4

Au pied d'une des tours du château

(Entrent Arkël, Geneviève et Pélléas.)

ARKËL: Le vent est trop violent du côté de la mer. Il me secouait comme une plante . . . Asseyons-nous ici à l'abri de la grande tour; le veilleur nous avertira s'il aperçoit quelque chose au large . . . Le vent m'a fatigué comme si j'avais gravi une montagne.

PÉLLÉAS: Il est dur comme une barre de fer. Il souffle du sud sans reprendre haleine un instant. On dirait qu'il a peur de perdre une minute de cette nuit. Ils auront vent arrière tout le temps . . .

GENEVIÈVE: Es-tu sûr que le vent n'éteindra pas la lampe, Pélléas?

PÉLLÉAS: J'ai monté tout à l'heure à la tour; la lampe est à l'abri du moindre souffle.

GENEVIÈVE: Tu n'as rien vu sur la mer?

46

PÉLLÉAS: Je n'ai vu que les vagues qui sont assez hautes cette nuit . . . La lune entrait déjà dans la mer.

GENEVIÈVE: Est-il vraiment si tard que cela?

PÉLLÉAS: Il y a longtemps que minuit est sonné.

GENEVIÈVE: Le veilleur, sait-il que nous sommes ici?

PÉLLÉAS: Il sonnera la cloche s'il aperçoit du navire.

GENEVIÈVE: Je crains qu'il ne s'endorme; il est très vieux . . .

PÉLLÉAS: Nous allons voir s'il s'est endormi . . . Claudius! Claudius! Holà! Claudius! . . ne vois-tu rien venir?

LA VOIX DU VEILLEUR: Il y a une clarté dans le ciel! . . .

PÉLLÉAS: De quel côté y a-t-il une clarté dans le ciel?

LA VOIX DU VEILLEUR: Du côté où le soleil va se lever . . .

PÉLLÉAS: Ce n'est pas par là qu'ils viendront. Il faut regarder vers le sud.

LA VOIX DU VEILLEUR: On ne voit plus bien loin . . . Il y a un brouillard sur la mer . . .

GENEVIÈVE: Ne faites pas de bruit; le roi s'est endormi contre la tour . . .

PÉLLÉAS: Où est-il? – Je le distingue à peine. – Il fait noir par ici. – C'est étrange, il n'y a pas d'étoiles de ce côté. Il a l'air malheureux quand il dort. – Il a l'air si vieux quand il est immobile! . . Regardez, regardez! – J'ai pitié de tout ce que je vois . . .

GENEVIÈVE: Il n'est pas à l'abri du vent. Voyez comme sa barbe blanche est agitée. Donne-lui ton manteau, Pélléas. Il n'est pas encore à l'abri du vent. On ne peut pas l'abriter du vent. – As-tu froid, Pélléas? Tu es bien pâle ce soir . . .

PÉLLÉAS: Non, non; ce n'est rien. C'est peut-être le sommeil. – Mes yeux se ferment d'eux-mêmes.

GENEVIÈVE: Va dormir un instant, mon enfant. Je veillerai seule; les femmes veillent mieux que les hommes.

PÉLLÉAS: Non, non; ce n'est pas la peine. Le soleil est sur le point de se lever. Je dormirai pendant le jour. Je dormirai tant que je veux, plus tard. – Ecoutez donc, entendez-vous des cris dans la fôret?

GENEVIÈVE: Ce sont des bêtes de nuit qui s'entretuent. Il fait noir de ce côté-là . . .

PÉLLÉAS: C'est une bête que d'autres poursuivent. Elle s'approche au lac . . . Je l'entends du bruit de la terre . . . Elle ne pourra plus leur échapper. – J'ai peur, maintenant, que la lampe ne s'éteigne. Il me semble que le vent a tourné. (On entend sonner une cloche.) – La cloche! la cloche! Ils sont là!

ARKËL (s'éveillant en sursaut): Oh! oh! Ils font trembler la tour! . . .

LA VOIX DU VEILLEUR: Un navire! un navire! Il entre dans le port! . . .

GENEVIÈVE: Allons à leur rencontre! Il est là! – Venez! Venez! Venez! (Elle sort avec Arkël.)

PÉLLÉAS: Où donc est mon manteau? – Je ne vois pas à deux pas devant moi. Il fait plus noir ici qu'au centre de la terre. – S'ils n'étaient pas venus cette nuit, je n'attendrais plus. Maintenant je ne reverrai plus celui qui va mourir ... Mes chevaux étaient prêts cependant ... Je ne parviendrai pas à boucler ma ceinture ... Claudius! Claudius! où en est le navire?

LA VOIX DU VEILLEUR: Il est dans le port! Il est dans le port!

PÉLLÉAS: Ils vont vite! Ils vont vite! Pourquoi n'as-tu pas averti plus tôt?

LA VOIX DU VEILLEUR: À cause du brouillard; on ne voit pas très loin ...

PÉLLÉAS: Vois-tu ce qui descend du navire?

LA VOIX DU VEILLEUR: Il en descend bien des choses; bien des choses ...

DES VOIX *(dans le lointain)*: Pélléas! Pélléas! Pélléas!

PÉLLÉAS: Je viens! je viens! je viens! ...

(Il sort.)

Pélléas et Mélisande

ACT I SCÈNE 4

At the foot of one of the castle towers

(Enter Arkël, Geneviève and Pélléas.)

ARKËL: The wind is too strong over by the sea. It shook me like a plant ... Let's sit here in the shelter of the main tower; the watchman will warn us if there's anything out to sea ... The wind has tired me as if I'd climbed a mountain.

PÉLLÉAS: It's as strong as an iron bar. It's blowing from the south without letting up to catch its breath. You might say it's frightened of losing even a minute of its force. They'll have the wind in their sails all the way ...

GENEVIÈVE: Are you sure the wind won't blow out the lamp, Pélléas?

PÉLLÉAS: I've just been up the tower; the lamp is sheltered from even the slightest breath.

GENEVIÈVE: You saw nothing out to sea?

PÉLLÉAS: I only saw the waves: they're very high tonight ... The moon has already gone down into the sea.

GENEVIÈVE: Is it really as late as that?

PÉLLÉAS: Midnight struck a long time ago.

GENEVIÈVE: Does the watchman know we're here?

PÉLLÉAS: He'll ring the bell if he catches sight of a ship.

GENEVIÈVE: I'm afraid he'll fall asleep; he is so old ...

PÉLLÉAS: We'll see if he's fallen asleep ... Claudius! Claudius! Holà! Claudius! Can you see anything?

VOICE OF THE WATCHMAN: There's a light on the skyline! . . .

PÉLLÉAS: On which side is there light on the skyline?

VOICE OF THE WATCHMAN: Over where the sun's about to rise . . .

PÉLLÉAS: They won't be coming from over there. You must look towards the South.

VOICE OF THE WATCHMAN: You can't see very far any more . . . There's a mist on the sea.

GENEVIÈVE: Don't make a noise; the king has fallen asleep by the tower.

PÉLLÉAS: Where is he? I can hardly make him out. – It's so dark over here. – It's strange, but there are no stars over on this side. How sad he looks when he's asleep. – He looks so old when he's still! . . . Look, look! – I pity everything I see . . .

GENEVIÈVE: He isn't sheltered from the wind. See how his white beard is trembling. Give him your cloak, Pélléas. He's still not sheltered from the wind. He can't be sheltered from the wind – Are you cold, Pélléas? You are very pale this evening . . .

PÉLLÉAS: No, no, it's nothing. Perhaps I'm tired – My eyes are closing of their own accord.

GENEVIÈVE: Go and sleep for a while, my child. I'll keep watch alone; women watch better than men.

PÉLLÉAS: No, no, it's not worth the trouble. The sun's about to come up. I'll sleep during the day. I'll sleep as much as I want later on. – Listen! Can you hear cries in the forest?

GENEVIÈVE: It's the night beasts killing each other. It's very dark in there.

PÉLLÉAS: It's one animal that the others are chasing. It's going towards the lake . . . I can hear their feet on the ground . . . It won't be able to escape. – Now I am frightened that the lamp will blow out. It seems to me that the wind has changed. *(The ringing of a bell is heard)* – The bell! The bell! They're here!

ARKËL *(waking brusquely)*: Oh! oh! The bells are making the tower shake! . . .

VOICE OF THE WATCHMAN: It's a ship, a ship! Coming into port! . . .

GENEVIÈVE: Let's go and meet them! He's there! – Come on! Come on! Come on! *(She goes out with Arkël)*

PÉLLÉAS: Where's my cloak? – I can hardly see two steps in front of myself. It must be darker here than at the centre of the earth. – If they hadn't come tonight, I wouldn't have waited any longer. Now I won't ever see him again – he who is going to die . . . My horses are ready, though . . . I can't seem to fasten my belt . . . Claudius! Claudius! Where is the ship?

VOICE OF THE WATCHMAN: It's in the harbour! It's in the harbour!

PÉLLÉAS: They've come so quickly! They've come so quickly! Why didn't you warn us sooner?

49

DAVID GRAYSON

VOICE OF THE WATCHMAN: It was because of the mist; you can't see very far . . .

PÉLLÉAS: Can you see who's coming off the ship?

VOICE OF THE WATCHMAN: A lot of things are coming off, a lot of things . . .

VOICES *(in the distance)*: Pélléas! Pélléas! Pélléas!

PÉLLÉAS: I'm coming, I'm coming! I'm coming!

   (He exits)

(*Translated by David Grayson and Richard Langham Smith*)

50

3 Sirens in the labyrinth: amendments in Debussy's *Nocturnes*

DENIS HERLIN

Among the orchestral works published during Debussy's lifetime, rare are those that escaped the changes he constantly made after publication. *La mer* even appeared in a second edition (*c*. 1910) while the composer was still alive. The *Nocturnes,* published in 1900 by Eugène Fromont, would no doubt have met the same fate had Debussy remained on good terms with the publisher, as he implied in a letter to Stravinsky dated 24 October 1915:

> Concerning the *Nocturnes.* . . I've made a great many changes. Unfortunately they're published by a publisher (Fromont, in the rue du Colisée) whom I no longer deal with. Another problem is that there are no copyists at the moment capable of doing this delicate work![1]

Of the three pieces in this symphonic triptych, 'Sirènes' was subjected to the highest number of amendments, as can be seen not only from Debussy's personal copy containing his autograph annotations (currently in the *Collection musicale François Lang* at Royaumont in France (subsequently referred to as the François Lang copy)[2] but also from the scores belonging to various friends of Debussy who were also conductors, such as those of Caplet[3] and Inghelbrecht,[4] all of which contain corrections not in Debussy's

---

[1] 'Pour les *Nocturnes* . . . j'ai fait de très nombreuses modifications. Malheureusement ils sont édités chez un éditeur (Fromont, rue du Colisée) avec lequel je ne suis plus en relations. Un autre ennui est qu'il n'y a pas de copistes, en ce moment, capables de faire ce travail délicat!' Letter of 24 October 1915 to Igor Stravinsky in Debussy, *Correspondance 1884–1918,* ed. François Lesure, (Paris, 1993), p. 362.†

[2] For full details see Denis Herlin, *Collection musicale François Lang* (Paris, 1993), p. 54.

[3] Now in the Bibliothèque Nationale de France, Paris (Musique), Ac. e10 684A.

[4] Currently in a private collection, Paris. The orchestral parts belonging to Inghelbrecht are in the library of Radio-France.

hand.

Only fifteen years later, a second edition of the *Nocturnes* came out, published by Jobert who had taken over the business from Fromont. This bore the added inscription '*New Edition 1930*'.[5] The reasons for this new edition are explained in a note from the publisher:

> In subsequent years, Claude Debussy revised the orchestration in his own score...
>
> With the consent of Mme Claude Debussy, we now present the definitive edition of this masterpiece.
>
> A comparative study of the previous edition with the present one will reveal profound differences, principally in 'Fêtes' and 'Sirènes', and will show Claude Debussy's evolution in the art of orchestration, an art that attains its height in the present work, one of the monuments of French orchestral music.[6]

It is this second edition that has prevailed and that is used in performance of this work in our times. Until very recently, it was assumed that the changes in the 1930 edition stemmed directly from the François Lang copy – this was what the publisher referred to as 'Debussy's own score' – and this annotated score was considered as the primary source for this new edition.

However, numerous corrections in the copies belonging to Caplet and Inghelbrecht, which were not in the François Lang copy, nevertheless appeared in this second edition. These changes in fact derived from a second annotated copy, discovered in October 1989 in France, among the effects of the heirs of Roger-Ducasse. Although a better understanding of

---

5   On 28 April 1922, Eugène Fromont sold his business to one of his clerks, Jean Jobert, for the sum of 450,000 francs.

6   'Au cours des années qui suivirent, Claude Debussy modifia l'orchestration sur sa propre partition.... Avec l'assentiment de Mme Claude Debussy, nous présentons aujourd'hui l'édition définitive de ce chef-d'oeuvre. Un examen comparatif de l'ancienne édition avec la nouvelle révèlera de profondes différences, principalement dans 'Fêtes' et 'Sirènes', et montrera l'évolution qui s'est opérée dans l'art d'orchestrer de Claude Debussy, art qui atteint son sommet dans le présent ouvrage qui constitue un des monuments de la musique symphonique française.' In 1964 Denise Jobert-Georges decided to bring out a revised edition of the *Nocturnes*. This work was undertaken by André Jouve and consisted only of the correction of the engraving errors.

the circumstances of the 1930 revision is gained from this copy, it nevertheless poses many other problems.[7]

In fact, the changes in the Roger-Ducasse copy, far from confirming those in the François Lang copy, were very often quite different, sometimes

[7] Letters between Jean Jobert and Emma Debussy in the Jobert Archives explain the circumstances of the 1930 revision: [Jean Jobert to Emma Debussy, 7 February 1930] Chère Madame, Vous savez sans doute qu'il existe une profonde différence dans l'orchestration des *Nocturnes* entre l'édition primitive (telle que je l'ai reçue de Fromont) qui est en vente et la version donnée actuellement par les Concerts Symphoniques Français qui ont modifié leur matériel d'exécution d'après les indications que le Maître leur avait données au cours des années qui ont suivi la première publication. Je possède une partition sur laquelle j'ai reporté moi-même les corrections d'après celle que possède Monsieur Roger-Ducasse. J'étudie en ce moment l'éventualité de publier l'édition correcte qui était celle voulue par le Maître et de la substituer à l'ancienne, mais je ne voudrais pas le faire sans votre approbation. Bien que cette substitution comporte une dépense importante, je pense que si ce sacrifice a pour résultat de se conformer aux intentions de Claude Debussy, il ne sera pas inutile. Vous remerciant à l'avance de vouloir bien me donner votre sentiment sur la question, veuillez croire, Chère Madame, à mes sentiments très respectueux.' (Dear Madame, You are no doubt aware, regarding the orchestration of the *Nocturnes*, that there is a great difference between the early edition (in the form in which I received it from Fromont) which is on sale and the version currently being performed by the Concerts Symphoniques Français, who have made changes in their material for performance according to the indications given to them by the composer in the years following the first publication. I own a score on which I myself have copied the corrections from the one owned by Monsieur Roger-Ducasse. I am at the moment contemplating publishing a corrected edition conforming to the composer's wishes, to replace the earlier edition, but I would not like to do so without your approval. Although this would entail a great deal of expense, I think the sacrifice would be worthwhile if it resulted in complying with the intentions of Claude Debussy. I shall be grateful if you will let me know your feelings on the matter. Thanking you in advance, Yours respectfully).

Emma replied as follows: [Emma Debussy to Jean Jobert, 9 February 1930] 'Cher Monsieur, Votre projet est louable de toutes les façons et je ne puis que vous en remercier. Ne croyez-vous pas que la partition du Maître sur laquelle il a apporté au fur et à mesure des répétitions les corrections nécessaires, vous serait utile? Voulez-vous venir Mercredi entre 2 et 3 heures pour que nous en parlions? Croyez, je vous prie, à mes sentiments sincères.' (Dear Sir, Your project is commendable in every way and I can only thank you for it. Would the composer's score on which he marked all the necessary corrections while he was rehearsing not be useful to you? Will you come on Wednesday between 2 and 3 o'clock so that we may discuss it? Yours sincerely.)

even contradictory. A brief description of the sources of this work enables us to understand the nature of the changes and divergences between the two annotated copies and to see to what extent it is possible to trace the chronology of the different corrections made by Debussy.

Apart from these two copies of the first edition, annotated by Debussy, two manuscript sources currently exist for 'Sirènes', firstly, the autograph short score, at present held in the Library of Congress, with the vocal parts noted in full and with some indications of instrumentation,[8] and secondly, the complete autograph full score, dedicated to Georges Hartmann, currently in the possession of Madame Jobert-Georges.[9]

In addition to these two manuscript sources, there also exists a second set of proofs for 'Sirènes', the first and third sets never having been found. Dedicated to Pierre Louÿs, these remained for some thirty years in the collection of Pierre Monteux in Hancock (USA) before being acquired in 1988 by the Bibliothèque Nationale in Paris.[10]

In 1900, the first edition of *Nocturnes* appeared which, apart from one or two changes, followed the autograph manuscript. It was therefore on two copies of this edition that Debussy noted his amendments from 1901 until the end of his life, an indication of his desire to perfect a work with which he was never satisfied.

The François Lang Copy

In December 1933, at the time of the sale of Debussy's library, the pianist François Lang, a great collector of first editions and music manuscripts, acquired almost all the scores annotated by the composer. For researchers interested in the genesis of the works, these annotated scores

---

[8] Library of Congress, Washington, ML 96. This short score was bought in 1927 from Lily Texier, to whom it was dedicated. See Marie Rolf, 'Orchestral Manuscripts of Claude Debussy: 1895–1905', *Musical Quarterly*, 70 (1984), 538–66.

[9] When Georges Hartmann, who had been a music publisher since 1870, sold his business to Heugel in 1891, Fromont became no more than a name. Debussy dedicated the *Nocturnes* to Hartmann.

[10] Bibliothèque Nationale de France, Paris (Musique), Rés. Vma. 354. It is inscribed with the following dedication: 'Nocturnes / pour la fanfare du Roi Pausole / et aussi pour / Pierre Louÿs / son / Claude Debussy.

constitute a source of prime importance.[11] Among them, currently held in the Abbaye de Royaumont, is a first edition of the *Nocturnes* bound in half-vellum with the dates of composition: 'December 1897 to December 1899' on the reverse of the third end-page.

Although 'Nuages' and 'Fêtes' contain amendments, the most substantial changes occur in 'Sirènes', with the annotations variously marked in lead pencil; black pencil and black ink; blue pencil and blue ink; red pencil and red ink; and green pencil and green ink. In most cases, Debussy indicates these amendments by deleting in pencil and correcting in ink. One of the difficulties of this multicoloured copy arises in trying to date the different corrections, as these are sometimes superimposed in layers.

The Roger-Ducasse Copy

Bound in half-vellum like the François Lang copy, this score includes on the cover the following autograph annotation: 'Claude Debussy/80 av: du Bois/de Boulogne'. Below this is the signature of Roger-Ducasse. The circumstances in which the latter came into possession of this copy as well as an annotated edition of *La Mer* remain mysterious. In fact, the friendship between Roger-Ducasse and Debussy developed rather late, even though their first exchange of letters dates from the first performance of *Pelléas* in 1902.[12] It was only towards the end of the composer's life that he seems to have become a close friend, although very little correspondence between them exists. A pupil and friend of Gabriel Fauré, Roger-Ducasse was well acquainted with Emma Debussy who on 2 January 1923 offered him a score of the orchestration of four unpublished pages of one of the *Proses lyriques*, 'De Grève'.[13]

[11] See Herlin, *Collection musicale François Lang*, pp. 53–9, 230-1, and 249–50.

[12] This information comes from an unpublished text by Roger-Ducasse in a private collection: 'Profondément troublé par *Pelléas*, je ne puis, après la 1ère représentation m'empêcher d'écrire mon enthousiasme. Sa réponse ne se fit attendre et, de ce jour, naquit une affection mutuelle que seule devait dénouer la mort.' (Deeply moved by *Pelléas*, I simply had to write to express my enthusiasm after the first performance. He lost no time in replying and, from then on, a mutual affection blossomed which came to an end only at his death.)

[13] Currently in a private collection in France. The orchestration of the 25 bars of the beginning of 'De Grève' is unfortunately incomplete.

Might it therefore have been Emma Debussy who presented him with the two annotated scores of Debussy? In two letters to Ernest Ansermet, Roger-Ducasse refers to the copies of *La Mer* and the *Nocturnes* in his possession,[14] although he never mentions the fact that Debussy gave him these scores, an omission which would seem to confirm that he received them from Emma Debussy.

The corrections contained in this copy are manifold. As in the case of the François Lang copy, the most substantial amendments occur in 'Sirènes'. The changes made by Debussy are generally written very carefully in red ink, while the deletions are made in blue pencil, more rarely in black pencil. Beside these autograph amendments in two colours, there are a number of corrections not by Debussy, mainly in green ink but also in lead pencil and black ink, in an unidentified hand.

These were the two copies used by conductors to correct their own scores when including the *Nocturnes* in their programmes, as was also the case with the scores used at the *Concerts Colonne*[15] and the *Concerts Lamoureux*,[16] as well as to those belonging to Caplet,[17] Inghelbrecht,[18]

---

[14] In a letter of 24 March 1939 to Ernest Ansermet, Roger-Ducasse wrote: 'J'aurais aimé vous apporter aussi l'édition précieuse des *Nocturnes* et de *La mer*, où Debussy, à chaque audition, se corrigeait lui-même, non pas en ajoutant, mais, au contraire, en émondant, à l'encre ou au crayon rouges, un nombre impressionant de mesures.' (I should also have liked to bring you the precious edition of the *Nocturnes* and of *La mer*, in which Debussy, at each new performance, corrected his own work, not by adding anything but, on the contrary, by thinning out in red ink or red pencil an impressive number of bars.) Ten years later (2 June 1949), Ducasse wrote to Ansermet again: 'Je possède les *Nocturnes* et *La mer*, les deux partitions appartenant à Debussy et revues, corrigées de sa propre main, chaque fois qu'il les réentendait. "Mon cher maître lui disais-je, si vous vivez encore vingt ans, il ne restera plus de ces deux oeuvres que les portées!"' (I own the *Nocturnes* and *La mer*, the two scores that belonged to Debussy, revised and corrected in his own hand each time he heard the compositions performed. 'My dear Maître', I said to him, 'if you go on living for another twenty years, nothing will remain of these two works except the staves!') These two letters were published by Claude Tappolet, *Lettres de compositeurs français à Ernest Ansermet* (Geneva, 1988), pp. 139–41.

[15] Bibliothèque des *Concerts Colonne*, Théâtre du Châtelet, Paris.

[16] Bibliothèque des *Concerts Lamoureux*, Salle Pleyel, Paris.

[17] See note 3.

[18] See note 4.

Ansermet,[19] and Godet.[20] No trace has been found of those belonging to Doret and Pierné. Although only secondary sources, these scores are nevertheless of great interest and constitute a major element in dating and documenting the evolution of the various amendments.

With the help of the letters, various recollections, and the copies discussed above, it is possible to date the amendments with a degree of precision. In the case of the François Lang copy, the corrections in blue and red ink are referred to very early on. In an unpublished letter dated 31 December 1903 to an unknown recipient in charge of rehearsals for the *Nocturnes* which were to be conducted by Eugène Ysaÿe, Debussy wrote as follows:

> You will receive a corrected copy of the *Nocturnes* with my apologies in advance for the trouble these corrections will undoubtedly cause you.[21]

The multiple corrections in red and blue ink and red and blue pencil are also to be found on the copies in the libraries of the *Concerts Colonne* and the *Concerts Lamoureux*. These orchestras included the *Nocturnes* in their programmes from 1904 onwards.

The corrections in green ink on this same copy seem to date from much later, probably from the last years of Debussy's life. Accounts given by Ernest Ansermet and Robert Godet, a great friend of the composer, are of prime importance in this connection. Recommended by Igor Stravinsky and Robert Godet, the young Swiss conductor paid a visit to Debussy, probably on 19 May 1917, of which he gave the following account to Jean-Claude Piguet in 1961:

> And then, after a quick survey of all our common friends, we got round to his orchestral works about which I had a good many questions to ask. When it came to the *Nocturnes* he showed me a score covered in all sorts of corrections, in ordinary pencil, blue pencil, red ink and green ink. 'Which

[19] Bibliothèque musicale, Geneva. The annotations on the score were probably made by the librarian of the *Orchestre de la Suisse Romande* from the personal score of Ernest Ansermet, still unlocated.

[20] Bibliothèque publique et universitaire, *Archives Godet*, Geneva, Ib 3671(2) Rés. The corrections made by Godet on this score follow those of Ansermet.

[21] 'Vous allez recevoir un exemplaire corrigé des *Nocturnes* et je m'en excuse à l'avance de la peine que vont vous donner ces corrections.' Letter of 31 December 1903 (Pierpont Morgan Library, New York, Koch 5, box 1).

are the right ones?' I asked. 'I'm not actually sure', he replied, 'they are all possibilities. Take this score with you and use whatever you like from it.'[22]

Debussy's evasive, disconcerting reply concerning the corrections was no doubt due to extreme tiredness caused by his illness. Ansermet, however, was so perplexed by all these revisions that Godet wrote a long letter to Debussy, dated 23 January 1918, to ask him to be more precise:

> Ansermet – that young conductor of unsound baton but sound and very likeable personality whom you said you had seen and whose conversation you had enjoyed (on Stravinsky among others) – is going to conduct the *Nocturnes* . . . Well, the said Ansermet has, with great care, taken note of the corrections in red ink marked on the score you so kindly lent him last Sunday in Paris. But there were other corrections, he tells me, in green ink, at the end of 'Sirens' (whose sea-weed hair must surely have turned similarly green). Ansermet thought he had understood that the corrections in green were merely conjectures and represented for you no more than provisional reminders; on returning the score, however, he had the impression that he had been mistaken, that your mind was set on them, and that, far from committing an indiscretion by taking note of these changes, he would have been well advised to have done just that.[23]

[22] 'Et puis, après un tour d'horizon où il fut question de nos amis communs, nous en vînmes à ses oeuvres d'orchestre sur lesquelles j'avais mainte question à lui poser. Au sujet des *Nocturnes*, il me montra une partition couverte de toutes sortes de corrections au crayon ordinaire, au crayon bleu, à l'encre rouge et à l'encre verte. "Quelles sont les bonnes?" lui dis-je. "Je ne sais plus très bien, répliqua-t-il, ce sont des possibilités. Emportez cette partition et prenez-y ce qui vous semblera bon." See Ernest Ansermet and Jean-Claude Piguet, *Entretiens sur la musique* (Neuchâtel, 1983), p. 37.

[23] 'Ansermet – ce jeune chef d'orchestre à la baguette défectueuse, mais personnellement intelligent et sympathique, que vous m'avez dit avoir reçu et apprécié pour sa conversation (sur Stravinsky entre autres) – va faire les *Nocturnes*. ... Or le dit Ansermet a relevé avec grand soin les corrections à l'encre rouge notées sur la partition que vous aviez voulu lui prêter dimanche à Paris. Mais il y en avait d'autres (me dit-il) à l'encre verte, à la fin des 'Sirènes' (dont les cheveux d'algue doivent affecter ce coloris, c'est évident). Ansermet avait cru comprendre que ces corrections vertes n'avaient qu'un caractère conjectural et ne représentaient pour vous qu'une manière de provisoire memento; en vous rendant le cahier, il a eu l'impression qu'il s'était trompé et que vous aviez arrêté votre décision dans ce sens, et que dès lors, loin de commettre une indiscrétion en prenant note aussi de ces modifications, il aurait été bien avisé de le faire.' See François Lesure, 'Cinq lettres de Robert Godet à Claude Debussy (1917–1918)', *Revue de Musicologie*, numéro spécial (1962), 92.

Unlike the early corrections which are present throughout, those in green ink do not cover the whole score. Placed not only at the end, as Godet states, but also at the beginning of 'Sirènes', they are generally very difficult to read, sometimes merely outlined, and contain important thematic changes in both the vocal and orchestral parts, which recall those of the *Fantaisie pour piano et orchestre*.[24] This would explain why Ansermet interpreted certain illegible passages in a sometimes very debatable way.[25]

Regarding the Roger-Ducasse copy, one can deduce from the address on it that the amendments were made after January 1908. It was then that Debussy's number in the Avenue du Bois de Boulogne changed from 64 to 80. Inghelbrecht's recollections are also helpful in enabling one to assess when these corrections came to an end, namely in May 1913. Indeed, for the inauguration of the Théâtre des Champs-Elysées, Gabriel Astruc planned an original musical season from April to June 1913, calling notably on the talents of the American dancer Loïe Fuller who was enthralling Paris by her performances with multicoloured veils. She undertook to create a vivid choreography for Debussy's *Nocturnes*, under the direction of the young Inghelbrecht. The latter, in his book of recollections, recounts the impromptu visit of Debussy during rehearsals for this show which was due to have its première on 5 May 1913:

> At that time I was not yet part of Debussy's circle. I was in fact greatly in awe of him, having always feared becoming too close to those composers whose works I admired. One evening, alone in the studio with the orchestra, I was working on the *Nocturnes* when suddenly the door opened and in the doorway appeared the composer himself.

> 'Why did you not call me earlier? I have made countless changes to the score which you ought to have taken into account before going ahead'.[26]

24 See Teresa Davidian, 'Debussy's *Fantaisie*: Issues, Proofs and Revisions', *Cahiers Debussy*, 17–18 (1993–4), 15–33.
25 For Ansermet's version of this work, refer to his recording of 'Sirènes' made in 1958 with the Orchestre de la Suisse Romande (Decca 414040-2).
26 'A cette époque je n'étais pas encore entré dans l'intimité de Debussy. Je la redoutais même, ayant toujours craint d'approcher de trop près les auteurs des oeuvres que j'admirais. Un soir, seul au studio avec l'orchestre, je travaillais les *Nocturnes* quand, soudain, dans l'encadrement de la porte qui venait de s'ouvrir parut l'auteur. "Pourquoi ne m'avez-vous pas appelé plus tôt? J'ai fait dans cette partition de nombreuses modifications que vous deviez connaître avant d'aller plus loin.' See D.-E. Inghelbrecht, *Mouvement contraire* (Paris, 1947), p. 184.

Table 3.1. Manuscript corrections in the François Lang and Roger-Ducasse orchestral scores of the Nocturnes and their availability

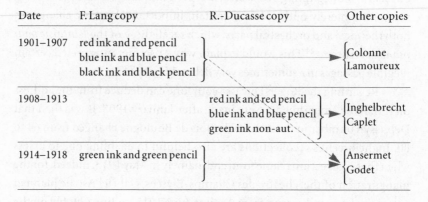

Date	F. Lang copy	R.-Ducasse copy	Other copies
1901–1907	red ink and red pencil blue ink and blue pencil black ink and black pencil		Colonne Lamoureux
1908–1913		red ink and red pencil blue ink and blue pencil green ink non-aut.	Inghelbrecht Caplet
1914–1918	green ink and green pencil		Ansermet Godet

A comparison of the changes in the Inghelbrecht and Caplet scores with those of the Roger-Ducasse copy reveals that the non-autograph corrections were equally carefully filled in. In brief, both the autograph and non-autograph corrections can be placed between 1908 and May 1913. It is certain that during this period the *Nocturnes* were included more and more frequently in concert programmes, although in general 'Sirènes', due to its 'prohibitively expensive and much sought after choir' as Debussy wrote with irony, was performed less often than the other two. [27] Debussy himself included the symphonic triptych in the programme for his concerts abroad and must certainly have felt the need to clarify these corrections. Would it not then follow that the François Lang score was a more experimental copy, while the Roger-Ducasse score was a fair copy of certain changes? Unfortunately, this tempting hypothesis brings us no nearer to an understanding of the contradictions contained in these two copies.

A summary of this complex chronology is contained in table 3.1 which shows the evolution of the corrections and the links connecting them to the scores belonging to Debussy's conductor-friends. This chronology of the different layers of corrections may enable us to follow the complex genesis of this perpetually reworked composition, but the funda-

[27] Letter of 2 June 1912 to Désiré-Emile Inghelbrecht (Bibliothèque Nationale de France, Paris).

mental question remains; that of the essential nature of the changes Debussy brought to the musical text.

Before analysing in detail the nature of these changes it is advisable to examine the reasons which drove Debussy to make the changes. Anxious that his intentions should not be betrayed, Debussy did everything possible to be present at the rehearsals of his works. It was in this spirit that he wrote to Edouard Colonne who was to conduct the *Nocturnes*:

> Dear Monsieur Colonne,
> You can count on me for Saturday morning at 11.00 ... There is still much to be done in the first Nocturne (Nuages) so as to bring out the soaring rhythm which gives it its particular character ... 'There is still a smell of oil' as mechanics say about an engine that hasn't been sufficiently well tuned ...[28]

Conductors did not always take kindly to this type of comment. But it is certain that Debussy was not satisfied with the resulting sound. Whether this was due to the state of his own orchestration or to the incapacity and technical inability of orchestras to produce what he wanted, remains an unanswered question.

In several articles, such as that by Pierre Boulez on the *Nocturnes* written in 1967,[29] this work – and 'Sirènes' in particular – is constantly discussed in terms of a process of lightening. On what is this impression based? By systematically recording all the changes it has been possible to classify the different kinds of corrections (see table 3.2). In this table, the corrections in green ink and green pencil on the François Lang copy have not been taken into account as these came later and are more problematic.

In studying this table, certain observations spring to mind. In both copies, changes involving the lightening of the instrumental parts constitute practically half the corrections. This seems to confirm the statements

---

[28] 'Cher Monsieur Colonne, Vous pouvez compter sur moi Samedi matin à 11h ... Il y aura encore à faire dans le premier *Nocturne* (Nuages) pour qu'il prenne un rythme planant qui en fait la particularité ... "Ça sent encore l'huile" comme disent les mécaniciens d'une machine qui n'est pas suffisamment réglée.' Letter of 3 December 1908 to Edouard Colonne in Charavay sale catalogue (1987), no. 93.

[29] This text was first published with the recording of *The Complete Orchestral Works* by Debussy (Columbia D 3M-32988); it was reprinted in Pierre Boulez, *Points de repère*, ed. Jean-Jacques Nattiez (Paris, 1985), p. 364.

Table 3.2. Comparitive table of different categories of correction in the François Lang
and Roger-Ducasse orchestral scores of the Nocturnes

Nature of the corrections	F. Lang copy	R.-Ducasse copy
PROCESS OF LIGHTENING	48%	53%
Elimination of an instrumental part	23%	26%
Reduction of duration by eliminating a note and adding a rest or by reducing the note value	18%	21%
Elimination of parts in fifths, or octave doubling in the same part	7%	6%
CHANGE OF INSTRUMENTATION	14%	9%
Transfer of a motif from one instrument to another	11.5%	5.5%
Doubling of a motif	0.5%	0.5%
Change of attack (*pizz., arco*, on the fingerboard)	2%	3%
CHANGE OF NOTES OR THEMATIC ELEMENTS	28%	24%
Note changes	6%	6%
Change of thematic motives	22%	18%
ADDITION OF INSTRUMENTAL PARTS	10%	14%
Extension of an existing part	3%	6%
Addition of instrumental or vocal parts in bars marked *tacet*	7%	8%

above. However, it must be acknowledged that the remaining half of the corrections are of an entirely different nature, concerned with thematic and harmonic amendments, changes of instrumentation, sometimes even additions to the parts. What is more, the divergence between the two annotated copies is clearly evident. It is striking to discover, for instance, that instrumental and thematic changes are more numerous in the François Lang copy, while the process of lightening is more considerable in the Roger-Ducasse copy.

In order to work out the percentages, the significance of the corrections for each instrument have been evaluated. The conclusion from this assessment is that four instruments are the subject of most modification, in the following decreasing order: bassoons, horns, double basses and clarinets. Furthermore, the three wind instruments and the double bass all belong to the middle or low register. This further element substantiates the idea of lightening stated above. It is also worth noting that instruments like the harp, the strings, the flute, the cor anglais and the oboe, as well as the vocal parts, are barely affected by this process of reduction.

As an illustration of the process, an example concerning the bassoon, the instrument subjected to the most numerous amendments, is illuminating. Bars 95–8 undergo a certain number of transformations. In the autograph manuscript, the writing for the three bassoons is extremely dense, with intervals of a fifth and a sixth (see ex. 3.1a). The 1900 edition reproduces the text of the autograph manuscript, except for the last two bars for bassoon 3. The duration of the note is shortened in bar 97, while bar 98 is entirely eliminated (see ex. 3.1b). It is certain that this amendment was made at the stage of the third proof (which has never come to light), since the text of the second proof is identical to that of the manuscript. In the Roger-Ducasse copy, the entire passage is eliminated with, however, an ambiguity in bassoon 1 at bars 95–6 (see ex. 3.1c). Are these two notes to be omitted? In Inghelbrecht's copy, they are retained, while in Caplet's copy and in the second edition of 1930, the parts for bassoon 1 as well as the two other bassoons are eliminated. Regarding the François Lang copy, the parts for bassoons 1 and 2 are eliminated at bar 95 as well as on the first two beats of bar 96; the durations are shortened at bars 97–8. In addition, the part for bassoon 3 – as in the Roger-Ducasse copy – is entirely eliminated (see ex. 3.1d). These corrections also appear in the Colonne and Lamoureux scores.

63

Example 3.1. Bassoon parts in A 'Sirènes' bars 95–8

Example 3.1a. Autograph MS

Example 3.1b. 1900 edition

Example 3.1c. Roger-Ducasse annotated copy

Example 3.1d. François Lang annotated copy

This example is interesting in more ways than one. In the first place, it shows that the process of lightening had already begun at the stage of the third proof, although naturally not to the same extent as the amendments made to the edition once it was published. What is more, it not only reveals

Example 3.2. Examples of middle/low register wind note shortenings in 'Sirènes'

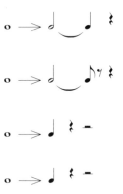

the divergence between the two annotated copies, but also shows that the omissions are far more radical in the Roger-Ducasse copy than in the François Lang copy. From this example, chosen from among many of its kind in 'Sirènes', it can be concluded that, in general, long note values for wind instruments of middle or low register are either purely and simply eliminated, or else shortened (see ex. 3.2).

Similarly for the double basses, doubling in octaves or fifths is generally eliminated, while certain note values are shortened, as in bars 26–37 (see ex. 3.3a [1900 edition], ex. 3.3b [Roger-Ducasse copy], ex. 3.3c [François Lang copy]) or as in bars 87–8 and 91–2 (see ex. 3.4a [1900 edition], ex. 3.4b [Roger-Ducasse copy], ex. 3.4c [François Lang copy]). Whether for bassoons, double basses or other instruments, a similar type of correction recurs in several other orchestral works such as *La Mer*, and it is possible that this kind of correction reflects Debussy's experience in working on that piece.[30] What is certain is that orchestras such as that of the *Concerts Lamoureux*, conducted by Chevillard who gave the first performance of the *Nocturnes*, were more accustomed to performances of Wagner than to the subtleties of the orchestration of 'Sirènes'.

---

[30] See the critical apparatus for *La mer*, in *Oeuvres Complètes* series 5, vol. V, ed. Marie Rolf.

Example 3.3. Elimination of double-bass doublings in 'Sirènes' bars 26–37
Example 3.3a. 1900 edition

Cb.

Example 3.3b. Roger-Ducasse annotated copy

Cb.

Example 3.3c. François Lang annotated copy

Cb.

Example 3.4. Lightening of double-bass in 'Sirènes' bars 87–8 and 91–2
Example 3.4a. 1900 edition

Cb.

Example 3.4b. Roger-Ducasse annotated copy

Cb.

Example 3.4c. François Lang annotated copy

Cb.

Other passages in 'Sirènes' also raise complex problems, such as bars 56–66, revealing the contradictory nature of Debussy's corrections. In this passage of static character, the thematic motif of 'Sirènes' (two quavers linked to a triplet) is transmitted to different instruments (horn, clarinets, violas, cellos, violas, cellos) in a middle or low register (see ex. 3.5a [1900 edition]). In the Roger-Ducasse copy, the instrumentation of the thematic motif remains the same. The corrections involve the lengthening of the note values for viola (bar 59) and the elimination of two bars for the same instrument (bars 60–1). These corrections are duplicated in bars 63 and 64, but not in bar 65. The part for double bass is altered by eliminating bars 59 and 64 and by changing the pitch in bars 60–1 and 64–5 (see ex. 3.5b). These corrections are also found in the Caplet and Inghelbrecht scores. The François Lang copy, however, contains instrumental modifications that differ from those of the Roger-Ducasse copy (see ex. 3.5c). There is a change of instrument in the thematic motif at bars 60–1 and 64–5: it passes from the cellos (low tessitura) to the clarinets, and so remains in the same tessitura as the violas; there is a margin note indicating the change to be engraved. The same amendments occur for the viola as in the Roger-Ducasse copy: lengthening of notes, elimination of two bars and duplication except at bar 65. In the double bass part, bars 59 and 63 are eliminated, as in the Roger-Ducasse copy, but contrary to this score, bars 62 and 66 are also deleted. The double bass part is also shortened without changing the pitch. The Colonne and Lamoureux scores follow this version. The second edition of 1930 also follows these amendments, with the exception of bars 60–1 and 64–5, where the double bass part remains the same as in the first edition.

In conclusion, it is evident that a thorough examination of all the amendments in Debussy's orchestral works and of their evolution through compositions such as *La mer, Images* and *Jeux* remains to be undertaken.[31] A study of this nature would test the hypotheses put forward in the course of this article. Through all these changes, Debussy was searching for a sound-ideal, as he himself indicated in an unpublished letter dated 31 December 1903:

[31] See the critical apparatus of *Jeux* in *Oeuvres complètes*, series 5, vol. VIII, ed. Pierre Boulez and Myriam Chimènes.

Example 3.5a. 'Sirènes' bars 55 ff. 1900 edition

E. 1417 F.

Example 3.5a. (*cont.*)

E. 1417 F.

Example 3.5a. (*cont.*)

Example 3.5b. 'Sirènes' bars 56 ff. Roger-Ducasse copy with manuscript corrections. Transcription of corrections in Roger-Ducasse copy

Example 3.5b. (*cont.*)

Example 3.5b. (*cont.*)

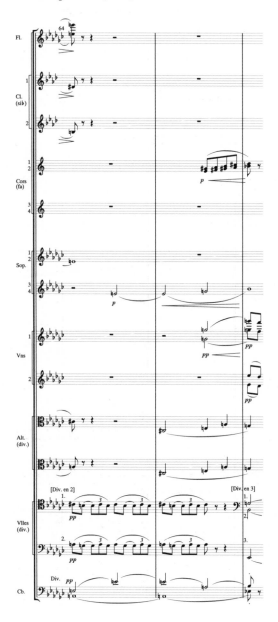

Example 3.5c. 'Sirènes' bars 56 ff. François Lang copy with manuscript corrections. Transcription of corrections in François Lang copy

Example 3.5c. (*cont.*)

Example 3.5c. (*cont.*)

With regard to the 3rd *Nocturne* (with women's voices) I would ask you to ensure that the singers are placed within the orchestra and not in front of it, otherwise the resulting effect would be diametrically opposed to the sound I had in mind: it is essential that the group of voices should not be more prominent than any other group in the orchestra; in short, it must not stand out, it must blend in.[32]

Between the sonority which he had in mind and the often disappointing performance of his works, Debussy was constantly in search of a kind of sound alchemy. The manifold amendments he brought to his scores bear testimony to this almost chimerical quest.

Some awkward questions arise in formulating a critical text of 'Sirènes' as well as the two other *Nocturnes*. It is obvious that the 1930 edition is to be avoided, since it comprises a mixture of the two annotated copies, together with the ensuing inconsistencies. The version of 'Sirènes' which is currently performed is therefore a sort of hybrid. In short, the François Lang and the Roger-Ducasse copies each have their own coherence. Therefore, rather than attempting a subjective and perilous mixture of these two versions, would it not be better to publish two different versions of 'Sirènes'?[33] But even if this were done, the chimerical nature of 'Sirènes' would nevertheless persist: in fact it seems that the complexities inherent in this work which, as Debussy himself admitted, caused 'more trouble . . . than the five acts of *Pelléas*',[34] impose on us this very state of incertitude.

(Translated by Sidney Buckland)

---

[32] 'A propos du 3ᵉ *Nocturne* (avec voix de femmes) je vous demanderai de veiller à ce que les choristes soient placées dans l'orchestre et non devant, sans quoi il en résulterait un effet diamétralement opposé à celui que j'ai cherché: il faut que ce groupe de voix n'ait pas plus d'importance sonore que tel autre groupe d'orchestre; en résumé, il ne doit pas avancer mais se mêler.' Letter of 31 December 1903 (Pierpont Morgan Library, New York, Koch 5, box 1).

[33] A new edition of the *Nocturnes* is currently in preparation by the author for the *Oeuvres Complètes*.

[34] 'plus de mal que les cinq actes de *Pelléas*', letter of 16 September 1898 in Debussy, *Correspondance*, p. 138.†

4   Debussy's piano music: sources and performance

ROY HOWAT

Commentaries on Debussy's piano music usually focus on its originality, taking the notation relatively for granted. By now we can probably
take its originality more for granted but his notation less so, since his precisely notated scores seem to spawn an extreme variety of performance
styles. How much of this variety is an essential part of his music?

One answer lies in the cluster of unverified performing traditions that
has attached itself to this repertoire, independent of Debussy's actual
markings. A subtler answer is that under his densely precise notation lie
several interpretative problems, paradoxes, and suspect readings that can
send performers off in different directions. Yet experience of editing his
piano music for the *Oeuvres Complètes*, plus years of performing it, have left
me particularly admiring of his notational care, a care far removed from
any loosely 'impressionistic' thinking.[1]

---

[1] The following editions are pertinent to the discussion in this chapter:
   Edition critique des Oeuvres Complètes de Claude Debussy:
   Series 1, vol. II, *Images (1894); Pour le piano; Children's corner*, ed. Roy Howat
   (Paris, forthcoming).
   Series 1, vol. III, *Estampes; D'un cahier d'esquisses; Masques; L'isle joyeuse;*
   Images I et II, ed. Roy Howat (Paris, 1991).
   Series 1, vol. V, *Préludes*, books I and II, ed. Roy Howat and Claude Helffer (Paris,
   1985).
   Series 1, vol. VI, *Etudes*, ed. Claude Helffer (Paris, 1991).
See also
   Howat, 'The New Debussy Edition: approaches and techniques', *Studies in music*,
   19 (1985), 94–113.
   Claude Debussy, *Préludes*, book I. *The autograph score*, intro. Roy Howat,
   Pierpont Morgan Library Music Manuscript Reprint Series (New York, 1987).
   Debussy, *Etudes pour le piano. Fac-similé des esquisses autographes (1915)*, intro.
   Roy Howat. Publications du Centre de Documentation Claude Debussy, no. 5
   (Geneva, 1989).

Three recurring observations stand out. First, his basic notation of notes is thoroughly classical in its economy as well as its polyphonic and structural clarity; in the latter respect his manuscripts are even clearer than the original printed editions. Second, when a notational problem does appear, it often proves impossible to devise a better notation without introducing a new problem or distortion. Third, the profusion of performing indications is something of an added layer in the notation, sometimes not completed until proof stage.

Undoubtedly the greatest variations in performance of Debussy's piano music exhibit themselves through tempo and dynamics. Some of this can be attributed straight away to misguided wilfulness, stemming from a mentality that regards French music as frivolous and its performing indications as optional toppings. The memoirs of pianists who worked with Debussy, such as George Copeland, Maurice Dumesnil, Marguerite Long and E. Robert Schmitz confirm that Debussy – like Chopin, Fauré and Ravel – regarded such treatment as anathema.[2] However, the case is more complex: Debussy's concentration on the low end of the dynamic scale often makes literal observation of his dynamics extremely difficult, and occasionally a tempo indication is in apparent conflict with musical details. More generally, the enormously varied rhythmic surface of his music makes it difficult to keep a steady tempo underneath, especially when we are accustomed to relying for tempo on the more motor-rhythmic patterns of older music.

On top of that come all the fluctuations Debussy indicates – *rit.*, *cédez*, *serrez*, *animez*, *rubato* and so forth. With the music's rhythmic surface already so varied, there's an understandable temptation to let such fluctuations proliferate, especially among performers brought up – like most of us in English-speaking countries – in the Germanic tradition of the expressive *rallentando*. The progressive incursion of this into performance of French music over the years is amusingly reflected by composers' progressive defences against it. Debussy, when wanting no *rallentando*, simply indicates none; Ravel, thirteen years younger, fore-

---

[2] See Marguerite Long, *Au piano avec Claude Debussy* (Paris, 1960), English edition *At the Piano with Debussy*, trans. Olive Senior-Ellis (London, 1972); E. Robert Schmitz, *The Piano Music of Claude Debussy* (New York, 1966); and Roger Nichols, *Debussy Remembered* (London, 1992).

stalls it by writing *sans ralentir*.[3] For Poulenc, a generation later, this becomes *surtout sans ralentir*. Probably a major 'secret' of playing French music is to convey its expressive nuances through voicing and colour – *sans rigueur* – without having to resort to audible tempo stretching except where indicated. A related issue is that indicated tempo stretching in this repertoire usually has a structural rather than a locally expressive function, and to confuse the two usages in performance risks structural damage – especially in works such as Debussy's *Préludes* or *Jeux*, where highly segmented structures rely on rhythmic continuity for their integration into larger forms.

Marguerite Long, who worked with not only Debussy but also Fauré and Ravel, emphasises Debussy's insistence on steady tempi, with recourse when necessary to the metronome.[4] In this respect the last two pages of 'Reflets dans l'eau' are revealing, leading from a very turbulent climax to an ending of extreme contemplative stillness, and with harmonic motion ranging from demisemiquaver to minim or semibreve. If this passage is played to a metronome, allowing only for the local *ritardandi* indicated at bars 64 and 79–80, and the slight reduction of tempo indicated for bars 65–70, its in-built rhythmic contrasts and progression of moods essentially emerge by themselves.[5] In particular, the musical effect of the long-term indications *en retenant jusqu'à la fin* from bar 71 and *Lent* at bar 81 is embedded in the notation, and any attempt to impose them only obscures them by distorting the underlying metre that sets them off. Walter Gieseking, recognising this, advised pianists to count bar 81 onwards in six, in order to maintain the underlying tempo 'in absolutely strict time' against the notated crossbeats.[6]

[3] Regarding Ravel's extreme aversion to unmarked *ritardandi*, see comments by Gaby Casadesus in D. Elder, *Pianists at Play* (Evanston, USA, 1982), p. 74, and V. Perlemuter and H. Jourdan-Morhange, *Ravel according to Ravel* (London, 1988), p. 7 and *passim*.

[4] See Long, *Au piano avec Claude Debussy*, pp. 38, 41–2, 46, 74. Pierre Monteux also recalled, 'And he [Debussy] wanted everything exactly in time.' See Nichols, *Debussy Remembered*, p. 186.

[5] Bar numbers are as in the *Oeuvres Complètes*, 1/III; some other editions number differently because they introduce an extra bar line in the cadenza-like bar 23.

[6] See Elder, *Pianists at Play*, p. 227.

The relationship that emerges there is of a prescriptive rhythmic notation (which in itself assures the effect), allied to descriptive indications of the effects that emerge. A good proportion of Debussy's indications make clearer sense when viewed in this light – even the notorious *Le double plus lent* four bars before the end of the 'Toccata' from *Pour le piano*. Since a double augmentation is already written into the notation in that case, it causes absurd results if one reads the indication as a further doubling, and Marguerite Long confirms that Debussy warned her to ignore the indication.[7] It remains interesting, though, to know how it got there, especially as it is absent from all sources up to and including the first print.[8] Although Debussy apparently claimed ignorance of its provenance, it is unlikely to have been added by anyone else, especially in view of how much publishers dislike such late changes. Possibly it was a later descriptive indication Debussy added to warn pianists against rushing the augmentation, over-looking its contrary effect if read as a prescriptive instruction.[9]

Observation of those tendencies can alert the eye and ear more generally. In the *Etude* 'Pour les sixtes' at bar 33, the indication *Molto rit.* appears above a rhythmic augmentation into quavers of the previous bar's semi-quaver figuration. The augmentation already assures the effect, and ironically we can best bring out the relationship by momentarily counteracting it in metronomic terms – that is, by starting bar 33 with a marginally faster crotchet, thus leading the quavers out of the preceding semiquavers. Debussy does this in his recorded performance of the song 'L'ombre des arbres' (of which more below), in the penultimate bar where the syncopated rhythm is similarly augmented; he thus creates a sounding *rallentando* rather than instant augmentation. A similar notated relationship can be seen between bars 77 and 79 of the *Étude* 'Pour les quartes'.

A corollary to this appears earlier in 'Pour les quartes', in the shape of a semiquaver triplet figure marked *stretto* at bars 7 and 37 (ex. 4.1). Relative to

[7] See Long, *Au piano avec Claude Debussy*, p. 43.

[8] An exemplar is in the Bibliothèque Nationale de France, Paris (Musique), Vm7 17827. This, complete with a slightly misprinted cover, may even be a final proof used by the publisher as a legal deposit copy.

[9] This idea is corroborated by Marcel Ciampi, who recounted that Debussy told him to play those last bars in the main tempo but *rallentando poco a poco* (communicated to the author by Vlado Perlemuter).

Example 4.1. 'Pour les quartes' bars 6–9

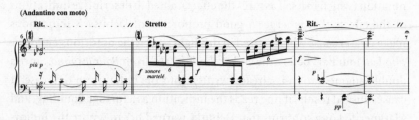

the basic tempo of the piece (as defined by Debussy at bar 1 or bar 49), the *stretto* effect is mostly built into the notation (as is the following *rit.*), needing only a slight nudge from the performer. The problem is now that, through over-prescriptive reading of the indication, a tradition has established itself, as can be heard on numerous commercial recordings, of racing the *stretto* off at almost double speed. Ironically this undermines the *stretto* by making the quaver of bars 6 and 36 seem to lead into a slower following crotchet instead of a faster quaver.

Not all nuances can be expected to activate themselves within the notated metre, but it is often a useful rule of thumb to test, against a constant pulse, how much of an indicated tempo nuance is already written into the notation. A similar method often applies for *rubato* indications: the music will rapidly tell us exactly where it needs the stretch. Indeed, nearly all the passages recalcitrant to a mechanical beat in Debussy's piano music are those already indicated by his tempo nuances. This accords with Debussy's reported advice to Maggie Teyte to sing the role of Mélisande 'as if it were Mozart; don't "do" anything to it except what I've indicated'.[10]

Sometimes an elusive *rubato* is betrayed by an oddity of notation – a good reason for editors not to correct them too hastily to grammatical normality. Ex. 4.2 shows bar 31 of the prelude 'Les sons et les parfums tournent dans l'air du soir' as it appears in both Debussy's autograph and the first edition, in a 3/4 context. Several later editions amend bar 31 to 4/4, probably by reading it similarly to the last two beats of bar 33. However, bar 33 differs from bar 31 in having a minim in the top voice, and by reaching the bass on the beat with an upward stem (in the autograph, as in ex. 4.2; the first edition prints the stem downward as in bar 31). Attention to these

---

[10] Recounted by Maggie Teyte to the pianist Nina Walker, and hence to the author.

Example 4.2. 'Les sons et les parfums' bars 31–3

small distinctions, and to the indication *Rubato*, suggests that in bar 31 the alignment may be Debussy's way of specifying the *rubato* necessary to reach the last beat, as an effective third beat, without rushing. The *Oeuvres Complètes* (1/V:16 and 164), reluctant to perpetuate a grammatical solecism, adapt this reasoning by maintaining 3/4, aligning the bass crotchet under the chord above, lengthening the bass tie to make the same visual point, and exploiting the luxury of an explanatory critical commentary.

Similar evidence comes elsewhere from the *Préludes*, whose autographs show some notations like ♩, sometimes though not always normalised in the first editions. Even if the grammatical solecism may be largely the result of midnight oil, consciously or not it may have a message, warning us not to scramble the short notes. A more complex case is bars 17–20 of 'Ce qu'a vu le Vent d'Ouest' (ex. 4.3a). To understand the obviously faulty notation of bars 19–20, we first have to observe that the double-dotted notation of bars 17–18 is theoretically inexact (as also in bars 15–16), since each demisemiquaver (an eighth of a crotchet beat) would normally come before, not after the final semiquaver triplet (a ninth of a crotchet beat – this inversion of values is a quirk of western notation). On the one hand, Debussy obviously intends the demisemiquaver to come after; on the other hand, to 'correct' the notation by re-notating in triple dots would cramp the last note; in sum, Debussy's 'faulty' notation actually tells us exactly what to do, in a notated *rubato* across the voices.

Bars 19–20 add to the problem. Though they are usually 'corrected' as in the two possibilities of ex. 4.3b, comparison with bars 17–18 suggests that the source of the problem lies more in the main dotted voice: correction of this, as in the two alternative notations of ex. 4.3c, then minimises the intervention necessary for the running voice. Unfortunately ex. 4.3a has no space for the tied notation, and the equivalent, triple dots, is a nota-

Example 4.3. 'Ce qu'a vu le Vent d'Ouest'
Example 4.3a. Bars 17–20

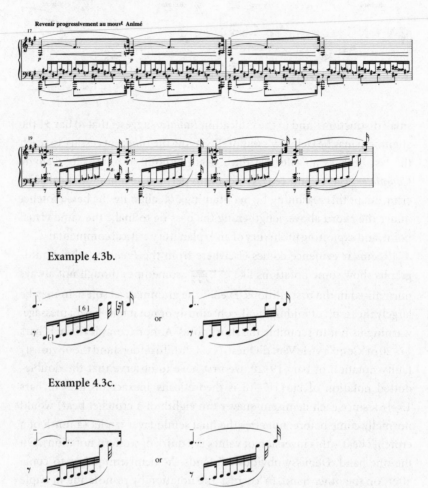

Example 4.3b.

Example 4.3c.

tion Debussy never used (strangely, as it can be found in Schubert and Liszt). Even if partly attributable again to midnight oil, his notation throughout this passage suggests that, as with older music even up to Schumann, Debussy still regarded value dots and double dots as approximate.

All this illustrates the fluid surface of Debussy's music, like Chopin's, relative to its underlying firm structure, and his efforts to convey this all in as simple notation as possible. Debussy's own comments to performers show him balancing as necessary: Marguerite Long, who could be needle-fingered, was told 'Seule compte le plaisir de l'heure!'[11] whereas Ricardo Viñes's playing of the second series of *Images* was faulted because 'he doesn't yet feel their architecture clearly, and despite his incontestable virtuosity is distorting their expression'.[12] (Viñes's recording of 'Poissons d'or' does betray architectural inaccuracy, letting the intensity collapse before the focus of the main climax.)[13] Debussy's comment is the more revealing for linking expression so directly with architecture.

A sidelight on Debussy's notational philosophy emerges from some of his autographs, particularly of *Children's corner* and first book of *Préludes*, which show that many performing indications were added only at proof.[14] Do the late additions imply that his concept of the music had changed, or do they merely map the music more exactly? Experimentation at the piano usually points more to the latter conclusion.

One exception is betrayed by a manuscript bass tie across the last two bars of 'Pagodes' (from *Estampes*), which Debussy removed at proof, replacing it by the indications *Retenu* and *laissez vibrer*, plus the pause and final bass *tenuto* dash (all absent from his manuscript). Such a large adjustment suggests musical rethinking rather than just notational polish, and a likely reason can be seen by comparing the piece's whole last page with that of Ravel's *Jeux d'eau* published the year before. The analogies are so striking that Debussy may have deemed it wise, at the eleventh hour, to vary at least the final gesture – especially as his revised reading profits by coming nearer the rhythmic patterns of Indonesian gamelan.[15] (As it happened, a resem-

---

[11] See Long, *Au piano avec Claude Debussy*, p. 103.
[12] 'Il n'en sent pas encore clairement d'architecture, et malgré son incontestable virtuosité il en fausse l'expression.' See letter of 1908 to Georges Jean-Aubry, quoted in Margaret G. Cobb, 'Debussy in Texas', *Cahiers Debussy* 1 (1977), 45–6.
[13] Columbia LF41, recorded 1930, reissued on EMI Pathé Marconi LP 1731791.
[14] The first book of *Preludes* is a complex case, with many indications added to the autograph after engraving, and then copied into proof. See Claude Debussy, *Préludes*, book I, ed. Howat, p. vii.
[15] Regarding the relationship of this piece to gamelan, see Howat, 'Debussy and the Orient', in C. A. Gerstle and A. Milner (eds.), *Recovering the Orient* (London, 1994), pp. 45–81.

blance in the following *Estampe*, 'La soirée dans Grenade', to Ravel's earlier *Habanera* did cause a scandal.)

Debussy's descriptive indications of nuance stand further in relief when compared with Ravel's more laconically prescriptive habits. For example, at bars 12–14 of the prelude 'Feuilles mortes' Debussy makes a descriptive change from 3/4 to 2/4 metre to draw our attention to a delicate hemiola, whereas Ravel embeds strings of hemiolas and inverse hemiolas in the 'Forlane', 'Rigaudon' and 'Toccata' from *Le tombeau de Couperin* without changing the notated metre. Debussy's indication to bar 1 of 'Des pas sur la neige' – *Ce rythme doit avoir la valeur sonore d' un fond de paysage triste et glacé* – contrasts similarly with Ravel's terse prescription *sans expression* for the hushed climax of 'Le gibet'. While Debussy aims to guide the player completely into the feeling, Ravel goes straight for the effect, using stealth if necessary to prevent performers from botching the expression by emoting.[16] Not that Debussy is averse to notational stealth. Alternating accents and *staccato* dots at bars 51 and 63 of the prelude 'General Lavine', marking burlesque allusions to 'Camptown Races', automatically ensure the appropriate ragtime swing without need for further comment. The device recurs, using dots and dashes, in the similar ragtime rhythm of the *Etude* 'Pour les notes répétées'.

There is a major perspective on this whole topic which we easily lose by looking back at Debussy's music relative to what followed it, rather than hearing it in its balletic soil of Massenet, Delibes and Chabrier, as well as of Debussy's own early works. Some dance rhythms or gestures in his piano music elude exact notation; nowadays, with the dances less fashionable, we have to rely on external sources. Marcel Ciampi, who worked with Debussy, recounted that in 'La soirée dans Grenade' and 'La Puerta del Vino', both headed *Mouvt. de habanera*, Debussy wanted the ostinato rhythm 'overdotted'.[17] Debussy's recorded piano roll of 'La soirée dans Grenade' (of which more below) supplements this by revealing an analogous stretching of the rhythms ♫., ♫♩ and ♫♩ at bars 33–6 towards ♫♩, ♫♩ and ♫♩ respectively. It is understandable that Debussy, to avoid com-

---

[16] For further discussion of this passage see Perlemuter and Jourdan-Morhange, *Ravel*, p. 34.

[17] Information kindly supplied by Ciampi's former pupil Julie Hennig.

plicated notation in what was still a widely popular dance genre (and in pieces he wanted to sell), regarded their heading *Mouvt. de habanera* as sufficient to convey the message.

Debussy's stepdaughter Madame de Tinan (the former Dolly Bardac) also recalled that Debussy used to make a characteristic sarabande 'lift' before the long chords in the 'Sarabande' of *Pour le piano* (bars 2 and similar) and in 'Hommage à Rameau' (bars 8 and 64), a nuance only partly implied by the notated *staccato* dots and tenuto dashes.[18] As this is a characteristic gesture of the sarabande, and the genre is specified in each piece's heading, he may have assumed performers should recognise the gesture. Debussy's dots and dashes there have a particular allusion, and it pays us to relate any unusual articulation to context, as with the dashes above the repeated right-hand C♯ crotchets at bar 38 of 'Pagodes'. Our western conditioning to subdue those to the melody underneath has to be forgotten here, in a context where Debussy's emphasis is on the entirely different textural balance and colours of gamelan.

Debussy loves turning the tables in such ways, as with the explosive offbeats in 'Golliwogg's cake-walk', or bar 11 onwards of its fellow cake-walk 'General Lavine' where the offbeat accompanying chords are deliberately marked louder than the *pp* melody underneath. A more daring example again of the latter device is the drowning of the right hand melody on the last page of 'La cathédrale engloutie' by the left hand waves, sounding like a peal of cathedral bells. Again those effects play themselves, provided we don't unthinkingly try to 'stop the accompaniment drowning the melody'!

Some popular idioms have also changed since the 1900s: Blues for example have become slower, and ragtime faster (see Scott Joplin's repeated exhortations never to play ragtime fast). Recognition of the latter, with its sung and danced form of cakewalk, puts a more moderate complexion on not only 'Golliwogg's cake-walk' but also the preludes 'Minstrels' and 'General Lavine', linking them to the moderate ragtime tempi indicated for the central movements of the Cello and Violin Sonatas, and thence to the

---

[18] Communicated to the author, *c.* 1979, by Mme de Tinan (1893–1985). From 1904 (aged 11) 'Dolly' – her real name was Hélène – lived in the Debussy household, and later claimed very clear memories of how Debussy played. Bar 64 of 'Hommage à Rameau' also has the indication *Poco rit.* to help the sarabande 'lift'.

most misunderstood of them all, the *Etude* 'Pour les notes répétées'. (Satie's *La Diva de l'Empire* also provides an obvious tempo standard for cakewalk of the time). According to Jacques Février, Poulenc's performances of 'Minstrels', played very strictly in time at a moderate cakewalk tempo, were a revelation – perhaps a legacy from Poulenc's teacher Ricardo Viñes, who premièred the piece.[19]

Probably the commonest misconception is of Debussy's indication *Lent* in the context of a waltz. In particular, *La plus que lente* is not really a slow piece: 'lente' refers only to the fashionable *valse lente* genre (the object of Debussy's irony) as opposed to the very fast waltz, and his title is a compaction, in the style of French classical music, that can be only approximately rendered in English as 'The slow waltz outwaltzed'. True slow waltzes, where any indication *Lent* is still qualified by the underlying lilt, include 'La terrasse des audiences du clair de lune' (with its allusions on the last page to the end of Chabrier's *Valses romantiques*), and – slower again – 'Feuilles mortes' and 'La cathédrale engloutie' (once the latter's notational tempo problem is solved, of which more below), analogous in movement to the 'Epilogue' of Ravel's *Valses nobles et sentimentales*.[20] A café waltz underlies 'Les sons et les parfums tournent dans l'air du soir', a *valse bleue* according to Alfred Cortot,[21] whose inebriated metrical lurches match the ironic tale of Baudelaire's poem ('Le violon frémit comme un coeur qu'on afflige; Valse mélancolique et langoureux vertige!'). In turn, 'La fille aux cheveux de lin', at Debussy's indicated $\quarternote = 66$ and free of uninvited *rubato*, becomes a gentle antique minuet, appropriate to the song of a shepherd wooing a shepherdess.[22]

[19] Information communicated to the author by Jacques Février during a masterclass in Salzburg, summer 1975.

[20] An unpublished orchestration of 'La cathédrale engloutie' by Debussy's colleague Henri Busser, dated January 1921 (Bibliothèque Nationale de France, Paris (Musique), Ms.18837), indicates $\quarternote = 66$ at bar 1.

[21] Alfred Cortot, *Cours d'interprétation*, ed. Jeanne Thieffry (Paris, 1934), p. 57.

[22] Lecomte de Lisle's poem 'La fille aux cheveux de lin', from the collection *Chansons écossaises*, clearly takes its title from Robert Burns's 'Lassie with the lint-white locks', a shepherd's love song to a shepherdess. This context is less clear from de Lisle's poem which is more interested in her cherry-red lips. The character and allusions of Debussy's *Prélude* (like the shepherd taking a breath on his flute in bar 2) suggest that Debussy, too, knew Burns's poem. The minuet relates further to the second of Debussy's Mallarmé songs of 1913, set as a 'menuet lent' ($\quarternote = 56$), an ode to a painted princess on a teacup, ending with a request to be 'the shepherd of your smiles'.

Mention of Debussy's metronomic indications opens another topic, one which with many composers can be a Pandora's box of problems. Up to 1904 Debussy's only works to show metronomic indications are the song *Mandoline* (published 1890), the String Quartet (published 1894) and the piano piece *Masques* (1904). From 1905, with *La mer*, metronomic indications suddenly increase, perhaps as a result of the firm of Durand becoming Debussy's sole publisher that year (of the three Debussy works published by Durand in the 1890s, two were *Mandoline* and the String Quartet; Durand also published *Masques*). His metronomic indications remained sporadic: the first series of piano *Images* (1905) has none, the second series (1907) has them in unusual detail; *Children's corner* (1908) has none, though the autograph shows some incomplete indications lacking numbers; eight preludes from Book 1 (1909–10) have them, but only one prelude from Book 2 (1911–13). Among the last works, *En blanc et noir* and the Cello and Violin Sonatas have them, but not the Sonata for flute, viola and harp, nor the *Etudes*. On 9 October 1915 Debussy wrote to his publisher Jacques Durand, 'You know my opinion of metronomic indications: they work for a bar, like "the roses, the space of a morning", only there are those who don't understand music and use the lack [of indications] to understand even less of it!'[23] This needs some consideration in the face of all Debussy's reported insistence on rhythmic directness. The closest tally comes from his indications to the *Image* 'Et la lune descend sur le temple qui fut' of 1907, which change every few bars, varying between $\downarrow$ = 66 and 52, then slowing to 46 for the last bars. The fluctuations clearly have a structural role in delineating alternating formal segments, but even so they indicate a more unified basic tempo than most current performances of the piece. Our first example in this chapter, the last part of 'Reflets dans l'eau', actually allows a similar degree of give and take (as at bars 65–70), and the range Debussy marked in 'Et la lune descend' may well encapsulate all those different aspects of his rhythmic thinking.

---

[23] 'Vous savez mon opinion sur les mouvements métronomiques: ils sont justes pendant une mesure, comme "les roses, l'espace d'un matin", seulement, il y a "ceux" qui n'entendent pas la musique et qui s'autorisent de ce manque pour y entendre encore moins!' Cited in Jacques Durand (ed.), *Lettres de Claude Debussy à son éditeur* (Paris, 1927), p. 158, translated Roger Nichols: *Debussy Letters* (London, 1987), p. 305. Often assumed to refer to the *Etudes*, this letter more probably relates to the Cello Sonata or *En blanc et noir*, both published in December 1915; the *Etudes* did not go to engraving until 1916.

Another issue stems from the fact that very few performances of 'Et la lune descend' (or any of his slower pieces) keep up with Debussy's metronomic indications, though the latter are quite feasible and structurally very cohesive. The problem mainly seems to lie again in misinterpreting *Lent*. It could conversely be argued that Debussy's metronome was reading falsely fast. This, however, is unlikely, as many of his metronomic indications are very moderate – for example those to the preceding *Image* 'Cloches à travers les feuilles'; the 6/8 section in the first movement of *La mer*; the *Préludes* 'Voiles' and 'Les sons et les parfums' (where his indications if anything seem on the slow side); the central movements of the Cello and Violin Sonatas, the finale of the former; the list can go on. In general – apart from some isolated problems discussed below – we have to assume that his indications for the most part reflect what he intended.

Two of his piano pieces, however – *Masques* of 1904 and 'Poissons d'or' of 1907 – have metronomic indications so fast as to be virtually unplayable. *Masques* is almost physically manageable at the printed $\downarrow. = 104$, whereas in 'Poissons d'or' the opening demisemiquavers combined with melodic snatches in thirds (ex. 4.5a below), and the arpeggio figurations in bars 14–15, are certainly impossible at the indicated $\downarrow = 112$. Probably for that reason, most performances at least pursue the metronomic indication of *Masques*, but make no such attempt in 'Poissons d'or'. I would suggest that Debussy's intention was more the contrary, and the reasons for this involve a major issue, orchestral versus purely pianistic notation. Starting with *Masques*, the main reasons for ignoring the metronomic indication are that, first, it completely swamps the piece's rich rhythmic detail, especially its alternations of 3/4 and 6/8 patterns; second, in the autograph the indication is pencilled in a hand clearly not Debussy's;[24] third, it makes musical nonsense of Debussy's *sans retenir* on the last page. To those reasons can be added the close polar relationship between *Masques* and *L'isle joyeuse* – initially intended as the outer pieces of a triptych – manifest not only rhythmically through their main themes (ex. 4.4) but also on a larger scale through a similar congruity in structural dimensions and proportions.[25]

[24] See Debussy, *Oeuvres Complètes*, 1/III, p. 160. The hand is that of one of the house editors at Durand.

[25] See Roy Howat, 'En route for *L'isle joyeuse*: the restoration of a triptych', *Cahiers Debussy*, 19 (1995), 37–52, particularly 39–40.

Example 4.4.

Masques, bars 1–4

L'isle joyeuse, bar 7

By contrast, in 'Poissons d'or' ♩ = 112 is both technically feasible and musically desirable for the central part of the piece, especially bars 57 onwards, and it seems probable that Debussy set the indication with this part, rather than the beginning, in mind. Yet too large a tempo discrepancy from the opening strains the architecture (see Debussy's comment above about Viñes), and we have to dare to ask whether Debussy's opening notation (ex. 4.5a) is really intended literally, or whether it is rather a sort of orchestral (or descriptive) notation of the effect he wants to hear. Before crying sacrilege, we may well ask how else he could notate the effect and then, in an analogous case, ask how two hands are meant to encompass bar 96 of 'Feux d'artifice' (ex. 4.5b). In the latter passage common sense tells us not only to 'fake' the bass at bar 96 by pedal, but also to interrupt it at the end of bar 90 to make space for the three descending semitones (ex. 4.5c) – and moreover to read the bass demisemiquavers as *tremolando* if they are not to sound absurd; in sum, to treat the whole passage like an orchestral reduction. Many other contexts corroborate that Debussy often used demisemiquavers as equivalent to *tremolando* or trill – for example, at bar 126 onwards of 'Jardins sous la pluie' where the notated demisemiquavers, in that rapid tempo, can hardly be played faster than semiquavers.[26] (The reason for writing demisemiquavers here rather than a trill may simply have been to indicate the upper note start.) All this accords with Maurice

[26] See this passage and further source evidence in Debussy, *Oeuvres Complètes*, 1/III, pp. 26 and 158.

Example 4.5a. 'Poissons d'or'

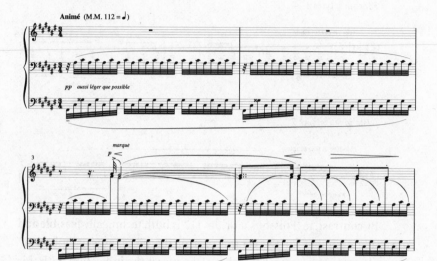

Example 4.5b. 'Feux d'artifice'

Example 4.5c. 'Feux d'artifice'

Dumesnil's recollection that 'Debussy often thought in terms of orchestration';[27] in this respect a direct comparison with ex. 4.5a can be found in 'Jeux de vagues' from *La mer* (two bars before figure 30), similarly in 3/4 metre indicated ♩ = 112, and mixing trill and demisemiquaver notation.

More support comes from 'La danse de Puck', where Debussy's left hand demisemiquavers in bars 63–6 are clearly equivalent in structural and textural function to the trills of bars 87–90 (ex. 4.6a and ex. 4.6b). As in ex. 4.5a, the probable reason for demisemiquaver notation is simply that the interval is wider than trill notation allows. Both trills and demisemiquavers share a further shorthand in 'La danse de Puck' (ex. 4.6c): the voice leading implies that the left hand auxiliary D and D♯ at bars 55–6, and D♮ at bars 67–8, have an analogous role to the crotchets in ex. 4.6a and ex. 4.6b, and need to be 'orchestrally' read and voiced (easily done by sounding them almost simultaneously on the beat, a standard technique of playing orchestral reductions).

Probably the most explicitly orchestral (or vocal) single indication in Debussy's piano music is the pair of *portamento* lines in 'La Puerta del Vino', at the middle of bars 35 and 36.[28] In purely pianistic terms the effect is unobtainable, but he clearly wants us to sense the allusion, and perhaps hint at it as best we can through agogic stretching and voicing. Orchestral or vocal notation is equally clear from the frequent places where pianists have to rearrange from one hand to the other, with Debussy more intent on showing the music's polyphony and voicing, as in the opening bars of 'Cloches à travers les feuilles'. His use of three-stave notation is sometimes more a visual luxury than a technical necessity; like his mania about the visual presentation of his editions, though, it is still descriptively functional, helping to set the evocative scene. The autograph of the second book of *Préludes* pushes this to an extreme by bracketing four staves to a system throughout the first four preludes, though the music never uses more than three at a time.[29]

Orchestral thinking of this sort carries other pianistic implications, regarding not only tempo – orchestras can't pull music around as pianists

[27] See Nichols, *Debussy Remembered*, p. 160.

[28] The Durand edition misprints these as broken lines: in the autograph (see note 29 below) and the *Oeuvres Complètes*, 1/III they are unbroken.

[29] Bibliothèque Nationale de France, Paris (Musique), Ms.1006.

Example 4.6. 'La danse de Puck'
Example 4.6a. Bars 63–4

Example 4.6b. Bars 87–9

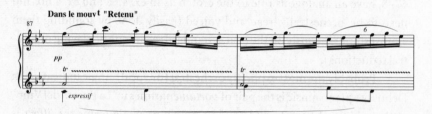

Example 4.6c. Bars 55–7 and 66–8

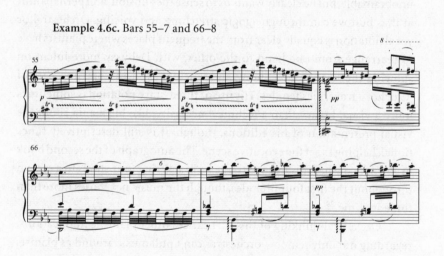

habitually do – but also pedalling. Walter Gieseking observed that 'often the pedal sign in Debussy is the bass note'.[30] *Staccato* or *portato* phrasing above long bass notes often has to be pedalled or half-pedalled through in order not to lose the bass, but this has degenerated to a false 'impressionistic' habit of pedalling through *staccato,* phrase ends, bass and other rests and all, for as long as the harmony can bear. Ironically, after what has just been argued about the opening of 'Poissons d'or', a more orchestral reading of his notation often demands more attention to note values and rests. This has strong implications for the first 20 bars of the prelude 'Voiles', habitually pedalled through in a whole-tone haze, but actually notated very differently from the sustained bass of bars 21 onwards. A similar contrast within the bar distinguishes the *portato* (gently *staccato*) outer voices at the beginning of 'Danseuses de Delphes' from the legato chromatic inner melody (a voicing borrowed verbatim from the end of Chopin's Bᵇ prelude).

A more orchestral reading of Debussy's notation also directs our attention to lifting at phrase ends (why otherwise did he mark such detailed phrasing?) especially at breathing points like bars 2 and 9 of 'La fille aux cheveux de lin', or at *staccato* lifts such as bar 22 of the same piece, bars 25–6 of 'Danseuses de Delphes' (whose ♩= 44 indicates the piece as a sarabande, not a dirge), and bars 8, 10 and similar of 'Canope' (whose autograph includes an analogous *staccato* dot at bar 23). Likewise to observe the rests *subito* as notated in bars 29–30 of 'Brouillards' can be as dramatic in this macabre prelude as the sudden silences in Ravel's 'Scarbo'. Debussy's indication to clear the pedal for the last bar of 'Voiles' confirms his interest in such effects,[31] and in the following prelude, 'Le vent dans la plaine' he again clears the pedal in the last bar, holding only the left hand Bᵇ, on a piano roll recording further discussed below. A more unusual *staccato* indication, the wedge to the *pp* bass crotchets at bars 96 and 98 of 'Pour les accords', is incomprehensible unless read as a timpani-like articulation (requiring a touch of pedal to emulate the timpani's resonance).

As this issue was opened up by a dubious tempo indication, it remains to deal with another. *D'un cahier d'esquisses* of 1903–4, contemporary with

---

[30] See Elder, *Pianists at Play,* p. 12, and Debussy's comments to Dumesnil on pedalling, quoted in Nichols, *Debussy Remembered,* pp. 160 and 162.

[31] This indication, missing from some reprints, is clear in the autograph and all prints issued during Debussy's lifetime.

La mer and sharing some of its melodic and textural ideas, remains one of Debussy's less-played pieces. Its heading *Très lent* probably plays a major role in the neglect, for it is hard to get any rhythmic life out of the piece thus, nor is its harmonic rhythm suited to a very slow tempo. A further problem emerges at the coda (bar 45), where the metre switches from 6/8 to 6/4, with the indicated equivalence ♩. = ♩. Taken literally, this would make the coda more than funereal. If, however, we read *Très lent* at bar 45 instead of bar 1, and then work backwards, carrying the indicated tempo equivalence back into bars 1–44, the whole piece transforms into a flowing barcarolle. This also makes sense of its notation, relating the 6/4 coda more to slow 6/4 passages in 'De l'aube à midi sur la mer' (the opening, then after figure 13), and the piece's opening nearer to the 12/8 entry of the cellos in 'De l'aube à midi' (before figure 9). Since the piece's autograph is lost, and its main source a magazine publication of 1904, it may be that Debussy had less control than usual over proofing, and that a sub-editor innocently moved a tempo indication from bar 45 to where it could be more easily seen at bar 1! (Experience of editing has shown that worse things happen.)

The problem extends beyond just this piece, for there is evidence that it was once intended to go (probably with a different title) between *Masques* and *L'isle joyeuse*. At this faster pace its barcarolle rhythm relates to the central part of *L'isle joyeuse*, its cadenza figure (bar 43) more clearly announces the jubilant ostinato figure in the coda of *L'isle joyeuse* (bar 220 onwards), and its final chord leads perfectly into the otherwise rather odd opening of *L'isle joyeuse*. The net result is a magnificent triptych matching all the others, rescuing *Masques* and *D'un cahier d'esquisses* from the neglect inflicted by their suspect tempo indications, and making better sense of *L'isle joyeuse* as a finale.[32]

There remains the issue of dynamics, an aspect often rendered inaccurately in Debussy's printed scores. In 1907, sending his second set of

[32] For more detail of the pieces' relationships and history see Howat, 'En route for *L'isle joyeuse*' and Debussy, *Oeuvres Complètes*, 1/III, pp. xvii–xviii. Besides the musical evidence, in January 1904 – the date written on the now-lost autograph of *D'un cahier d'esquisses* – Debussy played Ricardo Viñes the three pieces of a new suite, beginning with *Masques* and ending with *L'isle* (or *L'île*) *joyeuse*. The suite's overall title was then *Suite Bergamasque*, a title lost to Debussy shortly afterwards when he was forced to allow publication of his earlier (1890) suite of that name.

Images to Jacques Durand, Debussy writes: 'Would you please beseech your engraver to respect the exact placing of nuances – it's of extreme and pianistic importance.'[33] Comparison between his manuscripts and printed editions reveals what was troubling Debussy: his dynamics, often attached to particular voices, are sometimes moved in print as a result of engraver's conventions or attempts at visual clarity. For example, hairpin crescendos which Debussy carefully placed above the top staff at bars 5–6 and 22–4 of 'Des pas sur la neige', and under the lower staff at bars 244–7 of *L'isle joyeuse*, were moved by Durand's engraver to between the staves, obscuring Debussy's careful polyphonic voicing; and the *subito pp* at bars 137 and 170 of the 'Toccata' in *Pour le piano*, like the *subito p* at bars 166 and 170 of *L'isle joyeuse*, were 'tidied' to the beginning of the bar, instead of immediately after the first chord as Debussy had carefully written them. Hairpins were also sometimes 'squared off', climaxing on the wrong note of a phrase, or starting earlier or leading further than indicated in the manuscript. As numerous examples of this post-date 1907, it seems that Debussy's plea to Durand had only limited success.

Analogous misreadings sometimes iron out subtle distinctions between similar bars. A telling example from 'Jardins sous la pluie' is shown in ex. 4.7, where Debussy's autograph dynamics clearly bring up first the left hand alone, then both hands to climax at bar 88. The engraver – who presumably viewed the visual difference between the two bars as accidental (and would not have liked the *crescendo* inside the slur, a grave violation of engraving rules) – simply averaged out the two bars, oblivious to the resulting distortion.[34] On paper the difference may look trivial; in performance, though, it is crucial, for such illogicalities quickly sap the pianist's confidence in the composer's notation, to the point where one begins to apply one's own ideas of dynamics instead.

A priority of the *Oeuvres Complètes* has been to correct such distortions, sometimes in the teeth of engraving convention; the necessity of pla-

---

[33] 'Voulez-vous être assez aimable pour adjurer votre graveur de respecter la mise en place des nuances – cela a une importance extrême et pianistique'. Cited Debussy, *Oeuvres Complètes*, 1/III, p. xii.

[34] Bars 126 and 130 of the same piece are another case where the engraver equated two bars that Debussy had differentiated in manuscript: see Debussy, *Oeuvres Complètes*, 1/III, pp. 26 and 158.

Example 4.7. 'Jardins sous la pluie'
Autograph nuances

Durand edition (1903)

cating the present-day engraver in this regard has sometimes proved the point of what originally went awry. Stem directions are another example. In order to indicate polyphony on a large scale, Debussy's manuscripts often maintain a consistent stem direction for a voice regardless of whether it climbs high or low on the staff. The resulting visual clarity of architecture stands out in a piece like 'Mouvement', where the bass stems point down throughout bars 40–66, and similarly throughout the last two pages of the piece, indicating large architectural lines that encompass the the bass F♯s leading into and through the central section (see *Oeuvres Complètes* 1/III, 84–95). The importance of this is not just to show architectural breadth. When stems are partly inverted, as in the first editions, voices become mis-related – for example at bar 48 in 'Mouvement' where the tenor line appears to come out of the octave G of bar 47, instead of entering as a new voice. When dynamics are attached to specific lines (as in that case), it risks further confusion. Alert pianists can often spot the musical sense, but the repeated notational misrepresentation inevitably implants a false view of Debussy's musical thinking. Although it was quickly agreed, in view of the evidence, to give priority to Debussy's manuscript logic in the *Oeuvres Complètes*, experience elsewhere has shown that most publishers, even of

98

'Urtexts', will not yet accept such flouting of notational or engraving conventions widely regarded as musical 'grammar' or 'laws'. In cases where the conventions inadvertently distort or conceal a composer's indications, musical Urtext editing still has a major issue to confront. The issue extends beyond purely musical or European contexts, to the classical clarity of Debussy's beloved oriental art: his comparison in 1915 of the manuscript notation of his *Etudes* to the intricacy of a Japanese *estampe*, like his set of musical *Estampes* in 1903, is eloquent.[35]

Another notation of Debussy's sometimes distorted is the ⦃ arpeggio indication. In several contexts where he carefully used this across only part of a chord, the engraver extended it across the whole chord: for example, the autograph left hand arpeggio sign at bars 48 and 50 of 'Mouvement' covers only the top two notes, indicating sensibly that the bass octave sounds together. Conversely at bars 2 and similar of the 'Sarabande' of *Pour le piano*, the autograph sign covers the two lowermost notes, so that only the bass need sound before the rest of the chord. This exactitude also affects bars 81–6 of 'Reflets dans l'eau' (ex. 4.8a), where Debussy's right hand arpeggiation (correctly printed in the first edition) is virtually always misread as an arpeggiation across three octaves. Durand's engraver was also inexact with the first chord of bar 85: Debussy's separate arpeggio sign for each hand (as in ex. 4.8a) was misprinted as a single sign across both hands. Awareness of that misreading helps to solve a problem in the piece's second last bar, where the first edition's arpeggio sign seems incompatible with the *tenuto* dashes (ex. 4.8b). In the autograph the *tenuti* are present but not the arpeggio sign, which must have been added at proof. If we surmise, by analogy with bar 85, that Debussy's proof addition (now lost) was more probably a separate sign for each hand (ex. 4.8c), the effect makes complete sense to the *tenuti*. The resultant echo of 'Clair de lune' is equally apt, for Debussy had revised and proofed 'Clair de lune' for publication only a few months before completing 'Reflets dans l'eau' in summer 1905.

It is known that Debussy liked both Bechstein and Blüthner pianos. In addition to the upright Bechstein on which he composed, Debussy had a

---

[35] 'Hier soir, à minuit, j'ai copié la dernière note des "Etudes" . . . Ouf! . . . La plus minutieuse des estampes japonaises est un jeu d'enfant à côté du graphique de certaines pages, mais je suis content, c'est du bon travail!' Debussy to Jacques Durand, 30 September 1915. Cited Durand (ed.), *Lettres*, p. 156.

Example 4.8. 'Reflets dans l'eau'
Example 4.8a.

Lent *(dans une sonorité harmonieuse et lointaine)*

Example 4.8b. Durand edition (1905)

Example 4.8c. Conjectural proof reading

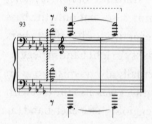

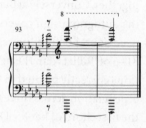

Blüthner boudoir grand, with the Aliquot system of added resonating strings, which he had bought in 1904 or 1905.[36] One clear indication of the Blüthner's influence is the final line of 'Les sons et les parfums', whose bass As give off a particularly rich but transparent resonance on a Blüthner, quite distinct from any other make. His liking for the richer sound of German pianos also suggests his Wagnerian side, distinguishing him from Fauré and

[36] According to Mme de Tinan (in conversation *c.* 1979), Debussy bought the Blüthner in Jersey in 1904; Maurice Dumesnil (Nichols, *Debussy Remembered*, p. 158) claimed that Debussy bought it after renting it during a stay in 'Bournemouth' (more probably Eastbourne where Debussy spent summer 1905). Alfredo Casella specified that Debussy normally had the Bechstein in his studio and the Blüthner in the salon (ibid., p. 172). According to Mme de Tinan the Bechstein was sold after Debussy's death to an American buyer; the Blüthner is now in the municipal museum of Brive (Périgord). The 'Chronique' in *Cahiers Debussy*, 16 (1992), 71, states that the Blüthner bears the date 1909, but

Ravel whose music reflects the lighter touch and more immediate tone of their Erards. It also suggests an affinity with Chopin, who similarly preferred the darker range of the Pleyel to the brighter, more ready-made tone of the Erard. This accords with Marguerite Long's and Alfredo Casella's accounts[37] of how profoundly Chopin lay at the basis of Debussy's pianism, and with Debussy's own memories of his first piano teacher Mme Mauté, a claimed pupil of Chopin.[38]

How did Debussy play? His only audio recordings, accompanying Mary Garden in 1904 in an extract from *Pelléas et Mélisande* and three *Ariettes oubliées*, though hard to hear in detail of colour, indicate masterly voicing combined with an entirely 'unimpressionistic' strictness of rhythm (unusual for that era, including hands mostly together), and considerable virtuosity when called for ('Green' goes impeccably at a very fast lick).[39] This tallies with Stravinsky's reminiscence of Debussy in 1912 or 1913 playing him *Jeux* in piano reduction: 'How well that man played!'[40] There are also the rolls Debussy recorded for Edwin Welte's reproducing piano system, of 'La soirée dans Grenade', *D'un cahier d'esquisses*, the complete *Children's corner*, *La plus que lente* (Welte rolls 2733–6), and the preludes 'Danseuses de Delphes', 'Le vent dans la plaine', 'La cathédrale engloutie', 'La danse de Puck' and 'Minstrels' (rolls 2738–9) – fourteen pieces in all. The inclusion of preludes from Book 1 but not Book 2, plus the issue of some of the rolls in 1913, suggests that Debussy recorded them around 1910–12.

What the rolls can tell us is mixed. Although Welte's system is in some respects very sophisticated, including a fair degree of reproduction of

this figure is more probably a case number (Blüthners are not generally dated). Copeland described the upright as a Pleyel, possibly in error (Nichols, *Debussy Remembered*, p. 166); while there is a Parisian verbal tradition that the firm of Pleyel lent Debussy an upright, this may refer to the Pleyel 'piano démontable' sent to him at Pourville for the summer of 1915. See Durand (ed.), *Lettres*, p. 140.

37 See Long, *Au piano avec Claude Debussy*, pp. 25–6, 36–7 and 74; and Nichols, *Debussy Remembered*, pp. 96–7.

38 See Debussy letter to Durand 1, September 1915, in Durand (ed.), *Lettres*, p. 150, trans. Nichols, *Debussy Letters*, p. 301; also J-J. Eigeldinger, *Chopin, Pianist and Teacher* (Cambridge, 1986), note 129 (regarding Mme Mauté and Chopin).

39 Reissued on EMI Références compact disc set CHS 7 61038 2.

40 Stravinsky, *An Autobiography* (New York, 1936), p. 49.

dynamics, successful playback depends on two factors. One is the quality and adjustment of the playing-back instrument in relation to the one used for recording. The other factor is how decisively the artist played in terms of touch and pedalling. This is because the Welte mechanism operates in a binary way: first, by identifying each note and pedal as either up or down at any moment, and second, by identifying dynamics as either static, increasing or decreasing. In that way a pianist who played with a very decisive touch and pedalling can be well reproduced without much difficulty; many of Welte's recordings of virtuosi attest to this. However, what if a pianist's touch plays with subtle half-tints, half-pedalling, and all sorts of voicings within parts and chords, responding to the inner balance points of the action, and sometimes using a *Bebung* touch that operates on half-escapement? This was the sort of playing for which Debussy was remembered: a pianist whose fingers 'never left the keys',[41] uninterested in velocity or cold clarity *per se*, and who preferred to explore all shades of colour and nuance in a piano, as his music does. Even if replayed on the original instrument used for recording (which is long gone), such playing strains the possibilities of such a recording mechanism by playing constantly on its binary dividing points.[42]

These are probably the reasons why those who remembered Debussy's playing were disappointed by the rolls, notably Mme de Tinan in whose estimation only the roll of 'La soirée dans Grenade' came near the subtlety she remembered from his playing.[43] To be fair, it should be added that Mme de Tinan's opinion was based on the 1960s Telefunken LPs recorded from the rolls on instruments not in the best of condition; some more recent recordings from the rolls reveal considerably better results.[44] Problems remain, though, and the best results obtainable still fall well short

---

[41] The violinist Egon Kenton, present at one of Debussy's performances around 1912, related this to Carl Schachter (who communicated this information to the author). See also Nichols, *Debussy Remembered*, pp. 96, 157, 159, 171, and 177.

[42] For further discussion of Debussy's Welte rolls and their problems and characteristics, see Howat, 'Debussy and Welte', *The Pianola Journal*, 7 (1994), 3–18.

[43] Information communicated to the author *c.* 1979 by Mme de Tinan.

[44] For details of audio recordings made from the Debussy rolls see D. Hall: 'The player piano on record – a discography', *The Pianola Journal*, 3 (1990), 25–39. The Telefunken LPs were GMA 65 and 75.

of the rhythmic clarity on the audio recordings. For example, scrappy rhythm seems to be ineradicable in the most exposed parts of 'Minstrels' (of all pieces), suggesting the roll's inability to reproduce something Debussy was perhaps doing in half-touch – for example, imitating the timbre of a banjo?

On the positive side, the rolls are vital in confirming details like presumed accidentals missing in other sources; in this respect the *Oeuvres Complètes* are the first Urtext edition, to my knowledge, to take corrections from a recorded source. A larger correction of this nature is the roll's series of left-hand offbeat chords in bars 8–9 of 'Danseuses de Delphes' (F and G an octave below the right thumb); comparison with bars 16–17 makes their necessity obvious. Naturally, variants from the rolls cannot be taken unquestioningly, and for the *Oeuvres Complètes* there has had to be careful selection into categories of plausibility, with variants of musical interest given on auxiliary staves (*Oeuvres Complètes*, 1/II, 1/III and 1/V).

A factor not digitally encoded on the rolls is the original tempo (though machines are set to a standard playback speed) and the roll of *Children's Corner* (roll 2733) yields some very fast tempi quite at odds with Debussy's moderate tempo headings – for example, $\quarternote$ = *c.* 160 for 'Modérément animé' in 'Doctor Gradus ad Parnassum' and up to $\halfnote$ = 208 for 'Allegretto ma non troppo' in 'Serenade for the Doll'! These improbable tempi are quoted without query in some recent editions and literature. Maurice Dumesnil, however, relates that Debussy insisted that both 'Doctor Gradus' and 'The Snow is Dancing' should not be played too quickly – in the latter case 'not fast at all'.[45] Further evidence comes from an early 1920s reissue of the roll (in 'licensee' format for modified machines), which spaces the perforations proportionally further apart and in playback yields tempi approximately 30 per cent slower. Besides making more sense of the pieces above, this produces especially interesting results in 'Golliwogg's cake-walk', now at around $\quarternote$ = 80, instead of $\quarternote$ = 112 from the original issue. Not only does this relate better to Debussy's metronomic indications for the ragtime central movements of his Cello Sonata and Violin Sonata; also the right hand syncopations are more audibly snapped,

---

[45] See Nichols, *Debussy Remembered*, p. 162.

and the off-beat dynamic explosions emerge as marked in the score.[46] The importance of this last detail relates to the pneumatic mechanism of the Welte machine: a faulty playback speed causes distortion or misplacing of the nuances encoded on the roll, and in this respect the later reissue of *Children's corner* is clearly more accurate. Although it too is not above suspicion in some respects, the point is clear that the tempi from the faster roll, which has always served as reference, are not to be believed.[47]

Of all the variants from Debussy's Welte rolls the most radical is the tempo relationship in 'La cathédrale engloutie', where the minim pulse of bars 7–12 and 22–8 is made equal to the surrounding crotchet pulse, producing a continuity of triple metre.[48] Despite the caveat above about overall tempi from the rolls, there can no doubt that this tempo doubling is authentic, corroborated as it is by independent sources including recordings by Alfred Cortot and George Copeland, the memories of Mme de Tinan and others who heard Debussy play the piece in concert, and Henri Busser's orchestration (see note 20). (Two Debussy associates who did not know about it were E. Robert Schmitz and Marcel Ciampi, who perhaps never studied this Prelude with Debussy; Marguerite Long, who did not record the piece, leaves the topic unmentioned.) For added interest, the tempo transitions on Debussy's roll are accompanied by other variants, including a particularly arresting triplet quaver bass descent to bar 22 (C – B♭ – A♭ – G), answering the bass E – D – C – B of bars 13–15 (see *Oeuvres Complètes* 1/V, p. 43). Unfortunately Debussy's own printed score of the piece (which he may have corrected) is lost, and his autograph shows only a minimum of implicit evidence of why he left the piece with this confusing notation.[49] We should remember, though, that Debussy was used to similar notational

---

[46] The mechanical aspects of all this are discussed in Howat, 'Debussy and Welte'.

[47] The problem may have been because of a compression on the unusually long roll 2733, to accommodate all six pieces; (see Howat, 'Debussy and Welte'). The slower 'licensee' reissue, by contrast, was divided into three rolls (2733, 2733a and 2733b).

[48] This is documented in more detail elsewhere (Debussy, *Oeuvres Complètes*, 1/V, p. 167; C. Burkhart, 'Debussy plays "La Cathédrale engloutie" and solves metrical mystery', *The Piano Quarterly*, 65 (autumn 1968), 14–16; and Roy Howat, *Debussy in Proportion, a Musical Analysis* (Cambridge, 1983), pp. 159–62 and his introduction to Debussy, *Préludes*, book I, pp. vii–viii).

[49] See Howat's introduction to Debussy *Préludes*, book I, pp. vii–viii.

augmentations in Rameau's scores, for example through his revision a few years earlier of *Les Fêtes de Polymnie*.[50]

The phenomenon alerts us to the possibility of similar problems elsewhere, and a related case, only partly solved by Debussy and not yet taken further in any edition, emerges from 'Pour les quartes', a piece that mixes 6/8 and 3/4 metres but in a (fairly) constant quaver tempo. In an early working draft Debussy notated bars 25–36 in half their final value, and made a fair copy like this up to bar 28 (ex. 4.9a), before observing that this no longer matched the opening tempo of the piece (*Andantino con moto*).[51] His final fair copy (ex. 4.9b) solves the problem from bar 25 onwards, relative to bars 1–17, but leaves a problem in between, with bars 18, 22 and 24 still implausibly scrambled at their notated tempo. Indeed, the earlier reading (ex. 4.9a) makes more sense of the continuity across bars 24–5, even if its *stretto* and lack of *rit.* in bar 24 show that Debussy was already thinking in slower quavers. Unfortunately, doubling note values through bars 18–24 is not the answer, as it leaves most of the passage too slow, including the middle of bar 24. Indeed, the oddly long central hiatus of bar 24 between two fast flurries of demisemiquavers is part of the problem, suggesting an inadvertent mixing of two notations within the bar.[52] A solution comes from Debussy's early working draft, in which the opening demisemiquavers of bar 24 are changed to semiquavers – probably a late amendment, perhaps even during the last recopying stage, as it makes sense only to the final reading in ex. 4.9b. Why this was not carried through to the final fair copy is unknown – perhaps just the tiredness of copying at a moonlit hour.[53] Practical experiment, combined with the evidence of Debussy's draft, suggests a solution of re-notating bar 24 in one of the two ways shown in ex. 4.9c. This can explain

[50] The intricate metrical rules for setting French speech in Rameau's time (to which Debussy often referred when championing Rameau), coupled with an archaic avoidance then of 2/4 notation in operatic recitative, necessitated the augmentation of values to 2/2 in duple bars.
[51] The two respective early manuscripts are reproduced in facsimile in Debussy, *Etudes pour le piano*, intro. Roy Howat (Geneva, 1989), pp. 13–14, and Debussy, *Oeuvres Complètes*, 1/VI, p. 116.
[52] An analogous mix of notations within a bar, in the manuscript and proofs of 'La cathédrale engloutie', is reproduced in facsimile in Debussy, *Oeuvres Complètes* 1/V, pp. 180–1.
[53] See note 35 above.

Example 4.9. 'Pour les quartes'

Example 4.9a. Abandoned fair copy

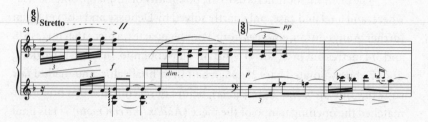

Example 4.9b. Final fair copy

Example 4.9c. Possible renotations of bar 24

Debussy's *stretto* in ex. 4.9a, and relates the triplets logically to ex. 4.1 above.

Indeed, comparison of ex. 4.1 and ex. 4.9 suggest that the whole problem springs from the fact that the rhythmic relationship across bars 17–18 is much the same as across bars 6–7, but that Debussy uses quaver beats in bar 18 for virtually the same purpose as he used crotchet beats at bar 7. The re-notation of bar 24 could thus be matched by augmenting bars 18–19 into three bars of 3/4 (retaining *Stretto*), and adding *Rubato* above bar 22 (or augmenting it into 3/4 with *Stretto* above). This would allow the triplet group of bar 18 time to register and bite (relating it again to ex. 4.1), and the fast-moving harmonies of bar 22 time to be heard. Whatever solution is adopted, the need for qualifying indications in all three bars concerned (18, 22 and 24), together with the source confusion, suggests that the passage involves a tempo somewhere between two notations. Once again Debussy's notational solecisms, if read carefully, have important information to impart.

In sum, Debussy's notation seems designed to sensitise us and guide us to the fullest feeling for both the music he heard and the feelings that underlie it. 'How much we have first to find, then to discard, to arrive at the bare flesh of emotion', he once wrote to Robert Godet.[54] The clarity of his notation suggests a similar process on paper. If isolated problems remain, we have to be well enough in touch with his notational thinking to recognise problems without confusion, and deal with them without wilfulness. The inevitable subjectivity of intervening in such cases is much less than the subjectivity of ducking the problem, or of dull, uncomprehending obedience.

---

[54] 'Combien il faut d'abord trouver, puis supprimer, pour arriver jusqu'à la chair nue de l'émotion . . .' Debussy to Robert Godet, 18 December 1911. See Debussy, *Correspondance*, p. 298.

5   Portrait of the artist as Roderick Usher

JEAN-MICHEL NECTOUX

> I dared to say to him that people had tried to shake off the dust of tradition, some in poetry and some in painting (only with great difficulty could I add the names of any musicians) and that the only result of this was that they were treated either as Symbolists or as Impressionists, terms of which kind are to be despised.[1]

This ironic statement of Debussy, from his 'Conversation with Monsieur Croche', may serve as a starting point if not as a warning. In common with many other critics, Emile Vuillermoz convincingly put forward the idea of Debussy as a 'landmark of musical Impressionism': a thesis which has for a long time prevailed. In another work, subtle in approach and admirably documented, Stefan Jarocínski perceptively allied the composer's work with the aesthetic of suggestion: more a property of Symbolism than of Impressionism.[2] The 1984 Rome exhibition and the recent monographs of François Lesure have also followed this line of approach.[3]

Far be it from my intention to re-open a debate which can never be conclusive owing to the elusive nature of what constitutes either Symbolism or Impressionism in musical terms, I wish merely to present

---

[1] 'J'osai lui dire que les hommes avaient cherché, les uns dans la poésie, les autres dans la peinture (à grand-peine j'y ajoutai quelques musiciens) à secouer la vieille poussière des traditions, et que cela n'avait eu d'autre résultat que de les faire traiter de symbolistes ou d'impressionnistes; termes commodes pour mépriser son semblable.' Debussy, 'Entretien avec M. Croche', *La Revue blanche* (1 July 1901); reprinted in François Lesure (ed.), *Monsieur Croche et autres écrits*, rev. edn. (Paris, 1987), pp. 48–53. English version, Richard Langham Smith (trans. and ed.), (London and New York 1977, repr. Cornell, 1988).

[2] Stefan Jarocínski, *Debussy, impressionnisme et symbolisme* (Warsaw, 1966); French trans. (Paris, 1970); Eng. trans. (London, 1976).

[3] Exhibition catalogue, *Debussy e il simbolismo*, by François Lesure and Guy Cogeval (Rome, 1984); François Lesure, *Claude Debussy avant 'Pelléas', ou les années symbolistes* (Paris, 1992), and *Claude Debussy* (Paris, 1994).

certain new facts and bring to the foreground certain works of art which fascinated Debussy, leaving aside his relatively well-known predilection for Monet, Turner and Whistler. Rather do the present reflections concentrate on the aesthetics of a group of artists whom he knew personally: in the first case Henry Lerolle whose art lay outside the boundaries of both Impressionism and Symbolism and in whose home Debussy admired Degas; secondly the Norwegian Frits Thaulow; and finally two particularly idiosyncratic personalities, Henry de Groux and Camille Claudel.

This done, I have attempted to isolate what the composer's closest friends tell us about the sources of the composer's personal tastes and as far as is possible to reconstruct the circumstances in which the composer enthused about such works of art, whether paintings or sculptures. References to the fine arts are relatively rare among his published correspondence: Debussy preferred to keep to himself the more intimate cross-currents of his intellectual life. As a guide, the testimonies of several people privileged to be close to the composer must therefore be followed: Robert Godet; Louis Laloy; Mme Gérard de Romilly; Pasteur Vallery-Radot and René Peter; all of whom were friends of the composer at one time or another and who open up paths of enquiry in this domain, to date relatively little explored.

Debussy left Rome definitively in 1887 and thus returned to Paris when the vogue for Symbolism was at its peak: the manifesto of Jean Moréas dates from 1886, the year of the last Impressionist exhibition, and it is thus in the triumphant years of the Symbolist movement that the composer's artistic tastes were formed and refined. In a questionnaire of 1889 he indicated among his favourite painters Botticelli (remembered from his Italian stay) and Gustave Moreau, an artist of whom we find no further mention. It was at this time that he visited several important collections, among them the Louvre where in the company of Pierre Louÿs he was deeply struck with admiration for Titian's *Jupiter et Antiope*. It may be assumed that he paid still more visits to the Musée du Luxembourg which exhibited the works of contemporary artists. Similarly, he could hardly have failed to visit the annual Salons of the newly founded *Société Nationale des Beaux-Arts*, rival of the old-established *Société des Artistes français*. He frequented both antiquarians and bookshops, in particular that of Edmond Bailly, the Librairie de l'Art Indépendant, which was a veritable rendez-vous of poets and artists, as well as art galleries such as those of Georges Petit and Durand-Ruel where, from about 1890, he had admired the *Nocturnes* of Whistler and, in 1900, the first *Water-lilies* of Monet.

Debussy, however, was not of sufficient means to be able to adorn his walls with the pictures of the contemporary artists whom he admired: Whistler, Degas or Monet. Pasteur Vallery-Radot mentions that coloured reproductions of Turner and Whistler hung in the composer's comfortable apartment in the Avenue du Bois in 1910: a sign of the composer's fidelity to the artists whom he had admired twenty years earlier.[4] Even before this, he was already the proud possessor of several originals, owing to the generosity of certain artistic friends. The most remarkable of these was undoubtedly a work by Odilon Redon which the artist had given him in April 1893, after a performance of *La Damoiselle Elue*.[5] This work, probably a lithograph, has unfortunately been impossible to identify, nor has its whereabouts been ascertained among the many objects, manuscripts and archives which belonged to the composer.

In her evocation of the tiny apartment inhabited by the Debussys at 58, rue Cardinet in the last years of the nineteenth century, Mme Gérard de Romilly notes: 'there was a divan and several oriental rugs, as well as pictures by Lerolle, Jacques Blanche and Thaulow, and drawings showing Lilo Debussy, still at that time in the full flower of her beauty'.[6]

Lerolle, Degas, Thaulow

The importance of the friendship between Debussy and Henry Lerolle (1848–1929) is well-known, especially during the early 1890s. Lerolle was one of the first confirmed enthusiasts of the as yet incomplete *Pelléas* and in 1893 dedicatee of *De Soir* from the *Proses Lyriques*.

---

[4] See the introduction to Pasteur Valléry-Radot (ed.), *Lettres de Claude Debussy à sa femme Emma* (Paris, 1957), p. 35. It would be interesting to know precisely which works, as few possessions of Debussy survive.

[5] See the letter of thanks Debussy sent Redon, in Debussy, *Correspondance 1884–1918*, ed. François Lesure (Paris, 1993), p. 75.

[6] 'il y avait aussi un divan, quelques carpettes d'Orient et aux murs, des tableaux peints par Lerolle, Jacques Blanche, Thaulow, et des dessins représentant Lilo Debussy alors dans tout l'éclat de sa beauté.' G. de Romilly, 'Debussy professeur par une de ses élèves (1898–1909)', *Cahiers Debussy*, 2 (1978), 5 and 10.

'Debussy told me that there was only one painter who understood music, and that it was me', wrote Lerolle to his brother-in-law Ernest Chausson. 'Perhaps he has good reason for saying that, the rascal!. . . I see only Debussy and occasionally Bonheur', he goes on, 'and even though the artistic ideas of musicians are those which I like best, they don't appear to be sufficient as painters for me to be entirely confident in them.'[7]

In Parisian society of the fin-de-siècle, Lerolle as much as Chausson represented the type of bourgeois artist living within a traditional family according to Catholic principles far from the disorder of the Bohemian artist. Comfortably off, he resided in the Avenue Duquesne near the Invalides, keeping up with the latest in literature, music and the fine arts in their most refined manifestations. Retaining his distance as much from the conventions of official academic teaching as from the radical audacity of the avant-garde, Lerolle's art, delicate and sensitive, provides an example of a sort of well-tempered modernity. 'It is through the artists of the official salon that the still discussed innovations of our grand inventors have been propagated', wrote Maurice Denis. 'Lerolle was one of those who contributed to the transformation of French painting, while still remaining accessible to the public who appreciate Gérôme and Cabanel'.[8]

In his fine portrait of his mother, first shown at the *Société Nationale des Beaux-Arts* in 1895 and now in the Musée d'Orsay in Paris, we can observe the artistic qualities of Lerolle: his taste for a fluid style; the delicacy of his application; the slightly dry style of his drawing – a distinction which places him in the lineage of Whistler and of certain of the early works of Degas. An excellent draughtsman and even more remarkable as an

[7] 'Debussy m'a dit qu'il n'y avait qu'un peintre qui s'y connaisse en musique, et que c'était moi. Peut-être a-t-il des raisons pour cela, le mâtin . . . Je ne vois plus que Debussy et quelquefois Bonheur. Et quoique les idées artistiques des musiciens soient celles que j'aime le mieux, ils ne me paraissent pas tout à fait assez peintres pour que j'aie entière confiance en eux.' Letter of 5 February 1894, quoted C. Oulmont, *Musique de l'amour I: Ernest Chausson et la 'bande à Franck'* (Paris, 1935), p. 79.
[8] 'C'est par ces artistes du Salon officiel que furent propagées les innovations des grands inventeurs, encore discutés. Lerolle a été de ceux qui ont contribué à cette transformation de la peinture française, tout en restant accessibles au public de Gérôme et de Cabanel.' Maurice Denis, *Henry Lerolle et ses amis* (Paris, 1932), p. 14.

engraver, Lerolle had, like Degas before him, been a pupil of Louis Lamothe, a disciple of Ingres.

'We would meet Degas at Lerolle's house', testified Maurice Denis, 'in front of some of his finest pictures: nudes, dancers, women doing their hair, jockeys.'[9] These may either have been a dozen works acquired by Lerolle from Durand-Ruel or those obtained directly from Degas himself. In 1883, Lerolle had won Degas's imagination, the latter being both surprised and charmed that a canvas of horses and jockeys (*Avant la course*, oil, *c.* 1882, L.702, Clark Art Institute, Williamstown, Massachusetts) had been able to impress a painter he described as 'entirely given to decoration, in the space left free in between the exhibitions of the *Société Nationale des Beaux-Arts* and the triennial exhibitions', according to a letter from Degas to Madame Bartholomé.[10] Having become a regular at his salon in the Avenue Duquesne, Degas confided in the young painter who had nothing of the official artist about him, despite his participation in the massive project of decorating the latest temples to the Republic: the Sorbonne and the Hôtel de Ville de Paris.

The collection of Degas's works which Lerolle assembled within a few years was remarkable. Among them, the most noteworthy were perhaps the following, since acquired by major international collections: *Women combing their hair* (*Femmes se peignant*, peinture à l'essence, [oil mixed with turpentine] *c.*1875, L.376, Phillips collection, Washington); *Reclining bather* (*Baigneuse allongée sur le sol*, pastel, 1886–8, L.854, *Musée d'Orsay*, Paris) and *Woman in bathtub* (*Femme au tub*, pastel, L.738, Tate Gallery, London). It may be added that Ernest Chausson, another close friend of Debussy around 1893–4, had followed the example of his brother-in-law Henry Lerolle in acquiring a fine series of pastels by Degas, as well as an oil portrait (of Bellet du Poisat).[11]

---

[9] 'Degas, on le rencontrait chez Lerolle devant quelques-uns de ses plus beaux tableaux, des nus, des danseuses, des femmes qui se coiffent, des jockeys'. ibid., p. 5.

[10] 'tout à fait en train de se faire décorer, dans l'espace laissé libre entre le Salon et l'Exposition Triennale ou Nationale'. Quoted in H. Loyrette, *Degas* (Paris, 1991), p. 481.

[11] Loyrette gives the complete list of Degas belonging to Lerolle and Chausson, ibid., p. 765.

Debussy admired this supreme artist, according to Robert Godet 'for the unique gracefulness of his rhythms in the movements of dance and the intense accuracy with which those working are portrayed, as well as, in the figures themselves, the sense of fatality inscribed in destiny which the models portray'.[12]

In Degas there is an originality of vantage point; a correctness of proportion; a delicacy in tonal intensity and an audacity in the composition which is often asymmetric and foreshortened and which has, above all, that sense of arabesque which Debussy sought after in his own works. The parallel with Degas seems to me quite as striking as those already observed with Whistler and Turner, moreover, it is all the more remarkable because at this time Degas was relatively unknown and had exhibited very little. In the autumn of 1892, and subsequently that of 1894, he had, however, agreed to present about 20 landscapes painted on monotype at Durand-Ruel's. These may be counted as among his finest and most forward-looking works, already pointing towards abstraction. Debussy was enthusiastic about these extreme works where he no doubt encountered a fluid imagination and the sense of mystery of certain Turners, allied to the subtle tones of Japanese art. These are imaginary landscapes and more than 'states of souls'; 'states of seeing' (états d'yeux) to quote the phrase of Degas.

It is thus not surprising to read in Godet's words that 'the only artist constantly on Debussy's lips at this time was one whom it is believed that he never met: Degas, and, more precisely, that side of Degas who was the landscapist of some rare pastels which fascinated and at the same time disciplined Debussy's mind'.[13] It may therefore be deduced with certainty that Debussy visited at least one of these exhibitions of landscapes which were no doubt intensely appreciated in the Lerolle–Chausson circle.

[12] 'pour la grâce unique de ses rythmes dans les mouvements de la danse ou leur intense justesse dans ceux du travail, et pour le sens, dans ses figures, des fatalités ataviquement inscrites dans le destin qu'apportent avec eux les modèles'. Robert Godet 'Entretien préliminaire' (with G. Jean-Aubry), in Debussy, *Lettres à deux amis* (Paris, 1942), p. 43.

[13] 'Le seul artiste que Debussy nommât constamment à cette époque était celui dont on croit être sûr qu'il ne le rencontra jamais: Degas, même le Degas paysagiste des trop rares pastels – une fascination et, à la fois, une discipline pour son esprit.' Robert Godet, 'En marge de la marge', *La Revue musicale* (1 May 1926), 71.

Debussy was deeply attracted by this upper-middle-class milieu where life was sufficiently carefree to allow an artistic exchange of ideas to be the main subject of conversation. Moreover, the resolutely anti-academic stance of Lerolle could hardly have failed to appeal to the disgruntled former *pensionnaire* of the *Académie de France* in Rome. It was in these circumstances that Debussy played the first version of the scene of Pelléas's death one evening in October 1893, and subsequently, in February 1894, the first act of *Parsifal*: 'It went very well', Lerolle wrote to Chausson, 'and I think everyone was happy even though some people said you could not hear the words sufficiently clearly. That was certainly true! You know what his diction is like when he sings: it was fine, for sometimes he merely sang "tra ta ra ta ta"! All in all the admirable Debussy went about it all just as other people carry round a suitcase to earn a bob or two. But I think he's happy enough in the knowledge that we've collected a thousand francs for him.'[14]

Maurice Denis described the setting for these recitals: 'Neither antiquarian bric-à-brac, nor an operating theatre: a harmonious blend of family heirlooms and modern furniture along with scrupulously selected works of art. Apart from the Degas, there were canvases by Fantin; Puvis; Besnard; Corot and Renoir; and some fine old pictures; all exhibited on walls hung with lightly coloured William Morris papers.'[15] A famous Renoir preserves the memory of this music room which must have been most welcoming to the young Debussy: *Yvonne and Christine Lerolle at the piano* (oil, 1897, Musée de l'Orangerie, Paris); while on the wall two works by Degas could be distinguished: *Before the race*, already cited, and *Dancers under a tree* (pastel, c. 1878, L.486, Norton Simon Museum, Pasadena, USA).

[14] 'Ça a très bien marché, et je crois qu'on a été content, quoique certains ont trouvé qu'on n'entendait pas assez les paroles. Je crois bien! Tu sais comment il prononce en chantant. Et encore heureux quand il ne disait pas seulement: tra ta ra ta ta. En somme ce brave Debussy fait cela comme d'autres portent une malle, pour gagner quelque chose. Mais je crois qu'il est assez content de penser que nous avons à peu près un millier de francs pour lui.' Letter of 5 Feb 1894, quoted C. Oulmont, *Musique de l'amour I*, pp. 79–80.

[15] 'Ni bric à brac d'antiquaire, ni salle d'opération: un ensemble harmonieux de meubles de famille et de meubles modernes, d'oeuvres d'art très choisies: outre ces Degas, des toiles de Fantin, de Puvis, de Besnard, de Corot, de Renoir, quelques bons tableaux anciens, sur des murs tapissés de papiers clairs de William Morris.' Maurice Denis, *Henry Lerolle*, p. 5.

Yvonne Lerolle, then aged seventeen, exerted a certain attraction over Debussy: he dedicated his three *Images* for piano of 1894 to this young lady, including a mysterious piece entitled *Souvenir du Louvre* recalling, perhaps, a visit there made in her company.[16] In February 1894, he copied out for her some fragments from *Pelléas*, notably the section evoking the appearance of Mélisande on the terrace by the sea, 'her hands full of flowers', the music most artistically written out on a fan made from Japanese paper, itself decorated with flowers in the Japanese style, and accompanied by the dedication "To Melle Yvonne Lerolle, in memory of her little sister Mélisande", a gallant gesture of some refinement whose idea he had no doubt borrowed from Mallarmé.[17]

Among the works which Debussy particularly admired at Lerolle's home there was also a very fine snow-scene in pastel, received from its painter Frits Thaulow in 1883: *Winter on the banks of the Simoa* (pastel, 1883, private collection).[18] Debussy was particularly fond of the works of Thaulow (1847–1906), an artist whose position could be compared to that of Lerolle himself in that it bordered the movements of both Impressionism and Symbolism. Having begun as a painter allied to the most detailed realism, he achieved a certain success in exhibiting snow-scenes or waterside scenes which became specialities of his, repeated extensively and amounting to a considerable output.

An exuberant personality, a devotee of music and something of a cellist in his time, Thaulow was well-known in the artistic circles of Paris where he was held in sufficient esteem to be offered, either as gifts or exchanges, works by Rodin, Camille Claudel and Gauguin (admittedly his brother-in-law) and Jacques-Emile Blanche who painted in 1895 a monu-

---

[16] Published in the suite *Pour le piano*, the Sarabande had already been included in the unpublished *Images* of 1894. On its publication in 1901, Debussy dedicated this piece to Mme E. Rouart, i.e. Yvonne Lerolle.

[17] 'A Melle Yvonne Lerolle, en souvenir de sa petite soeur Mélisande'. Reproduced on the cover of the volume Claude Debussy, *Correspondance, 1884–1918* (Paris, 1993).

[18] A work probably received by way of an exchange: Thaulow's pastel is inscribed 'A mon ami Lerolle' while the Norwegian painter owned a canvas by Lerolle, *Les Saintes*, bearing the inscription 'A mon ami Thaulow'. See. no. 140 of the sale catalogue immediately after the artist's death (*Atelier Frits Thaulow*, Galerie Georges Petit [6 and 7 May 1907]). No. 141 of the same catalogue is another painting of Lerolle: *Pivoines et rhododendrons*.

mental portrait of the Thaulow Family, now in the Musée d'Orsay, Paris: a painting which accurately places Thaulow as kind and generous, and overflowing with energy and enthusiasm.[19]

One may reasonably suppose that the work of Thaulow which hung on Debussy's wall (according to Mme de Romilly) was given to him by the Norwegian artist as a mark of kindness and respect to the young musician who had, in turn, shown him admiration, in the company of Lerolle.[20]

Two fringe artists: Henry de Groux and Camille Claudel

Somewhat more surprising is Debussy's attraction to the particularly idiosyncratic life and works of the painter and sculptor of Belgian origin Henry de Groux (1866–1930). His life, as well as his works, is coloured by various scandals such as his exclusion from the group of Brussels artists known as 'les XX' in 1890 for having refused to allow his work to be shown alongside 'the inane vase of suns of M. Vincent and all the other *agents provocateurs*', as he expressed himself to Octave Maus, referring to works in the neo-Impressionist style and particularly the famous *Sunflowers* by Van Gogh.[21]

De Groux delighted in vast cycles on epic themes, done in oil or pastel, which drew from him highly charged fantasies: Napoleonic epics; biblical events or the heroes of musical history, and above all Beethoven or Wagner

---

[19] See the catalogue noted above. Two of Thaulow's works are in the Musée Rodin in Paris; see the catalogue of the exhibition 'Frits Thaulow, un norvégien français' (Paris, 1994).

[20] The Thaulow specialist Vidar Poulsson has ascertained that it is impossible to follow the relationship between the painter and the musician much further. Thaulow, who was widely travelled, did not keep any of the letters he received. Neither has it been possible to identify precisely which painting Debussy owned from among his prodigious output. With only a few exceptions it has been difficult to locate the works in the possession of Debussy which were dispersed among the children of Emma Bardac: Raoul Bardac and Dolly de Tinan. The sale of his collection in 1933 contained only two works of visual art: the 'Wave' of Hokusai, and a lithograph of Steinlen. (See sale catalogue published by Georges Andrieux, Paris [Nov.–Dec. 1933], in the Département de la musique, Bibliothèque Nationale de France.)

[21] Quoted by Rodolphe Rapetti: 'Un chef-d'oeuvre pour ces temps d'incertitude: *Le Christ aux outrages* d'Henry de Groux', *Revue de l'art*, 96 (1992), 42–50.

whom he idolised. In 1890, in Brussels, his monumental work *Le Christ aux outrages* (oil, Palais du Roure, Avignon) caused a sensation owing to the audacity of its conception. Brought to Paris on the order of King Leopold II, this giant canvas was refused by the jury of the *Salon du Champs de Mars*, and his subject matter was referred to as libertarian art. The work was exhibited in Paris in February 1892 in a rustic location: a barn open to the winds, where hens wandered freely, at the end of the rue Vaugirard in the 15th *arrondissement*; his expressive audacity as well as the tumultuous and exaggerated nature of his composition attracted numerous celebrities, among them Mallarmé, Hérédia, Puvis de Chavannes and Debussy, who saw the work in the company of Robert Godet.[22]

At the time of his meeting with Debussy, a journalist from *Le Figaro* sketched a portrait of this unique artist: 'One would see him outside Tortoni's without recognising him. Perhaps you have noticed this very young man of that type who is at the same time gentle and energetic, with eyes grey like the sea, long straight blond hair, and a vague look with a remarkable inner quality. His hand is covered in rings and he wields a cane whose tip is ornamented with decorative gold, his thin, frail frame bending beneath a sky-blue overcoat'.[23] (See fig. 5.1.)

Debussy was impressed by the *Christ aux outrages* and kept in touch with this budding young artist, five years his junior, who so bravely and deliberately ignored conventional rules and the opinions of official juries. De Groux, on the other hand, despite his dreams of grandeur and passionate love of music, seemed to experience only pity for Debussy's aesthetic before *Pelléas*, as is testified by a fragment of his unpublished diary from 1897: 'I love the storms in sound evoked by Richard Wagner, and the sublime torrents of J. S. Bach. Do I really have to content myself with the feeble stutter-

[22] Robert Godet 'Entretien préliminaire' (with G. Jean-Aubry), in Debussy: *Lettres à deux amis*, p. 45. Godet is mistaken in placing the episode during the rehearsals for *Pelléas*. See Rapetti, 'Un chef-d'oeuvre . . .' to whom I am grateful for generous assistance.

[23] 'On l'a vu au perron de Tortoni sans le connaître. Peut-être a-t-on remarqué ce très jeune homme au type à la fois énergique et doux, les yeux gris de mer, le regard vague, ce regard *en dedans* qui étonne, des cheveux longs, blonds et plats. La main chargée de bagues, tourmente une canne à poignée d'or ciselée; la taille, frêle et mince, se courbe sous un pardessus bleu azur.' Charles Buet, 'Au jour le jour', *Le Figaro* (11 May 1892).

Figure 5.1. Henry de Groux in 1901 (de Groux archives)

ing of brother Debussy or the corny tunes of father [Ambroise] Thomas and Gounod, those elderly followers of the chaste Susannah?'[24]

In the first years of the new century, de Groux had substantially to modify his opinion, allowing himself to be won over and even seduced by the evolution of the composer whose aesthetic, in *L'isle joyeuse* and *La mer*, he may have seen as having become more passionate and vigorous.

This change of heart may be seen in a pastel inspired by the musician done by de Groux in 1909 (Maison Claude Debussy, Saint-Germain-en-Laye). (See fig. 5.2.)

This image, entirely characteristic of de Groux's extreme lyricism, reveals an aspect of Debussy far from the distant, rigid aesthetic which is often held to be his dominant characteristic. The de Groux archives also reveal the existence of another pastel until now unknown, probably contemporary with the known pastel: the pose is only slightly different, the subject being viewed entirely in a left hand profile, and the clothes are the same even if the likeness of Debussy is less apparent. It is possible that it is a first sketch which remains undated, known now only through one of a number of photographs taken in the artist's studio some twenty years after his death. (See fig. 5.3).[25]

In the knowledge of these, it is less astonishing to read in the composer's hand the following eulogy, in a letter to Godet dated December 1911:

> Yesterday at the *Salon d'Automne*, attracted by an exhibition of Henry de Groux, I rediscovered a moment of the past!
>
> This is an admirable exhibition! . . . Napoleon leading the Russian retreat[26] which freezes you more severely than all the snowdrifts in the world, and where you feel all the horror of his next fall from grace. There's a bronze of Tolstoy (see fig. 5.4) a considerable work, which seems to be marching

---

[24] 'J'aime les tempêtes . . . sonores de Richard Wagner ou les torrents sublimes de Sébastien Bach – Faut-il que je me contente des balbutiements atoniques du frère Debussy ou des rengaines des pères Thomas et Gounod, ces vieux suiveurs de la chaste Suzanne musicale?' Archives de Groux, private collection.

[25] Now in a private collection, the photographs reproduced come from this source.

[26] De Groux executed numerous works on this theme which obsessed him. It is impossible to ascertain the exact picture to which Debussy refers. The catalogue of the *Salon d'Automne* of 1911 is very vague, saying only that among them no. 16, *La retraite de Russie*, belongs to a M. Barreau. Two versions of this subject are reproduced in the issue of *La Plume* devoted to de Groux in 1899 (nos. 239–40).

Figure 5.2. Henry de Groux: *Claude Debussy* (pastel, 1909, Saint-Germain-en-Laye, Maison Claude Debussy)

Figure 5.3. Henry de Groux: *Claude Debussy* (pastel, 1909, unknown version; taken from a photograph from the de Groux archives, present whereabouts unknown)

Figure 5.4. Henry de Groux: *Tolstoy* (bronze, from a photograph from the *Albums Maciet*, Paris, Bibliothèque des Arts décoratifs)

against fate, much finer than those clever distortions of Rodin. There's a portrait of Wagner which has that face of a cynical old magician who is keeping something secret. . . In all this there are so many images, forms which haunt you without respite. I saw Henry de Groux there, he has hardly changed at all. As always with the air of a genial buffoon and, in his eyes, all the dreams in the world.

It seems to me most apt that it was with you that I first saw *Le Christ aux outrages*, wasn't it in a sort of barn on the outskirts of Vaugirard? . . .

This de Groux, who seems to disappear in such a way that one would have thought him dead, is a fine example of moral courage – I know others too. . . He teaches us that we should shun the evil smoke of censers and that occasionally there's no harm in spitting in them.'[27]

In the dialogue between Georges Jean-Aubry and Robert Godet, one reads in relation to Henry de Groux:

And it is the sculptor, above all, that Debussy appreciated in him. The letters of Claude prove this, as well as the fact that he himself exposed himself, it seems, to the whims of this passionate sculptor. Two busts should have been the result, but I have never seen them having left Paris long ago. I can illuminate this point no further.[28]

[27] 'Hier, étant au Salon d'Automne attiré par une exposition de Henry de Groux, j'ai retrouvé du Passé!
Cette exposition est admirable! . . . Un Napoléon menant la retraite de Russie qui vous glace plus profondément que toute la neige amoncelée et où l'on sent toute l'amertume des prochaines déchéances. Un Tolstoï en bronze, considérable, qui semble marcher contre la Destinée, beaucoup plus beau que les adroites mutilations de Rodin! Un portrait de Wagner avec cette face de vieux magicien cynique qui garde son secret . . . Tout cela autant d'images, de formes qui vous hantent sans relâche. J'ai vu là H. de Groux, à peine changé. Toujours l'air d'un pitre génial, et dans les yeux, tous les rêves du monde.
Il me semble bien que c'est avec vous que je vis pour la première fois *Le Christ aux outrages*, dans une sorte de grange au fond de Vaugirard? . . .
Ce de Groux, qui consent à disparaître si soigneusement qu'on a pu le croire mort, est un bel exemple de courage moral – j'en connais d'autres . . . Il enseigne qu'il faut dédaigner la mauvaise fumée des encensoirs et qu'au besoin il n'est pas inutile de cracher dedans'. Debussy, *Correspondance*, pp. 296–7.

[28] 'Et c'est le sculpteur, surtout, qu'apprécia en lui Debussy. – Les lettres de notre Claude en témoignent, et le fait qu'il exposa, paraît-il, sa personne aux entreprises de ce passionné modeleur. Il doit en être résulté deux bustes, mais je ne les ai pas vus (où sont-ils ayant alors quitté Paris pour assez longtemps. Je n'en sais pas davantage sur ce point.') Debussy, *Lettres à deux amis*, p. 46.

The unpublished documents in the archives of the artist permit us to confirm that there were not in fact two busts, but one bust and a monument.

When, after the death of Debussy, a committee of musicians was formed with the aim of erecting a monument to his memory, Henry de Groux was contacted by the composer Carol-Bérard (1881–1942), a pupil of Albéniz who knew de Groux and was an admirer of his work. It was at that time planned either to commission a bust of the composer or a monument on a grander scale if the collected funds permitted. When asked to submit an outline drawing, it seems that de Groux was inspired by the project and unheeding of the recommendation to be prudent, launched straight into the project without waiting to be officially designated. In his studio in the rue Chaptal, he modelled a bust of the musician (see fig. 5.5) most probably inspired by one of the photographs taken at Pourville that Emma Bardac had sent him (see fig. 5.6). The work was cast in the autumn of 1919, according to a letter from the sculptor to his daughter Marie-Thérèse.[29]

To be truthful, it is hardly a good likeness of Debussy: a resemblance to his model does not seem to have been the primary concern of the artist who noted with regard to his portrait of Wagner: 'My wish was to do a sort of triumphant portrait which is not simply a physical portrait, but which encompasses his genius, commemorating it in the noblest of poses which captures his art exactly. It's a sort of monumental art.'[30] Emile Baumann,

---

[29] Paris, 31 Oct 1919, 'Je suis encore très occupé à l'usine, à la fonderie *où toutes mes oeuvres sont à la fonte.* C'est trop important pour que je ne fasse pas les plus grands sacrifices pour réaliser une sorte de trésor et prendre rang comme sculpteur avec des pièces magnifiques. – Notre petit poilu en bronze est magnifique. Il est tiré à trois exemplaires – de même tous les bustes: Clemenceau, Mallarmé, Debussy etc. tous remaniés et achevés – Labeur énorme.' (I am still very busy in the factory, more precisely in the foundry where all my works are in the melting pot. It is so important that I am prepared to make any kind of sacrifice to produce works which are really precious and take my place as a sculptor known for magnificent pieces. Our little bronze soldier is magnificent. 3 copies have been done of him, in fact of all the busts, Clemenceau, Mallarmé and Debussy, all re-done and complete – a mammoth task!) This letter, as all those of de Groux quoted here, is unpublished.

[30] 'Ma volonté a été de faire une sorte de portrait triomphal, qui n'est plus le simple portrait physique, mais la configuration de son génie, commémoré dans une suprême attitude qui en précise la formule définitive. C'est une sorte d'art monumental'. Emile Baumann, *La vie terrible d'Henry de Groux* (Paris, 1936), p. 282. This probably refers to a diary extract of de Groux.

Figure 5.5. Henry de Groux: *Claude Debussy* (bronze, cast in 1919, Paris, Bibliothèque-Musée de l'Opéra)

Figure 5.6. Claude Debussy at Pourville, June 1904, copy sent to de Groux by Emma Debussy (de Groux archives)

son-in-law and biographer of Henry de Groux, discovered in de Groux's Debussy 'a young bearded God, exerting an ecstatic Dionysiac force, the mouth half open as he lends his ear to the sound of invisible flutes. The bliss of musical creation has never been better captured in this face of pagan happiness.'[31] It is in effect the creator, in particular, of the *Prélude à l'après-midi d'un faune* and *Sirènes* that de Groux chose to evoke, his bronze reverie, charged with lyricism, represents the composer in a strangely contorted pose which hardly explains the connections with the project for a monument on which de Groux worked in 1920, noting in his diary:

'The Debussy monument

According to the character of his art and his physique resembling a young druid or beautiful hierophant, I had wanted to recreate the figure of Debussy

[31] 'un jeune dieu barbu, exultant d'une force dionysiaque, extasié, la bouche entr'ouverte en prêtant l'oreille à des flûtes invisibles. L'ivresse du verbe mélodique n'a jamais été mieux transcrite dans un visage païennement heureux.' Ibid., p. 253.

126

by flanking him with a young or old aegypan tuning his pan-pipes to the noises of the water or the flowery banks, set amongst precious stones as if it were near a waterfall kindling a rainbow. A Bacchante, singing his song of freedom, would give way to a cloven-hoofed infant attracted by curiosity and pleasure.

This group, of which I have already done a model, is extremely well composed – the gesture made by the hand of the hierophant is one where he points to his ear, in the manner of an orchestral conductor, while the other seems to be silencing all other earthly or heavenly voices. None of this is in the least like Rodin's Victor Hugo, although perhaps inspired by the same idea of genius and the love of nature. It is very likely that they will be compared to my work, in a disparaging and hostile way, and that my individual conception will be seen against what is seen as a plausible influence. I couldn't care less!'[32]

[32] 'Le monument Debussy
Selon le caractère de son art et aussi de sa physionomie de jeune druide ou de bel hiérophante, j'eusse volontiers édifié la figure de Debussy, flanquée de celle d'un jeune ou vieil aegypan accordant sa syrinx aux rumeurs passant sur les eaux ou les berges en fleurs – dans un endroit de gemmes et de présences près d'une chute de cataracte génératrice d'arc-en-ciel. Une ménade écarterait de sa chanson émancipatrice un bambin aux pieds fourchus stimulé par la curiosité et le plaisir. Le groupe dont j'ai déjà fait la maquette se compose très bien aussi – le geste qui ramène la main de l'hiérophante, donc une main vers l'oreille tendue – à la manière d'un chef d'orchestre, – tandis que l'autre semble imposer silence à toutes autres voix de la terre ou des cieux, – ne rappelle nullement celui du Victor Hugo de Rodin, inspiré peut-être de la même idée de génie et d'amant de la nature! – et il est fort probable qu'on les rapprochera dans un esprit hostile à mon oeuvre, à ma conception personnelle si libre cependant de cette plausible influence; je m'en fiche, donc!' – Unpublished diary of de Groux, fragment dated 29 October from a volume inscribed on the back 'Henry de Groux: Les Sigillaires 1908' (private collection). Rodolphe Rapetti has confirmed that de Groux noted down thoughts and observations in these ledgers without any exact chronology. It may be assumed to date from 29 October 1920 as it appears to be taken from an unpublished letter from the sculptor to an unidentified Belgian correspondent, written from Vernègues and clearly dated August 1920: 'J'ai fait aussi assez bien de sculptures outre le Clemenceau que vous avez vu jadis à mon atelier. J'ai les premiers éléments de ma statue de Debussy – Un Mallarmé; un lord Byron; un Shakespeare, un Balzac et un Edgar Poë. J'oubliais un Maréchal Foch – fondu récemment et qui le venge, je crois, de ses innombrables effigies sans caractère.' (I have also done quite a lot of sculptures apart from the Clemenceau that you have already seen in my studio. I have the first elements of my Debussy statue, a Mallarmé, a Lord Byron, a Shakespeare, a Balzac and an Edgar Poe. I forgot to mention a Maréchal Foch, recently cast and which avenges the innumerable characterless effigies of him.) De Groux's chaotic punctuation has here, as in all other quotations, been preserved.

Figure 5.7. Henry de Groux: Project for the Debussy Monument (charcoal, Paris, private collection)

At the beginning of 1921, relations between the sculptor and the monument committee turned to one of confrontation: de Groux set himself against the tardiness of their decision even when he himself had not submitted any of the required designs. These projects Carol-Bérard wanted to publish in the special Debussy number of the new *Revue Musicale*, under the editorship of Henry Prunières, which appeared in December 1920. But since July of that year, de Groux had left Paris for the South, wandering from Vernègues to Avignon and then going on to Marseilles where he for some time camped out in the burnt ruins of the Opera.

Still absorbed in the project, de Groux produced more designs, sketches and plans[33] and made a substantial plaster mock-up. In January 1921 he sent a photograph of the plaster to Carol-Bérard but forbidding him to show it to the committee: an action which arouses the suspicion that the artist was not satisfied with what he had done. In a long and frank statement of his views, Carol-Bérard admitted his disappointment to the sculptor: '...the composition you have sent me does not really seem feasible. With respect, I am personally not enthusiastic about the way you have done it, but I will keep my opinion to myself. But let the heavens preserve us from a Debussy in a frock coat and bowler hat, could one really see him reduced to that, one who is still so vivid for us? I am thunderstruck, but I hope you will forgive me, and rest assured that I love sculpture and not at all in an old-fashioned way!'[34]

---

[33] See figs. 5.8–10: the charcoal drawing entitled *Le chant des sources, Claude Debussy* (fig. 5.9) figured in the Debussy exhibition at the Bibliothèque Nationale in 1962 (catalogue no. 211, dimensions 75 x 55 cm) belonging at that time to the artist's family. According to the letter of Carol-Bérard to de Groux cited below, d'Alignan, de Groux's Paris dealer, seems to have had in his possession several drawings pertaining to the Debussy monument.

[34] 'Eh! bien, la composition que vous m'avez envoyée ne me paraît vraiment plus possible ... Personnellement – dans sa réalisation – elle ne m'enthousiasme pas, je l'avoue humblement – et je garderai discrètement en moi cette opinion – ... Que Dieu nous préserve sans doute d'un Debussy en redingote et en chapeau melon ... mais le peut-on voir, lui si vivant encore pour nous tous, en si sommaire costume? Foudroyez-moi, mais pardonnez-moi tout de même ... et soyez certain que j'aime la sculpture et pas du tout comme un "pompier"!' Letter dated Sunday 30 January 1921 giving the precise history of the project.

Figure 5.8. Henry de Groux: Study of the aegypan for the Debussy Monument (from a photograph in the de Groux archives, present whereabouts unknown)

Figure 5.9. Henry de Groux *Le chant des sources, Claude Debussy* (Charcoal, after a photograph in the de Groux archives, present whereabouts unknown)

Figure 5.10. Henry de Groux, mock-up of the Debussy Monument (plaster, from a photograph in the de Groux archives. Original severely deteriorated, in a private collection, Paris)

The next stage of the Debussy monument project was one of pro-longed lethargy, the political and financial uncertainties of the 1920s unfavourable to its realisation. A new committee presided over by André Messager took up the idea again in 1926 and during the years 1928–1933 mounted numerous benefit concerts in France as well as abroad. De Groux was at this time working on a large-scale commemorative monument commissioned by the town of la Roque d'Anthéron and seems to have lost interest in the Debussy project, so much so that during his several changes of studio its mock-up was for some time mislaid.[35]

Now distant from the artistic milieux of Paris, the ageing de Groux no longer believed in the idea which had previously so strongly captivated his imagination. At his death, in Marseilles on 12 January 1930, it was left unfinished. The following year it was the brothers Jan and Joël Martel who were chosen for the cold marble edifice ceremoniously inaugurated on 18 June 1932 in the Bois de Boulogne, bordering on the Boulevard Lannes, while Aristide Maillol sculpted a fine female nude, placed in the park at

---

[35] Letter from de Groux to a certain Christine (surname unknown), assistant to Arthur Mangeot at the Ecole Normale de Musique in Paris, Avignon, 29 May 1929: 'Les travaux que j'achève ici et la nécessité prochaine de prendre possession de mon atelier de l'avenue du Prado à Marseille, mis à ma disposition par le maire tout récemment réélu – d'autres choses encore! – m'obligent à écarter provisoirement l'idée de la statue de Debussy à laquelle je me crois bien condamné, cependant, à devoir quand même renoncer . . . Quoiqu'il en soit, comment pourrai-je assez vous remercier de vouloir bien, avec l'aimable concours de votre cher directeur, monsieur Mangeot, éclairer de vos opportuns renseignements, un chemin que je pense bien être devenu pour moi, malgré tout, à jamais stérile . . . Dès que je serai à même de reconstituer un valable schéma de mon projet primitif, (que je ne parviens pas à retrouver) – je me ferai un tout particulier devoir de vous l'adresser, avec le commentaire dont il pourrait, fort plausiblement cependant, avoir besoin.' (The work I am finishing here and the subsequent need to retake possession of my studio in the Avenue du Prado in Marseilles, placed at my disposition by the recently re-elected mayor – and other things too! – oblige me temporarily to put aside or even renounce the idea of the statue of Debussy with which I had been encumbered. Be that as it may, I do not know how to thank you enough for having wanted, along with your director monsieur Mangeot, to open a path for me which, despite all, I think has become permanently sterile for me. As soon as I am in a position to put together a new and viable project from my first plan (that I can't succeed in finding) I will make a special point of contacting you, together with the plausible explanation it will require.)

Saint-Germain-en-Laye, as a tribute to Debussy, inaugurated on 9 July 1933.[36]

Only a few of the components of de Groux's Debussy project have to date been re-assembled: a charcoal drawing, actual size (2.02×1.36 m) corresponding to the above quoted description in de Groux's diary (see fig. 5.7); the plaster mock-up (Debussy and the aegypan) which represents a simplified version of the above drawing (see fig. 5.10); and above all the bronze bust (see fig. 5.5) of which one copy was sold at the somewhat lacklustre retrospective exhibition mounted by the artist's Paris dealer, d'Alignan, in May 1930.[37] Acquired, along with the pastel portrait of 1909, by the singer Paul-Henry Vergnes, this bust was added to the collections of the Musée de l'Opéra in Paris in 1975. La maison Claude Debussy at Saint-Germain-en-Laye was able to acquire the pastel portrait at a public auction in 1993.

De Groux, as we have seen, feared that his project would be compared to that of Rodin's monument to Victor Hugo and it seems that Debussy himself shared his aversion to that overrated work of the esteemed sculptor. According to Robert Godet, Debussy saw in Rodin's work only a 'gamey Romanticism' (Romantisme faisandé).[38] With regard to the single visit made by the composer to Rodin's studio, Godet remembered a maxim of the sculptor to which Debussy might have subscribed some years later: 'When you work a lot with your thumbs, you end up expressing certain ideas. It is better that they come as a result of this rather than being thought

---

[36] On this subject see the dossier on the *Monument Debussy* (1928–1933) in the archives of *l'Association française d'Action artistique* preserved in the Department of Music at the Bibliothèque Nationale de France, Paris, under the name *Fonds Montpensier*. Subsequently, the monument of Maillol has been housed in the *Mairie* at Saint-Germain-en-Laye.

[37] The modest catalogue with a preface by Arsène Alexandre lists 566 items including *Debussy* (pastel, item no. 65; probably the 1909 portrait) and the *Bust of Debussy* (no. 562, sculpture); item no. 70, a pastel entitled *Vision lyrique (Debussy)* has neither been identified nor rediscovered. Mention of the sale of the bust of Debussy is made in a letter to the artist's widow, Marie, signed 'Bella', the name of a friend, dated 14 May 1930, and highly critical of the disastrous effect of this unselective and massive presentation of de Groux's works. A letter to the same person of 21 May gives the price of 12,000 francs for the busts.

[38] Robert Godet, 'Entretien préliminaire' (with G. Jean-Aubry), in Debussy, *Lettres à deux amis*, p. 40

134

out before. To seek to express something in the work is to mistake the effect for the cause. The work which one puts into an object tends to bypass any idea of expression.'[39]

Without doubt, Debussy could hardly have considered Rodin's work other than benignly, being at that time at least a close friend of Camille Claudel – the unhappy pupil and mistress of the Faune of the Hôtel Biron [Rodin] – who must have revealed many little-known aspects of the great man.

Debussy had met this young woman in the years immediately following his return from Rome at Austin's, a café in the rue d'Amsterdam also formerly frequented by Baudelaire. Their initial encounter cannot have been easy, for Camille pronounced herself to be hostile to music. Sometimes playing the piano for her at Godet's, the young composer knew how to win her over and reassure her, as she was perhaps afraid of losing herself in the infinite variety of sounds: 'she ended up by listening with a concentration that was not at all an act of resignation', wrote Godet. 'And the time came when one would hear her say, when the pianist left the piano, his hands frozen, "No comment, Monsieur Debussy".'[40]

It is known that they went together to hear the Javanese musicians at the Paris World exhibition of 1889. Godet remembered the composer's liking for three works of Claudel: firstly *La valse* of 1891, exhibited at the *Société Nationale des Beaux-Arts* in 1893. 'Drunk and completely lost in the very substance of the music, in the storm and whirlwind of the dance', was Paul Claudel's description of this work.[41] Debussy kept a copy of it right up to the end of his life: he would have been able to admire a half-size bronze

---

[39] 'Quand on travaille beaucoup des pouces, on arrive à se faire, sans le faire exprès, quelques idées générales. Il vaut mieux qu'elles viennent après qu'avant. Y chercher le sens de l'oeuvre serait prendre l'effet pour la cause. Tout son effort tend à pouvoir se passer de commentaire.' Ibid., p. 40.

[40] 'elle finit par l'écouter avec un recueillement qui n'avait rien d'une résignation. Et le temps vint où on l'entendit, quand le pianiste quittait son piano les mains glacées, lui dire en le conduisant vers la cheminée: "Sans commentaire, Monsieur Debussy".' Ibid., p. 41.

[41] 'Ivre, toute roulée et perdue dans l'étoffe de la musique, dans la tempête et le tourbillon de la danse'. Paul Claudel, 'Camille Claudel, statuaire', *L'Art décoratif*, (July–Oct. 1913); cited in the catalogue of the exhibition *Camille Claudel*, Musée Rodin (Paris 1984), p. 18.

version, presented at the salon of *La Libre Esthétique* in Brussels, which he himself attended on the occasion of a festival of his works organised by Octave Maus (1 March 1894). Rather than one of the costly bronze reductions, which were made by Siot-Décauville after 1893, Debussy no doubt received from Camille Claudel one of the bronze patinated plaster reductions that the artist reserved for her closest friends such as Frits Thaulow and Robert Godet.[42]

Debussy also admired, although with 'a touch of dread' according to Robert Godet, the striking *Clotho*, an allegory of death whose idea obsessed the sculptress. The plaster version of this work (Musée Rodin, Paris) also featured in the salon of the *Société Nationale des Beaux-Arts* of 1893. The marble version (1895–9) bequeathed to the Musée du Luxembourg by a group of admirers has mysteriously since disappeared. Finally among the works about which Debussy was enthusiastic figures the highly expressive *Petite Châtelaine* of 1893 of which Godet owned a patinated plaster cast[43] as did his friends Frits Thaulow and Arthur Fontaine.[44]

According to Robert Godet, Debussy saw in the works of Camille Claudel 'the most perfect monuments to lyricism that sculpture has ever produced' admiring in her 'the genius of finding her style without owing anything to the Academy':[45] a declaration of some importance perhaps, for wasn't this the very goal pursued relentlessly by the composer himself? The remaining aloof from academic traditions; the refusal to sully one's art with careerist or financial considerations; the proud disdain for pre-existent systems clearly unite the young Debussy with Camille Claudel and Henry de Groux. The intransigence which characterised Debussy may be clearly seen from 'L'entretien avec M. Croche':

---

[42] Catalogue of the exhibition *Camille Claudel,* Musée Rodin (Paris, 1984), p. 109.

[43] Ibid., p. 113, According to an article by Mathias Morhardt 'Melle Camille Claudel', *Mercure de France*, March 1898, Thaulow also possessed at the time of his death, marble versions of *Causeuses* and of *La Petite Châtelaine* (Catalogue of the sale subsequent to the artist's death, nos. 173–4).

[44] Arthur Fontaine's copy figured in the second catalogue of the *Salon de l'Art Nouveau*, (Bing), (1896), no.788 (no indication of medium).

[45] 'Les plus parfaits monuments de lyrisme qu'eût produit la sculpture' . . . 'le génie d'arriver au style sans rien devoir à l'Académie'. Robert Godet, 'En marge de la marge' in 'La jeunesse de Claude Debussy', *La Revue Musicale* (1 May 1926), 71–2. These two phrases, placed in brackets by Godet, seem to be a transcription of Debussy's own words.

'Stay true to yourself . . . without blemish . . . An enthusiasm for his milieu ruins an artist.'[46] Here lies the key to why Debussy preferred Camille Claudel to Rodin, no doubt over-revered, too much surrounded by mundane sycophancy.

If an eye is cast over the artistic liaisons of Debussy's life, such as those considered above, it is surely the great genius of Degas who dominates the picture, but no doubt it is the composer's fascination for the complex figures of Camille Claudel and Henry de Groux which needs more careful attention because the connections were more personal and thus perhaps richer. More than the fact of their existence on the borders of society, Debussy would have found in their art an expression of personal torments which on occasion led them to madness.[47]

As André Schaeffner noted, there is with Debussy a well-spring of wildness and a certain taste for cruelty which caused him to respond to the *Histoires extraordinaires* of Edgar Allan Poe. Robert Godet testified to having learnt from Debussy of his obsession with the haunting feminine figures of Poe, Ligeia and Morella.[48] In addition, Debussy had accepted the idea of setting to music an esoteric play of Jules Bois published in 1890 entitled *Les noces de Sathan*.[49]

This attraction reveals the darker side of Debussy's personality and layers of psychological depth masked by the music, hidden unsuspected under a surface of ice. This inner torment; the fascination with the bizarre; the morbid impulses which come to fruition so sensitively in the works of Camille Claudel and Henry de Groux and render them so strange; their taste of ash and their brash violence are perceptible in Debussy in the prelude to the *Chambre magique* from *The Martyrdom of Saint Sebastian*, and still more, in *Pelléas*. We are reminded of the scene where Golaud is wounded, or that of the vaults apropos of which Debussy wrote to Henry Lerolle: 'And the vault scene is done, full of a sinister terror and with enough mystery to give vertigo

---

[46] 'Rester unique . . . sans tare. . . . L'enthousiasme du milieu me gâte un artiste, tant j'ai peur qu'il ne devienne par la suite que l'expression de son milieu.' Debussy, 'Entretien avec M. Croche' reprinted *M. Croche et autres écrits*, p. 52.
[47] Briefly in the case of de Groux and more permanently for Camille Claudel who was later interned for life.
[48] Debussy, *Lettres à deux amis*, p. 34.
[49] Edward Lockspeiser, *Debussy, his life and mind* (London, 1962), vol. I, p. 109.

to the most evil of souls'.[50] The two Poe operas on which the composer worked considerably would clearly have revealed this disturbing and unsuspected side of the composer had he succeeded in finishing them.

It was no doubt this side of the composer's sensibility which de Groux was able to perceive and which attracted him to Debussy. In his diary one reads the following admission, written several months after his encounter with the composer: 'I have always felt a strange attraction to horror, to excess, to the paroxysm which according to Nietzsche is a sign of the utmost decadence and which in me is certainly a sort of large-scale depravation of the sense of the aesthetic which drives me to paint and to seek to portray the maximum brutality, intensity, cruelty, and violence: things which I would certainly not be able to tolerate in the flesh.'[51]

In his letters to his publisher of 1909–1910, Debussy speaks of the 'sombre melancholy' of the neurasthenia of Roderick Usher and identifies himself with 'the progression into anguish which is the essence of the *Fall of the house of Usher*'.[52]

At the time when it pleased Debussy to return to the glaucous atmosphere of the *Histoires extraordinaires* of Poe, Henry Lerolle had all but abandoned painting; Degas was half blind; and Camille Claudel had been for a long time insane. As for de Groux, a passionate devotee of Poe whose bust he had modelled, he was then doing his pastel portraits of Debussy. Was it not the torments of Roderick Usher wandering in the dark corridors of his house that this highly perceptive painter captured, but with the features of the unknown side of Claude Debussy?

(*Translated by Richard Langham Smith*)

---

[50] 'Et la scène des souterrains fut faite, pleine de terreur sournoise, et mystérieuse à donner le vertige aux âmes les mieux trempées.' Letter of 28 August 1894, Debussy, *Correspondance*, p. 104.

[51] 'toujours j'ai éprouvé cet étrange attrait de l'horreur, de l'excès, du paroxysme qui est selon Nietzsche le signe des suprêmes décadences et qui fut certainement chez moi l'inclination d'une sorte de dépravation grandiose du sens esthétique qui me portait invinciblement à peindre, à chercher à reproduire dans leur maximum de brutalité, d'intensité, de cruauté et de violence, les choses dont je n'aurais certes pu supporter la vue'. Fragment of 7 June 1892, cited by R. Rapetti, 'Un chef-d'oeuvre . . .', p. 46

[52] Durand (ed.), *Lettres de Claude Debussy à son éditeur* (Paris, 1927), pp. 76–8, 81 and 95.

6 The reception of Debussy's music in Britain up to 1914

ROGER NICHOLS

For nearly the first forty years of his life, Debussy had to make his way without support for his music from England or any other part of Great Britain. If he was worried by this, it can only be said that he kept remarkably quiet about it. We know of his interest in English literature (most notably, of course, Rossetti's 'Blessed Damozel'), but this interest doesn't seem to have extended to learning the language. As Mme de Tinan told me, if he found an article in an English newspaper that he thought might be interesting, he would ask her to translate it for him. It's fair to say, I think, that he passed his eight visits to England between 1902 and 1914 in a fairly thick fog of incomprehension. More to the point, he was unable to do anything to promote his own music in the places where it mattered, and to a large extent it had to make its own way – even if, as we shall see, it had one or two champions whose names deserve to be remembered.

The first English notice of Debussy's music that I have discovered comes in *The Musical Times* of 1 February 1901 – the month when Henry Wood daringly included the 'Prelude' and 'Angel's Farewell' from *The Dream of Gerontius* in one of his Queen's Hall programmes. Among the notices of foreign performances, British readers could find that 'at the Lamoureux concert, on the 6th January, two very effective orchestral Nocturnes, by Mr Debussey . . . were much applauded novelties'. Just over a year later, *The Musical Times* had learnt to spell Debussy's name properly, but had to admit, in its issue of 1 June 1902, that 'the new lyrical drama Pelléas et Mélisande . . . recently brought out at the *Opéra Comique*, met with but a very qualified success'. This was the extent of Debussy's fame when he came over in 1902 with Mary Garden, and the following year when he reviewed the Covent Garden performance of *The Ring* for *Gil Blas*.

By the December of 1903, the situation had changed very slightly.

Debussy was no longer seen as an isolated phenomenon. 'M. Camille Chevillard announces his plans for the coming season of concerts . . . The young French school: de Bréville, Busser, Erlanger, Debussy etc.' I'm not sure Debussy would have approved that order, but the notice ends 'also Strauss will figure on his programmes' – which might have made up for it.

In any case, the first landmark in the promulgation of Debussy's music in this country was just around the corner. In August 1895, the 26-year-old Henry Wood had directed his first season of Promenade Concerts at the Queen's Hall. From the first, he made it clear that his programmes would include a quantity of less familiar items and, in the words of *The Musical Times*, 'it is gratifying to note that Jullien's British Army Quadrilles and vulgar effusions of every sort have been shelved'.[1] So it was that on Saturday, 20 August 1904, Wood conducted the first British performance of the *Prélude à l'après-midi d'un faune* – one of two novelties of which, according to *The Musical Times*, 'neither proved very interesting'. The composer had, apparently, 'attracted much attention in Paris by his operas, notably Pelléas et Mélissande, [*sic*], owing to the "advanced" character of the music'.[2]

Clearly *The Musical Times* critic had no pretensions himself to being advanced, a state generally regarded with deep suspicion in English society. And Henry Wood was wise enough to cater for the non-advanced (one would not wish to say 'retarded') who no doubt made up a large part of his audience. The programme for that concert on 20 August reads as follows:

Suite de ballet	Gluck-Mottl
Symphonic Dance in A	Grieg
'Divinités du Styx'	Gluck
'L'Après-Midi d'un Faune	Debussy
Symphony 1 organ/orchestra	Guilmant
Overture, Tannhäuser	Wagner
Funeral march of a Marionette	Gounod
'O tu, Palermo'	Verdi

---

[1] *The Musical Times* (1 October 1895), 668. Quoted Percy A. Scholes, *A Mirror of Music* (London, 1947), vol. I, p. 194.

[2] *The Musical Times* (1 September 1904), 600.

Overture, Carnaval Romain	Berlioz
Largo in G	Handel
March, Pomp and Circumstance in D	Elgar

– and that was just Part I. We may well wonder whether an audience accustomed to such gargantuan offerings could possibly have appreciated *L'Après-midi* in the middle of it all. Though certainly, whatever else the work was, it was not a 'vulgar effusion'. Puzzlement may have been compounded by the translation of the title in the programme book as 'The Afternoon of a Young Gazelle'.

During 1905, Britain seems on the face of it to have been Debussy-free. Of course, we have no means of knowing to what extent his songs and piano music were spreading, though I suspect it was slowly. In 1906, on 6 March, Henry Wood returned to the charge with *L'Après-midi* and again on 9 January 1907 ('Finlandia . . . was succeeded by Debussy's vague prelude...').[3] In saying that I have found no further notices of these performances, I should perhaps point out that *The Times* newspaper, 'the paper of record', did not have an arts page in these years, and did not see fit to mention Debussy until 1908. Of the other traceable manifestations of interest in Debussy's work in 1906, one came in the form of the first British public performance, given in Manchester, of the 'characteristic' String Quartet by the Ladies' Quartet of Edinburgh,[4] the other in a lecture given in Newcastle-upon-Tyne by Edward Clark – later to be closely involved with the BBC and in getting them to play music by Schoenberg and his pupils. On this occasion in 1906, W. Gillies Whittaker, later Professor of Music at Glasgow, acted as what was called a 'vocalist-illustrator'.[5]

But 1907 seems to have been the year when British interest in Debussy began to grow appreciably. There were, I think, three leading factors. The first was the foundation that year of *La Société des Concerts Français* by one of the most effective of Debussy champions over here, T. J. Guéritte – an engineer by training who lived in Newcastle and was, as his acute accent suggests, of foreign extraction. These concerts were organised first of all in the provinces as well as in London, but, as ever, it was those in London which

---

[3] *The Musical Times* (1 February 1907), 113.
[4] *The Musical Times* (1 December 1906), 837.
[5] Scholes, *A Mirror of Music*, vol I, p. 451n.

benefited from informed notices. The most valuable and influential of these was undoubtedly a review by Arthur Symons which appeared in *The Saturday Review* on 14 December 1907, of the last two of a series of five concerts, three given in Newcastle and two in London.

Nine composers featured in the London concerts, which boasted Ricardo Viñes as pianist and accompanist: Fauré, Chausson, d'Indy, Duparc, Debussy, Ravel, de Séverac, Roussel, and Florent Schmitt. Of these composers, 'two', writes Symons, 'stood out from the others with a definite superiority. These were Ernest Chausson, who seems to close the past, and Claude Debussy, who seems to open the future.' Symons is not so keen on Debussy's settings of Verlaine, thinking they add little if anything to the feelings evoked by the poetry. But Debussy's Quartet is a different matter, as played by the Parisian Quartet (whose cellist, M. Feuillard, was the teacher of Tortelier):

> Through this playing . . . I was able at last to enter into the somewhat dark and secret shadows of this wood. Here, if anywhere, is a new kind of music, not merely showy nor wilfully eccentric, like too much we heard at the two concerts, but filled with an instinctive quality of beauty, which can pass from mood to mood, surprise us, lead us astray, but end by leading us to the enchantment in the heart of what I have called the wood.

And he goes on:

> The whole point at issue is this: that here is an achievement of a new kind, which can be set somewhere in the same world of the old weightier kind, just as Villon has his place as well as Homer. You may begin by hating it, but you will surrender, while before Fauré and Ravel and the others you will find out that this genuine quality is not in them, or only here and there by accident. Fauré has a small and pretty talent, which will go the way of the stronger but not permanent talent of Saint-Saëns. Vincent d'Indy is without inspiration, Séverac scatters his fresher talent casually, Ravel does the worst possible things with a maddening energy.

Symons's finding of 'the somewhat dark and secret shadows of this wood' was surely a new note in British Debussy criticism – if you like, a Symbolist one, instead of an Impressionist or (as the English critics liked to say) an 'atmospheric' one. Debussy's music was not just vague vapouring. There were things going on in 'the dark and secret shadows' and, maybe, things you explored at your peril.

I think any reasonably musical reader of that article, noting that Symons also approved of Chausson's 'fine, simple vigour' and 'rich musical substance', might assume that Debussy's music was worth investigating further. If so, and if that reader lived in London, there was not long to wait – because the third, and perhaps the most important of the 1907 factors, was the decision by Henry Wood and Sir Edgar Speyer, the financial manager of the Queen's Hall Orchestra, to bring Debussy over to London. I find the actual wording of a passage in Wood's autobiography suggestive. Speyer, says Wood, 'wondered whether Debussy was anything of a conductor but concluded that, whether he was or not, London wanted him and London must have him'.[6] Since Debussy was to arrive in London at the end of January 1908, this conversation must have taken place in the autumn of 1907, at the latest – even given the relative immediacy of concert arranging in those far-off days. So Speyer and Wood must have decided to invite Debussy well before the appearance of Symons's article in mid-December. The statement 'London wanted him' must, therefore, have been prompted by a ground swell of opinion in the capital, to which the two impresarios naturally lent their profit-making ears.

With the turn of the year to 1908, the warmth of interest in Debussy turned into a veritable heat-wave. *The Musical Times* on 1 January, announcing that Debussy would conduct his three orchestral nocturnes on 1 February, described him as 'one of the most original and fascinating composers of the day', and in the following month's issue M. D. Calvocoressi contributed an accurate and level-headed account of Debussy's career so far, stressing that his music and his theories were closely allied: that rules were anathema to the creative artist, who must 'seek discipline in freedom'.

And on the very day Calvocoressi's article appeared, so did Debussy himself on the rostrum of the Queen's Hall. At this juncture, *The Times* included its first notice of him. Debussy's first public appearance, wrote its critic, 'of course, attracted a very large audience'[7] – the 'of course' suggesting that *The Times* had long been aware of this composer's pre-eminent genius. Debussy was not thought to have thrown any new light on *L'Après-midi* (an

---

6 Sir Henry J. Wood, *My Life of Music* (London, 1938), p. 157; repr. in R. Nichols, *Debussy Remembered* (London, 1992), p. 216.

7 *The Times* (3 February 1908).

implicit pat on the back for Henry Wood), and curiosity centred on the first British performance of *La mer*. Here, readers were told that:

> as in all his maturer works, it is obvious that he renounces melody as definitely as Alberich renounces love; whether the ultimate object of that renunciation is the same we do not know as yet. Instead of melodic subjects we have rhythmic figures, the interplay of which is extremely beautiful.

After further remarks about the importance of rhythm in this music, the writer turns to the question of form – one that exercised many of these early critics:

> For perfect enjoyment of this music there is no attitude of mind more to be recommended than the passive, unintelligent rumination of the typical amateur of the mid-Victorian era. As long as actual sleep can be avoided, the hearer can derive great pleasure from the strange sounds that enter his ears, if he will only put away all idea of definite construction or logical development . . . the practical result of this music is to make the musician hungry for music that is merely logical and beautiful, and many regrets were expressed by those who were obliged to leave the long concert before the Unfinished Symphony.

Some of these points were echoed in *The Musical Times* review on 1 March. After commenting on the warmth of Debussy's welcome, and the undemonstrative nature of his conducting, the writer tries to come to grips with *La mer*. Perhaps he'd read *The Times* review (perhaps he'd written it? – all the critics I am quoting from were anonymous). At any rate, we learn that

> such atmospheric strains, so unlike what one is accustomed to, must be listened to in a passive frame of mind, perchance in a darkened room. There can be no question as to the cleverness of the music or its poetic import; the only thing is to get one's ears educated, so to speak, in order to appreciate its strange idiom.

Today, we may have little patience with the 'darkened room' syndrome. More to the point, we may feel, was 'getting the ears educated'. But there was the major difficulty, in the case of *La mer*, of hearing the music enough times for that education to take place. As far as I know, *La mer* wasn't played again in Britain until after 1914, and no recording of it was made until the one by Piero Coppola in 1928. It was not given at the Henry Wood Promenade Concerts until 14 August 1934 (Wood conducting the

144

BBC Symphony Orchestra) – although this was a smarter response than the one accorded to *Jeux*, of which the same orchestra under Alexander Gibson gave the first Promenade Concert performance on 12 August 1960.

Henry Wood clearly felt that his sessions preparing *La mer*, for Debussy to take over, were strenuous enough to last him for some years – we know, incidentally, from Victor Segalen, that the strings had found the going rather less tough than the rest of the orchestra did: 'The brass, woodwind and percussion players had been at work from 10 o'clock till 1 o'clock. At first it was pitiful, despite their goodwill. It was "*La mer* broken into pieces", remarked Madame Debussy, who was with me ... At about 2 it was back to work, this time with the strings. This was much nearer the mark and with the right expressive nuances, in fact it wasn't far off being entirely satisfactory.'[8] Wood now turned his attention to what we may think the obvious work for an English audience, *La damoiselle élue*. The first British performance took place in the Queen's Hall exactly four weeks after *La mer*. *The Times* found *La damoiselle* much more to its taste. Comparing it with other settings which had been made of the Rossetti poem, the critic felt that:

> none has caught the rarefied atmosphere [again that word!] of the poem as finely as the French composer, whose opening phrases paint the quiet spaces of the celestial regions with exquisite insight. The themes, too, are beautiful in themselves and are combined with great skill, although the musical interest of the piece is almost entirely confined to the orchestra... the sung notes are almost always in contradiction to those which are played.[9]

The Musical Times was similarly impressed, again taking the 'atmospheric' line in suggesting that the cantata 'breathes that atmosphere which has become associated with the French composer's method. In this instance,

---

[8]   'Les cuivres, bois et batteries ont donc fonctionné de 10h. à 1h. D'abord, ça a été piteux, malgré leur bonne volonté. C'était '*La mer* en morceaux' disait Madame Debussy que j'accompagnais . . . Vers 2h., retravail, avec les cordes, cette fois; beaucoup plus d'apprêt, de nuances; pas loin d'une mise au point satisfaisante.' Cited Annie Joly-Segalen, André Schaeffner, *Segalen et Debussy* (Monaco, 1961), p. 91. Letter of Victor Segalen to his wife, 31 January 1908 (English trans. Nichols, *Debussy Remembered*, p. 219).

[9]   *The Times* (2 March 1908).

however, the air is less rarified than in his latest productions. Not only does the music reflect the tenderness of the poem but it makes a direct appeal to the listener by its sincerity and true beauty.'[10]

La damoiselle continued to be performed fairly regularly in this country right up until the First World War. I think it's worth abandoning the chronological approach for a moment, to look at a notice this work received four years later, when Sir Henry Wood (as he had since become) conducted a performance in Manchester at one of the Gentlemen's Concerts (to digress still further, I may say it was at one of these concerts the previous year – on 27 February 1911 – that Wood had given what I believe was the world première of Ravel's orchestration of the *Pavane pour une infante défunte*, beating the French première by 10 months). The performance of *La damoiselle* on 15 January 1912 received an interesting notice in *The Musical Times*. The choral parts were sung by the Ancoats Ladies Choir, trained by Miss Say Ashworth, and the *Musical Times* reviewer felt there was

> food for much thought in this juxtaposition of Lancashire mill-girls, Dante
> G. Rossetti's *Blessed Damozel* and Debussy's elusive music. What was the
> power that enabled these comparatively untutored girls to give us the very
> quintessence of such subtle music? Why should they succeed where more
> cultured folk entirely miss their way? [11]

What a pity Debussy, almost certainly, never saw that review! But it also raises a point about what the British in general saw in *La damoiselle*. It had been a custom in the mid–nineteenth century for music societies in London to bring down girls from Lancashire and put them up for the duration of choral festivals: the claims of North versus South over choral singing have never entirely subsided, but it was felt in many quarters that the open vowels of the North led to a fuller, purer tone. If we listen to the characteristic British soprano sound of the early years of this century – even the trained sound of singers like Isobel Baillie or Elsie Suddaby – and compare it with the sound of their French contemporaries like Ninon Vallin or Emma Luart, it's the sound of a flute as against that of an oboe. And clearly British audiences and critics saw *La damoiselle* as a perfect vehicle for this bright, pure, innocent, rather sexless sound – the work, if you like, enabled them to

[10]   *The Musical Times* (1 April 1908), 244.
[11]   *The Musical Times* (1 February 1912), 120.

prolong the Pre-Raphaelite movement beyond its natural historical limit. No dark and secret shadows in this wood; and certainly no need for passive, unintelligent rumination.

It seems possible that Debussy's music found particular favour in the North of England. The *Musical Times* reviewer of a choral concert given by the Manchester Vocal Society on 17 December 1910 had written: 'To Mr. Alfred Higson and his Sale and District Musical Society belongs the honour of singing for the first time in Manchester the new works by Delius and Debussy produced recently at the Blackpool Festival ... both pieces were rapturously applauded by an essentially popular audience, the Debussy chanson "Cold Winter" being doubly encored!'[12] Three weeks later, on 7 January 1911, the Blackpool Glee and Madrigal Society came to Manchester and again, 'had time permitted, both "On Craig Dhu" and "Cold Winter" might have been repeated – ultra-critical Manchester thus confirming the verdict of popular Manchester, as recorded here last month'.[13] On the other side of the Pennines, *L'enfant prodigue* had already been heard in Sheffield in 1908, conducted by Henry Wood, and *La damoiselle élue* at the Leeds Festival in 1910.

In 1908, the first two books in English were published about the composer: *Claude-Achille Debussy* by Louise Liebich, and *Debussy* by W. H. Daly. Daly's little book, published in Edinburgh, identifies the Strauss/Debussy dichotomy as being basic to the musical aesthetics of the time, and has things to say about Debussy's form, or lack of it. He writes:

> It has been laid to his charge that his forms and harmonies are alike vague and incoherent. There is, however, a conceivable stage in the mastery of form ... which may be so complete that form, in the sense of limit or restriction, disappears. Such, indeed, does the so-called 'formlessness' of Debussy reveal itself as one studies his music.[14]

This, I submit, is not bad going for 1908.

Liebich's rather longer book, published in London to coincide with Debussy's visit, also has some penetrating insights, claiming for instance that:

---

[12] *The Musical Times* (1 January 1911), 43.
[13] *The Musical Times* (1 February 1911), 121.
[14] W. H. Daly, *Debussy* (Edinburgh, 1908,), p. 11.

in the opening bars of *La damoiselle élue*, in parts of *Pelléas and Mélisande*, in the 'Songs of Bilitis', one comes across a quiet, restrained beauty of utterance, seeming to originate from an older source than even Gregorian chant, carrying one back to early Christian hymnology, which in its turn was taken either from the Hebrew temple service or from the Greeks.[15]

She mentions that Jacques-Emile Blanche's portrait of the composer had been shown at the New Gallery in London in 1907 and, more surprisingly, begins her second chapter with the sentence 'When as a youth M. Debussy was serving with his regiment at Evreux, according to his own statement he took great delight in listening to the overtones of bugles and bells.'[16] As far as I know, this has not been followed up by later biographers; it would be interesting to discover what form Debussy's 'own statement' took, since Mrs Liebich did not meet him until around 1910. And finally she mentions *Willow-wood* as being still among his current projects, in addition to *King Lear* and *Tristan*.[17]

Then came Debussy's last two public visits to this country, in February and again in May 1909. On the first of these occasions he conducted *L'Après-midi* again, and then the complete *Nocturnes*. Neither *The Times* nor *The Musical Times* gave the concert their unqualified approval, though for slightly different reasons. The fact that Debussy made a mistake in 'Fêtes' and that the orchestra refused to stop seems to have cheered everyone up enormously. But the Sirens failed to seduce. *The Musical Times* noted that 'the voices murmur melodious passages to the syllable "Ah!" – which incidentally solves that little problem – but felt they were too loud',[18] whereas *The Times* less kindly called it 'a persistent, wordless, wailing chant' and went on to make a rather more interesting general observation, that

> the worst of the kind of atmospheric music that M. Debussy writes so well is that the moment realism enters the whole is destroyed; and the song of the sirens, whether well or ill sung on the present occasion, strikes so realistic a note that it is impossible to regain the poetic atmosphere which need never have been disturbed.[19]

[15] Louise Liebich, *Claude-Achille Debussy* (London, 1908), p. 22.

[16] ibid., p. 14.

[17] ibid., p. 92.

[18] *The Musical Times* (1 April 1909), 258.

[19] *The Times* (1 March 1909).

148

This may remind us of the letter Debussy had written to his publisher just eleven months before, about creating 'realities, what imbeciles call "impressionism"'.[20] At least, *The Times* critic was aware of the distinction.

Debussy's music received further promotion in 1909 through the continuing efforts of *La Société des Concerts Français*, whose London concert on 26 February consisted entirely of works by him, including the String Quartet, various piano pieces played by Viñes (including the *Estampes*, 'Poissons d'or' and *L'isle joyeuse*) and a number of songs.[21] *The Times* by now had assumed a position of superiority where Debussy was concerned, and rather sniffily referred to the whole programme as consisting of 'very familiar works', while 'Mandoline' was definitely 'hackneyed'.[22] *The Musical Times*, with its nose twitching at the scent of snobbery, reported that

> the Debussy cult is making great progress in this country . . . It has reached that interesting stage when many people who are really desperately bewildered, affect to perceive beauties and wonderful meanings that have probably entirely escaped the attentions of the composer. [See note 18].

Meanwhile Herbert Hughes in *The New Age* that June could write that, even if London audiences had been slow to find out 'this most excellent society', at least they knew 'their Debussy pretty well by now (he has already entered the suburban drawing-room)'.[23]

We learn of Debussy's appearance, during one of his 1909 visits, at the 'Music Club' of London from the autobiography of Arnold Bax – in one of the best bits of musical knockabout I know.[24] I would add just one small rider to his hilarious description of the scene. Bax recalls that an address welcoming the composer was required, but that 'trouble began at once, for

20 'J'essaie de faire "autre chose" et de créer – en quelque sorte, des *réalités* – ce que les imbéciles appellent "impressionnisme".' Debussy to Jacques Durand, 24 March 1908. Quoted Claude Debussy, *Correspondance 1884–1918*, ed. François Lesure (Paris, 1993), p. 235.
21 Information given in Martha J. Stonequist, *The Musical Entente Cordiale* (Ann Arbor, 1972), pp. 169 ff.
22 *The Times* (27 February 1909), cited Stonequist, ibid., pp. 202–3.
23 24 June 1909, cited Stonequist, ibid., p. 185.
24 Arnold Bax, *Farewell, My Youth* (London, 1943), pp. 58–9; repr. Nichols, *Debussy Remembered*, pp. 222–3.

although Frederick Corder, who was a good French scholar, had been invited and had declared himself willing to make the address, he at the last moment failed to turn up, excusing himself on the plea of sudden sickness'.

Corder, then in his mid-fifties, was a professor at the Royal Academy of Music. It turned out that the reason for his absence was not sudden sickness, but rather long-standing prejudice; for which we have further evidence in a letter of July 1938 from a one-time pupil of Corder's at the Academy, the composer Benjamin Dale, who remembered that Corder 'used to execrate Strauss and pooh-pooh Debussy (both of whom I secretly admired!).'[25] My French dictionary translates 'pooh-pooh' as 'ridiculiser; traiter légèrement', and I think it about sums up the difference in attitude towards the two poles of musical modernism among the older British musicians.

Among these we must number Sir Charles Villiers Stanford. He, in August 1910, proposed, for the programme of a Leeds Festival to end all Leeds Festivals, the following line-up: Strauss's *Elektra* and *Sinfonia Domestica*, Mahler's *Choral Symphony*, Debussy's *Pelléas et Mélisande*, a new oratorio *The Black Country* by Rutland Boughton (Part 1 'Smoke'; Part 2 'The Pit Mouth'; Part 3 'The Explosion'); ending up with a Concerto for Penny Whistle and Tuba by A. Bax, after which all rise and sing 'God Help the Audience'... 'Receipts for the Festival £1.13s.4d'.[26]

And with that less than flattering reference to Debussy's opera, we come to the main item on the agenda – and one which in Britain, as in France, set the seal on his reputation. And yet, main item though it was, there is not much to say about the opera's reception except that it was hugely enthusiastic. Already by the revival at the end of 1910 (in which Maggie Teyte sang just once as Mélisande), it was being referred to as a 'great' opera. In *The Times* review of the Covent Garden première in May 1909, there are really only two small quibbles: one, that 'so rarely does any part move melodically except in the treble that the ear is apt to tire of the one sort of balance which goes on through all five acts' – which could, perhaps, be laid at the door of Campanini's conducting; and secondly, that

[25] Letter from Benjamin Dale to Patrick Piggott, 22 July 1938. Published in Lewis Foreman, *From Parry to Britten, British Music in Letters 1900-1945* (London, 1987), p. 211.
[26] Letter from Sir Charles Villiers Stanford to Herbert Thompson, 7 August 1910, ibid., p. 43.

Yniold's scene with the ball in act IV was left out – strange, when the performer of the part, Mlle Trentini, seems to have been excellent in all respects.[27]

The Musical Times was equally warm in its praises, calling the opera 'a remarkable and impressive work, and one which, as it becomes familiar, will grow in interest'[28] – again, a reminder that one had to work in those pre-electronic days to keep up with the latest developments, and that the wiser critics were content to bide their time before settling themselves in entrenched positions. *The Monthly Musical Record* would have liked more sung tunes ('that which hitherto has been considered the most powerful factor in music-drama plays altogether too insignificant a part') but conceded that in the opera 'the drama is the chief thing, and attention is never drawn away from it . . . It is a strong, wonderful work. Debussy's conception is new, but we feel that the earnest, vivid manner in which he has carried it out must and will be fully recognised.'[29] Later mentions in the same journal emphasised that supporters of the work would have to be patient: 'it is a work the merits of which can only gradually be appreciated'; 'owing to the uncommon and subordinate part played by the music in Debussy's work, it has not as yet been accepted by the public'.[30]

The view of *Pelléas* as a 'strong' work, though borne out by Maggie Teyte's memories of the Paris production in which she took over the role of Mélisande in 1908, was perhaps not widely shared. At all events, the perception seems increasingly to have been that the general 'insubstantiality' of Debussy's music, though perplexing, was a positive rather than a negative feature. Even Ricardo Viñes was on one occasion taxed with being 'inclined to be a trifle too strenuous',[31] while poor Hans Richter, conducting *L'Après-midi* at a Hallé concert on 22 October 1908, 'dealt with this delicate textile in a far too determinate spirit, like a square man in a round hole'.[32]

---

[27] *The Times* (22 May 1909).
[28] *The Times* (1 June 1909).
[29] *Monthly Musical Record* (1 June 1909), 136, cited Stonequist, *The Musical Entente Cordiale*, p. 210.
[30] *Monthly Musical Record* (1 January 1910, 3 and 2 January 1911), 1, cited Stonequist, ibid., p. 211.
[31] *Monthly Musical Record* (1 April 1909), 88 cited Stonequist, ibid., p. 171.
[32] *The Musical Standard* (31 October 1908), 288 cited Stonequist, ibid., p. 123.

Even so, in the years immediately before the War, there's the occasional whiff of 'we've heard all this before'. In 1913, the first British performances of 'Rondes de printemps' and 'Gigues', by the Orchestre Colonne under Gabriel Pierné, moved *The Times* critic to write that they

> ... do not add very much to what we already know of Debussy, except to make one feel that he has retired more completely into a region of his own imagination where musical sounds are related in ways which differ from normal standards... One easily admires the skill of his workmanship, but one leaves this work, at any rate, with the feeling that after all it expresses very little, much less, for instance, than Franck succeeded in expressing in his much less skilful tone poem *Le chasseur maudit* given in this programme.[33]

This time, I am glad to think Debussy did not see that article – battling with his own technical skill was a preoccupation of those pre-War years. But the author is surely right in saying that what was difficult about the music was not so much the vocabulary as the syntax.

Criticism of the 'atmospheric' school wasn't limited to the critics, either. In March 1912, Vaughan Williams wrote to E. J. Dent: 'Have you ever heard of a composer called Eric Satie – Ravel has, apparently, discovered him – he was doing *all the Debussy tricks* [my underlining] in 1887 before D. was interested.'[34] A couple of years later, on 29 March 1914, Gustav Holst wrote to Vaughan Williams, after hearing the first performance of the London Symphony at the Queen's Hall two days earlier:

> You have really done it this time. Not only have you reached the heights but you have taken your audience with you. Also you have proved the musical superiority of England to France. I wonder if you realised how futile and tawdry Ravel [the *Valses nobles*] sounded after your *Epilogue*. As a consequence of last Friday I am starting an anti-Gallic League the motto of which shall be 'Poetry not Pedantry'.[35]

---

[33] *The Times* (17 April 1913).

[34] Unpublished letter in the Dent Archive, King's College, Cambridge. I am grateful to Dr Hugh Cobbe for sending me a transcript of it.

[35] Ursula Vaughan Williams and Imogen Holst (eds.), '*Heirs and Rebels: letters written to each other and occasional writings on music by Ralph Vaughan Williams and Gustav Holst*' (London, 1959), p. 43. I am grateful to Dr Alain Frogley for drawing my attention to this letter.

We can hear from parts of the *Planets* suite that Holst didn't quite succeed in expunging the French influence: in short, Debussy and Ravel bid fair to become what Wagner had been to their own generations and were likely to be taxed, as he had been, with relying on 'tricks' to get them through.

Debussy himself paid one last visit to London in July 1914, to play *Children's Corner* at a private party given by Lady Speyer. He seems to have missed the performances of *Pelléas* at Covent Garden in June. Perhaps it was just as well, since the reviewer of the *Evening News* found that 'Signor Polacco, who conducted, did not always handle the delicate music with sufficient sympathy', and especially since, according to this review, 'M. Maguenat made a picturesque *Pelléas*.'[36]

So, overall, even if the British lion didn't immediately greet Debussy's music by rolling over and waving its legs in the air, its roars were at the worst muted and questioning, and at best welcoming and affectionate. Certainly, a grateful nod does not go amiss in the direction of Sir Henry Wood, 'to whose broad-minded enthusiasm', as W. H. Daly wrote at the head of his book, 'British appreciation of all that is most progressive in musical art is so greatly indebted'.[37]

---

[36] *Evening News* (25 June 1914).
[37] Daly, *Debussy*, p. 7.

7 Debussy and Satie

ROBERT ORLEDGE

Giving a comprehensive account of the unlikely yet enduring relationship between Debussy and Satie from Debussy's viewpoint is no easy task because, apart from a few references to Satie in letters to others, Debussy left no record of it.[1] We know that they met at least once a week, *chez* Debussy, over a period of more than 25 years (Satie says 30), and to have been a fly on the wall during these aesthetic exchanges is a tempting prospect indeed to the musicologist. We know that these otherwise secretive composers discussed their emergent compositions during these meetings, for Satie told his brother Conrad in June 1901 that 'If I didn't have Debussy to talk about things a bit above those common men discuss, I don't know what I should do to express my poor thoughts, if I do still express them'.[2] Then on 17 August 1903, Satie invited Debussy's opinion on his *Morceaux en forme de poire* in the third person, as follows: 'You who know him well, tell him what you think about it; surely he will listen to you more attentively than to anyone, so great is his friendship for you'.[3] But such discussions only took place when Satie was alone with Debussy, as a letter to Jean Lemoine in 1912 confirms,[4]

[1] An account with the focus on Satie can be found in chapter 4 of Robert Orledge, *Satie the Composer* (Cambridge, 1990), pp. 39–67, from which some of the material in this article is quoted.

[2] 'Si je n'avais pas Debussy pour causer de ce dont causent les hommes vulgaires, je ne vois pas comment je ferais pour exprimer ma pauvre pensée – si je l'exprime encore'. See Ornella Volta (trans. Michael Bullock), *Satie Seen Through His Letters* (London and New York, 1989), p. 145.

[3] 'Vous qui le connaissez bien, dites-lui ce que vous en pensez: sûrement, il vous écoutera mieux que quiconque, tant est portée son amitié pour vous'. The 'vous' is surprising, but authentic. Volta, *Satie,* p. 146.

[4] 'Je n'ai pu parler à Debussy de la chose dessus de la Critique: il n'était pas seul . . .' Letter of 17 June 1912, cited from a copy in the Archives de la Fondation Erik Satie, 56 rue des Tournelles, Paris. (Hereafter Archives FES). In it Satie writes: 'I have not been able to speak to Debussy of the above matter relating to [musical] Criticism, as he was not alone . . .'

and even though we know that Debussy replied to Satie during his holiday in Bichain in August 1903,[5] all his incoming correspondence was unfortunately destroyed during a fire at Conrad Satie's home during the last war.

This loss is a particularly unfortunate one for, as Satie recalled in his retrospective account of their relationship in 1922: 'I witnessed his entire creative development. The String Quartet [1893], the *Chansons de Bilitis* [1897–8], *Pelléas et Mélisande* [1893–1902] were born before me; and I still cannot forget the emotion this music produced in me.'[6] Here, we also learn that Debussy played Satie his own 'wonderful piano pieces...languishing and murmuring with tender melancholy'. He also played Chopin to him, being 'able to analyse and understand his music as few virtuosi can'. On rare occasions, Satie even ventured to the keyboard himself, as in early September 1908 when he played through the duet fugue from his *Aperçus désagréables* with Debussy, who most likely took the Primus part. As his extant letters to Debussy show,[7] Satie went to great pains to amuse and divert his now famous friend, and this fugue, with its humorous running commentary in the score, seems to have been composed specially for this occasion. As Debussy told his fellow composer Francisco de Lacerda on 5 September, 'your friend E. Satie has just finished a fugue in which boredom disguises itself behind wicked harmonies and in which you will recognise the influence of the methods peculiar to the aforementioned establishment [the Schola Cantorum, where Satie had been awarded a diploma for his contrapuntal studies that June]'.[8]

---

[5] Satie's three surviving letters to Debussy date from this summer. On 14 August 1903, in his second letter, Satie pressed Debussy for a reply to his letter of 20 July, and thanked him for it in his third letter of 17 August. See H. Borgeaud, 'Trois lettres d'Erik Satie à Claude Debussy (1903)', in 'Debussy 1862–1962', *Revue de Musicologie*, numéro special (1962), 72–3. Other letters to Debussy may one day emerge, but as they met so regularly there was little need for correspondence.

[6] 'J'ai assisté à tout son développement créateur. Le *Quatuor*, les *Chansons de Bilitis*, *Pelléas et Mélisande*, naquirent devant moi; & je ne puis encore oublier l'émotion que cette musique me donna . . .' From an article on Debussy written for *Vanity Fair* in August 1922, but never published. Cited in Erik Satie, *Ecrits*, ed. Ornella Volta (Paris, rev. edn. 1981), p. 68.

[7] Borgeaud, 'Trois lettres', 71–4.

[8] 'À ce propos votre ami E. Satie vient de terminer une fugue où l'ennui se dissimule derrière des harmonies malveillantes, dans quoi vous reconnaîtrez la marque de cette discipline si particulière à l'établissement cité plus haut.' Letter from Debussy to Francisco de Lacerda, 5 September 1908, cited in Claude Debussy, *Correspondance 1884–1918*, ed. François Lesure (Paris, 1993), p. 242.

If Debussy and Satie 'understood each other at once, with no need for complicated explanations, for it seemed that we had *always* known each other', as Satie claimed in 1922,[9] the 'E. Satie' above appears strangely formal, as does Satie's use of 'vous' (rather than 'tu') in his letters to Debussy. But Satie hardly ever used the familiar form of address, and if he did it was mostly to very close non-musical friends (like Vincent Hyspa, Henri-Pierre Roché (occasionally) or Léon-Paul Fargue) or to his brother Conrad. His relationship with Debussy was one of professional respect and sincere admiration, even though Debussy was less than four years his senior. Until 1908 at least, it was a case of a technically untrained musician meeting a *Prix de Rome* winner, albeit a self-educated one in all subjects but music. Like most intimate relationships it had its ups and downs: even Satie's retrospective account speaks of Debussy's 'outbursts of bad temper', though he explains that 'these were purely of the "explosive" type, leaving no bad feelings whatsoever afterwards'.[10] And if Satie's stance with his social superiors, wealthy patrons and musical peers tended to be timid and deferent,[11] it is most unlikely that this was the case when he and Debussy were alone.

Broadly speaking, until Satie began to emerge from his friend's shadow after 1911 things went relatively smoothly. But as Satie's fame grew, Debussy's incomprehension of his success caused growing friction between them, until Satie broke with the ailing Debussy over his attitude to *Parade* in 1917. And as Satie's temper was even more volcanic and unpredictable than Debussy's and he often broke with friends over trivial slights, it is perhaps surprising that his relationship with Debussy endured for so long. Probably the best summary comes from Debussy's friend, the critic and Chinese scholar Louis Laloy, even if he was Satie's arch-enemy. In 1928, Laloy recalled that:

> A tempestuous and yet indissoluble friendship bound Debussy to Satie. Or rather, it was like one of those family hatreds which was aggravated by the repeated shock of incompatible traits, without destroying the deep sympathy

[9] 'Nous nous comprenions à demi-mot, sans explications compliquées, car nous nous connaissons – depuis toujours, il semblait.' Satie, *Ecrits*, p. 68.
[10] 'ses mouvements de mauvaise humeur se montraient purement "explosifs", n'emmenant pas, à leur suite, la moindre rancune . . .' Satie, *Ecrits*, p. 68.
[11] See Jacques Guérin, 'Erik Satie: "Un dimanche à Luzarches"', *L'Optimiste*, 2 (June-July 1992), 8–9.

of the characters that was due to their common origin. They seemed like
two brothers, placed by the events of their life in very different situations,
the one rich and the other poor; the first welcoming, but proud of his
superiority and ready to make it felt, the second unhappy behind a jester's
mask, paying his share of things with witticisms to divert his host, hiding his
humiliation; each constantly on his guard against the other, without being
able to stop loving him tenderly. A musical brotherhood, yet a rivalry of
musicians.[12]

I doubt very much whether Debussy ever made Satie feel humiliated, or
whether any deliberate point-scoring went on, and as there are no known
gaps in their liaison it must be assumed that Debussy understood Satie's
curious logic and seriousness of purpose better than any of his contemporaries.

The reasons why their friendship was indissoluble are many and
varied. First of all, Debussy's treatment of Lilly Texier in 1904 earned him
the moral censorship of all but three of his earlier friends: Robert Godet,
Paul Dukas, and Satie. In reality, he was almost as lonely as Satie was, especially in his first years with the possessive Emma Bardac, and the constancy
of Satie's friendship must have been of great importance to him. Both composers were reclusive and disliked discussing their music with others, so it is
likely that their frank conversations provided a very necessary emotional
outlet.

Secondly, although Debussy's lifestyle appeared affluent on the
surface, his passion for collecting *objets d'art* and his need to keep Emma in
the luxurious style to which she had become accustomed proved way
beyond his means. In fact, he had far greater financial problems than the
impecunious Satie ever had, and both composers shared a common ground
in surviving on short-term loans from friends they knew they could never

[12] 'Une amitié rageuse et cependant indissoluble l'unissait à Satie. Ou plutôt,
c'était une de ces haines familiales qui s'exaspèrent par le choc répété de travers
incompatibles, sans détruire pourtant la sympathie des caractères, due à la
communauté de l'origine. On croyait voir deux frères, placés par les événements
de leur existence en des conditions très différentes, l'un riche et l'autre pauvre;
le premier accueillant mais fier de sa supériorité, prêt à la faire sentir, le second
malheureux sous un masque farceur, payant son écot en facéties pour divertir
son hôte, cachant son humiliation; toujours en éveil l'un contre l'autre, sans
pouvoir s'empêcher de s'aimer tendrement. Fraternité musicale, rivalité de
musiciens.' Louis Laloy, *La musique retrouvée: 1902–27* (Paris, 1928), pp. 258–9.

repay. At the same time, Satie badly needed congenial places of escape from the cluttered squalor of his room in Arcueil, and the meticulous order and bourgeois affluence of Debussy's home must have been especially attractive to him. Moreover, as Debussy was a gourmet the food was excellent, even if Satie's taste was more for well-cooked plain dishes in large quantities.[13] As Satie was never in a position to repay his friend's hospitality, it seems most likely that it was he who worked most assiduously at cultivating the relationship over the years.

Thirdly, both Debussy and Satie shared the common goal of carrying French music into the twentieth century. Even if their methods and technical expertise were on very different levels (especially as regards orchestration), both composers resolved at an early stage to abandon thematic development and to develop new formal approaches. They both sought to make their music restrained and exclusively French, as a reaction to Romantic excesses and the prevailing Austro-Germanic tradition. If Debussy found his way forward far earlier than Satie (in the *Prélude à l'après-midi d'un faune* and *Pelléas*), then it was Satie who unselfishly suggested the path that he was unable to take himself. As he recalled in 1922:

> When I first met him, at the beginning of our liaison, he was full of Mussorgsky and very conscientiously seeking a path which was not easy to find. In this respect, I had a great advance over him: no 'prizes' from Rome, or any other town, weighed down my steps . . . At that time [late 1891 – early 1892] I was writing my *Fils des étoiles* – to a text by Joséphin Péladan; and I explained to Debussy how we Frenchmen needed to break away from the Wagnerian adventure, which did not correspond with our natural aspirations. And I told him that I was not at all anti-Wagnerian, but that we needed our own music – without sauerkraut if possible.
>
> Why not make use of the representational methods of Claude Monet, Cézanne, Toulouse-Lautrec and so on? Why not make a musical transposition of them? Nothing simpler. Are they not alternative means of expression, too?[14]

---

[13] He told his brother Conrad in 1914 that he could eat 150 oysters or an omelette made with 30 eggs at a single sitting.

[14] 'Lorsque je me rencontrai avec lui, au commencement de notre liaison, il était tout imprégné de Moussorgsky & cherchait très consciencieusement une voie qui ne se laissait pas commodément trouver. Sur ce chapitre, j'avais, moi, une grande avance sur lui: les "prix" de Rome, ou d'autres villes, n'alourdissaient

Similarly, if Cocteau is to be believed, it was Satie who turned Debussy's attention towards Maeterlinck at this time, who advised him against Wagnerian realism on the stage, and who recommended the creation of a 'musical climate where the characters move and speak – not in couplets, not in *leitmotifs: but by the use of a certain atmosphere of Puvis de Chavannes*'.[15] Whilst Debussy by no means followed any of this advice to the letter and derived his inspiration more from Symbolist literature than art, Satie's fundamental challenge to nineteenth-century aesthetics came at a most opportune moment and must have given Debussy serious food for thought. Indeed, he referred to Satie as the 'the precursor' and was more influenced by his ideas than by those of any other living composer, with the possible later exception of Stravinsky.

Other factors which bound Debussy and Satie together were their shared interest in the occult, their love of children, and the fact that both found the process of composition difficult – Debussy more so than Satie, even if he never resorted to compositional systems to extricate himself from his creative blocks (his 'usines de néant'). Moreover, Satie never criticised Debussy: it was only Debussyism and the imitators of Debussy in the years after *Pelléas* that Satie objected to, and which made him resolved that Satieism should never exist. As his 1914 conversation with his brother Conrad shows, he called his friend 'Jupiter': a musical god, but one who scolded him when he ventured onto his manicured lawn in the Avenue du Bois de Boulogne as he played at 'bows and arrows' with his nine-year-old daughter Chouchou.[16]

pas ma marche ... J'écrivais, à ce moment-là, le *Fils des Etoiles* – sur un texte de Joséphin Péladan; & j'expliquais, à Debussy, le besoin pour nous Français de se dégager de l'aventure Wagner, laquelle ne répondait pas à nos aspirations naturelles. Et lui faisais-je remarquer que je n'étais nullement antiwagnérien, mais que nous devions avoir une musique à nous – sans choucroute, si possible.
    Pourquoi ne pas se servir des moyens représentatifs que nous exposaient Claude Monet, Cézanne, Toulouse-Lautrec, etc.? Pourquoi ne pas transposer musicalement ces moyens? Rien de plus simple. Ne sont-ce pas des expressions?' Satie, *Ecrits*, p. 69.

15 '[Il faudrait faire] un décor musical, créer un climat musical où les personnages bougent et causent. Pas de couplets, pas de leitmotiv – *se servir d'une certaine atmosphère de Puvis de Chavannes*.' Jean Cocteau, 'Fragments d'une conférence sur Eric [*sic*] Satie (1920)', *Revue Musicale* (March 1924), 221.
16 From notes taken by Conrad Satie after a tour round Satie's old haunts in Montmartre on 30 September 1914. Cited from a copy in the Archives FES. Chouchou called Satie 'Kiki' because she could not remember his then unusual Christian name.

Figure 7.1. (Left to right) Tosti Russell, Dolly Bardac, Satie and Debussy in the garden of 80, Avenue du Bois de Boulogne, Paris 16, in 1905 (photo, Archives de la Fondation Erik Satie, Paris)

A photo of 1905 shows Satie playing with Dolly (Hélène) Bardac, and the brothers Tosti and Sheridan Russell, with Debussy in the background,[17] and fig. 7.1 shows another photo taken on the same day. For part of each visit at least, Satie probably acted as a willing child-minder, and his letters to Mme Debussy and the dedication of 'Regrets des enfermés' to her in 1913 suggest that he had no trouble in retaining his welcome as a family friend. Indeed, Dolly later recalled that:

> Erik Satie came to lunch regularly. I always awaited his coming with impatience, so unexpectedly comical was his way of expressing himself and his repartee in conversation. His attitude towards Debussy was both curiously humble and lacking in spontaneity, in spite of a terrible malicious look from behind his pince-nez![18]

[17] Reproduced in Mme Gaston de Tinan (Dolly Bardac): 'Memories of Debussy and his circle', *Recorded Sound*, 50–1 (April–July 1973), plate 3 (between pp. 176 and 177).

[18] de Tinan, 'Memories of Debussy', 160 (original in English). Satie often wrote to Emma rather than Debussy, especially in 1916–17, in the knowledge that messages would be passed on. Debussy was a shy man, who was not given to informality. According to Sheridan Russell, ibid., 164, he always called Caplet, '"Cher André Caplet" or "Cher Caplet" – never "Cher André"'.

This reinforces other accounts of Satie's deference towards his peers and helps to explain why he felt more at ease with younger composers. But all such accounts reflect Satie's behaviour in the company of others, and again it is unlikely to have been thus when Debussy and Satie were alone. While Satie put a great deal of effort into amusing his hosts, and perhaps grew more careful in his remarks to Debussy as the latter attained celebrity status after 1902, their shared experiences of the 1890s meant that their friendship was far from one-sided and in the end it was Debussy who over-stepped the mark and caused Satie to sever the bond between them through a letter to Emma Bardac.

The chief problem lies in establishing exactly when their relationship began. Although Debussy and Satie were both students at the Paris Conservatoire between 1879 and 1884, they never met there. But as both of them hated this repressive institution, they must have spent as little time there as possible. This is confirmed by Satie's account in 1922, which says that 'As soon as I saw him for the first time, I felt drawn towards him and longed to live forever at his side. For thirty years I had the joy of seeing this wish fulfilled.'[19] If we date this back from their break in March 1917, it would imply that they met immediately after Debussy's return from Rome in February 1887. But, other than the above, there is no evidence to confirm this and it is unlikely that their weekly meetings would have begun before Debussy moved out of his parents' home in the rue de Berlin in early 1892. Similarly, we cannot assume that their meetings at Edmond Bailly's bookshop, the Librairie de l'Art Indépendant at 11 rue de la Chaussée d'Antin, took place before the early 1890s, for François Lesure has recently discovered that this bookshop was not established until October 1889.[20] Thus,

---

[19] 'Dès que je le vis pour la première fois, je fus porté vers lui & désirai vivre sans cesse à ses côtés. J'eus, pendant trente ans, le bonheur de pouvoir réaliser ce vœu.' Satie, *Ecrits*, p. 68. Although this sounds like a perfect marriage springing from love at first sight, all testimonies agree that there was no homosexual attraction on either side. Robert Caby says that Satie was 'only a *Platonist* completely divorced from sexual activity, as all the homosexuals who knew him have testified, beginning with those in Cocteau's circle' (letter to the author, 28 July 1988). In addition, Jacques Guérin told Steven Whiting in July 1993 that Satie 'hated homosexuals and often referred to them as "these corrupters" [malsains]' although he also hated and therefore repressed his own feelings of violence towards them.

[20] François Lesure, *Claude Debussy avant 'Pelléas'* (Paris, 1992), p. 99.

when Victor-Emile Michelet says that Debussy 'arrived almost every day in the late afternoon, either alone, or with the faithful Erik Satie'[21] in Bailly's bookshop and mentions Debussy's opera *Rodrigue et Chimène* in the same paragraph, we are still no nearer to a precise date, for Debussy was occupied with this project between 1890 and 1892. In fact, Satie's date of December 1891 or January 1892 (when he was working on *Le fils des étoiles*) is probably the most accurate, and the most likely place for their initial meeting would have been the *Auberge du Clou* cabaret in the Avenue Trudaine, where Satie had moved as pianist after his quarrel with Rodolphe Salis of the *Chat Noir* sometime during 1891.

The first dated evidence we have of their friendship comes in the reciprocal dedications of 27 October 1892. On this day, Debussy dedicated copy no. 45 of his *Cinq poèmes de Baudelaire* to 'Erik Satie, gentle mediaeval musician, who has strayed into this century for the joy of his good friend Claude A. Debussy',[22] and as these songs were published in February 1890, we can probably assume that Debussy's friendship with Satie only developed during 1892, otherwise the dedication would have occurred earlier. In response, Satie dedicated a copy of his *Trois Sonneries de la Rose+ Croix* 'to the good old son Cl.-A. Debussy, his brother in our Lord, Erik Satie', which tells us more about his religious obsessions at the time than about the nature of their relationship. Indeed, it may have been Satie who made the first dedication, as his *Sonneries* had only recently appeared in print from the Imprimerie Dupré. At this time, Satie was working on his curious ballet *Uspud*, and when his solo performance of it at the *Auberge du Clou* provoked hilarity and uproar, Debussy alone remained 'undisturbed' by its oddity.[23] This understanding of a serious purpose behind the anarchistic facade and the perceptiveness of his dedication helps to explain why Debussy's friendship was so important to Satie at this early stage in his

---

[21] 'Presque tous les jours, aux fins d'après-midi, il [Debussy] arrivait soit seul, soit avec son fidèle Erik Satie'. In Victor-Emile Michelet, *Les Compagnons de la hiérophanie: Souvenirs du mouvement hermétiste à la fin du 19ᵉ siècle* (Paris, 1937), p. 73.

[22] 'Pour Erik Satie, musicien médiéval et doux, égaré dans ce siècle pour la joie de son bien amical Cl. A. Debussy'. From the 150 copies published by subscription and put on sale at the Librairie de l'Art Indépendant. Copy no. 45, with its red ink dedication, now belongs to Mrs Margaret Cobb, New York.

[23] Contamine de Latour: 'Erik Satie intime', *Comoedia* (6 August 1925), 2.

career. Indeed, there was an anarchistic element in Debussy's temperament too, which shows most clearly in his dramatic satire *Les frères en Art* in 1898–1901. Although this is a 'pièce à clef', none of its artistic cast can be equated with Satie, just as Debussy does not appear in Satie's surrealistic play *Le piège de Méduse* in 1913. But one possible source for the sort of conversations they had around 1901 is in *Monsieur Croche Antidilettante*, for Debussy's cigar-smoking critic and Satie shared remarkably similar views about the *Prix de Rome* and Saint-Saëns, even though the model for Monsieur Croche is considered to have been Valéry's Monsieur Teste.

During the 1890s, Debussy helped Satie in several ways. After the failure of Satie's confrontational tactics to secure a performance of *Uspud* at the Paris Opéra in December 1892, Debussy approached his friend Ernest Chausson to try to get Satie's works played by the *Société Nationale* in 1893, as both of them were then on its governing committee. However, Chausson 'almost fainted' when he heard Satie's early works, and Debussy saw that the only way to achieve success would be by participating in the enterprise himself. To this end, he orchestrated Satie's third and first *Gymnopédies* sometime between 1893 and 1896 – the only occasion when he orchestrated the works of another composer – and thus Satie gained his first hearing at the *Société Nationale* in February 1897, when his *Gymnopédies* were conducted by Gustave Doret. Fig. 7.2 shows both composers during this period, as sketched by Satie's friend Augustin Grass-Mick. In 1896 Debussy also introduced Satie to the publisher Emile Baudoux, who published *Le fils des étoiles*, and to Jean Bellon of Bellon, Ponscarme et Cie., who later published Satie's popular songs *Je te veux*, *Tendrement* and *La Diva de l' 'Empire'* in 1902–4.

About this time, too, Debussy defended Satie's music at social gatherings, though there is no evidence in his manuscripts to support René Peter's allegations that Debussy 'spent entire afternoons crouched over his sketches', supposedly correcting elementary errors.[24] Rather, at a dinner in the home of the soprano Jane Bathori, Debussy 'vigorously defended Satie

---

[24] 'On le vit des après-midi entiers rester penché sur des croquis d'où l'auteur, en manière de protestation contre les antiques routines, avait exclu toutes inutilités comme, entre autres, le morcellement "par mesures" du texte musical.' René Peter, *Claude Debussy* (Paris, 1944), p. 71. This rather reflects the corrective work Debussy put in on Peter's youthful plays between 1896 and 1899, and his derogatory opinions of Satie are prejudiced and mostly inaccurate.

Figure 7.2. Augustin Grass-Mick: Debussy and Satie, 1896–7 (*Carnet de croquis* in the Archives de la Fondation Erik Satie, Paris)

164

against Willy [Henry Gauthier-Villars]', adding that 'no musician had *dared* openly to attack the powerful critic of the *Echo de Paris*, except Satie'.[25] And at another dinner *chez* Bellon around 1896, Debussy's enthusiasm for Satie's early work helped overcome Charles Koechlin's initial incomprehension of his Rose+Croix compositions.[26] In return, Satie helped Debussy find a suitable new apartment in the rue Gustave-Doré late in 1893, and acted as a witness at his marriage to Rosalie (Lilly) Texier on 19 October 1899.

By this time they were meeting on a regular basis, though again it is difficult to establish precisely when as the records conflict. René Peter says they met 'twice a week' in the 1890s 'to take coffee, smoke and talk about music',[27] to which Gustave Doret adds that Debussy 'came to my house every Monday night with Erik Satie during the period of the *Prélude à l'après-midi d'un faune*' (1892–4).[28] After Satie moved to the distant suburb of Arcueil in 1898, it seems as if the visits settled down to one per week. Pierre Bertin recalled that Satie spent 'every Saturday in the apartment of his friend Debussy in the rue Cardinet',[29] which would have been between September 1898 and 1905, apart from Debussy's summer holidays. It was the 'charming' meals that Debussy cooked for him in this period that Satie recalled in his article *À table* in 1922:

[25] '[Debussy] prenait vivement le parti de Satie contre Willy. Mais aucun musicien n'avait *osé* attaquer ouvertement le puissant critique de "l'Echo de Paris", *sauf Satie!*' Letter from Charles Koechlin to Rollo Myers, 27 December 1948. (Now in the Pierpont Morgan Library, New York, copy communicated to the author by Rollo Myers in 1970.)

[26] See Koechlin, 'Erik Satie', *Revue Musicale* (March 1924), 194. Koechlin admits that he 'did not in the least understand the harmonies of *Le fils des étoiles* (which were so new then)'. But he soon became one of Satie's staunchest admirers, thanks to Debussy's advocacy.

[27] 'pour distractions, deux fois dans la semaine il venait prendre son café chez Debussy, fumait de son tabac, causait musique'. Peter, *Claude Debussy*, p. 70.

[28] 'A l'époque de *l'Après-midi d'un faune*, tous les lundis soir, il arrivait chez moi avec Erik Satie.' Letter from Gustave Doret to Robert Godet, 31 March 1918, cited in Margaret G. Cobb, 'Further Debussy Souvenirs', *Cahiers Debussy*, 16 (1992), 60.

[29] '[Mais ces travaux divers ne l'empêchaient pas] de passer tous ses samedis dans l'appartement de son ami Debussy, rue Cardinet'. Pierre Bertin: 'Erik Satie et Le Groupe des Six', *Les Annales* (February 1951), 51.

Eggs and lamb cutlets were the main items at these friendly gatherings. But what eggs and what cutlets! ... I still lick my lips just thinking about them – inwardly, you understand.

Debussy – who prepared these eggs and cutlets himself – knew the secret *(the most absolute secret)* of these preparations. It was all washed down graciously with a delicious white Bordeaux wine which affected us a little and put us in just the right mood for enjoying the pleasures of friendship and of living far from 'Mutton Heads', 'Mummified Relics' and other 'Old Chaps' – those scourges of Humanity and of our 'poor world'.[30]

After 1905, we can only be certain that Debussy and Satie met once a week at or around the weekends. For Satie told his brother Conrad on 11 April 1911 that they met for lunch 'every Friday', whereas Emma Debussy said it was Saturdays (around 1913), and Jean Cocteau recalled (after Satie's death) that they met every Sunday.

The first watershed in their relationship came with the performances of *Pelléas et Mélisande* in April–May 1902, which proved to be a turning-point in the careers of both composers. For Debussy, everything hinged on the opera's success, and Satie was amongst the small band of enthusiastic supporters whose regular attendance at the initial run of performances helped this become a reality. So keen was he to hear his friend's *magnum opus* that we find him waiting with Robert Godet outside the Opéra-Comique in the Boulevard des Italians after the dress rehearsal on the early evening of 28 April while Debussy made the necessary alterations to act III, scene 4 to satisfy the objections of Henry Roujon, the Under-Secretary of

---

[30] 'Les oeufs & la côtelette de mouton faisaient les frais de ces réunions amicales. Mais quels oeufs & quelles côtelettes! ... Je m'en lèche encore les joues – intérieurement, vous le devinez.

Debussy – qui les préparait lui-même, ces oeufs, ces côtelettes, – avait le secret *(le secret le plus absolu)* de ces préparations. Le tout s'arrosait gracieusement d'un délicieux Bordeaux blanc dont les effets étaient touchants & disposaient convenablement aux joies de l'amitié & à celles de vivre loin des *"Doubles Veaux"*, des *"Momifiés"* & autres *"Vieilles Noix"* – ces fléaux de l'Humanité & du *"pauvre monde"*.' From *L'Almanach de Cocagne pour l'An 1922*, 169, cited in Satie, *Ecrits*, p. 51. According to Dolly Bardac, Emma banned Debussy from the kitchen after they had settled in the Avenue du Bois de Boulogne in October 1905 (see Satie, *Ecrits*, p. 257). 'Mutton Heads' was Satie's favourite description of music critics, whilst 'Mummified Relics' and 'Old Chaps' simply refer to professional colleagues who were useless and 'past it'.

State for the Fine Arts.[31] For Satie, who had tried experimenting with Debussyian harmonic progressions, extended forms and an orchestral conception in *The Dreamy Fish* in 1901, *Pelléas* proved just as much of a turning point. He was bowled over by the performances he saw and he told his brother Conrad on 27 June 1902 that it was 'very chic! Absolutely astounding. This appreciation is very short, but how well it expresses my thoughts!'[32] Later on he told Jean Cocteau how *Pelléas* led him to realise that 'nothing more can be done in this direction; I must search for something else or I am lost'.[33] Perhaps with *The Dreamy Fish* in mind, Debussy advised Satie to 'develop his sense of form',[34] which led to the *Trois morceaux en forme de poire* in 1903. Although Satie, anxious to find a parallel way forward, considered that these piano duet pieces marked 'a prestigious turning-point in the History of My life',[35] they mostly consisted of earlier material re-used, including cabaret songs composed for Vincent Hyspa (for whom Satie worked as an accompanist to keep body and soul together after 1898). The title may even have been a joke at Debussy's expense, as 'poire' also had the slang meaning of 'fool', and Satie may have been implying that Debussy was a fool if he expected him to use traditional forms. However, Vladimir Golschmann reports Satie as saying that:

> All I did . . . was to write *Pieces in the form of a pear*. I brought them to Debussy, who asked, 'Why such a title?' Why? Simply, *my dear friend*, because

[31] Information from 'En marge de la marge' in 'La jeunesse de Claude Debussy', *Revue Musicale* (1 May 1926), 83–4. After a while, Satie gave up waiting and Godet returned alone with Debussy as night fell for tea in the rue Cardinet. During this, they had the long discussion on Weber's operatic orchestration later recounted by Godet in *The Chesterian* (June 1926), 220-6. Whether the same discussion would have taken place had Satie been present is a matter for conjecture.

[32] 'très chic! Absolument époilant. Cette appréciation est assez courte; mais aussi combien elle exprime bien ma pensée!' Letter from Archives FES.

[33] 'Plus rien à faire de ce côté-là, il faut chercher autre chose ou je suis perdu.' Cocteau 'Fragments d'une conférence', 221.

[34] '[Debussy dit un jour à Satie qu'il devrait] développer son sens de la forme;' Pierre-Daniel Templier, *Erik Satie* (Paris, 1932), p. 26. Satie must have played his rambling piece *The dreamy fish* to Debussy for he mentions it in the same paragraph as the *Morceaux en forme de poire* in his letter of 17 August 1903.

[35] '[Je suis à] un tournant prestigieux de l'Histoire de Ma vie.' '*Recommendations*' (6 November 1903), with the MS of the *Trois morceaux* in the Paris *Opéra* library: *nouveaux fonds* Rés. 218, on verso of p. v of no. 6 ('En plus').

you cannot criticise my *Pieces* in the shape of a pear. If they are *en forme de poire* they cannot be shapeless.[36]

Whatever the true explanation is, Debussy still helped Satie check the proofs of these pieces in September 1911 before they were published by Rouart-Lerolle, and Satie remained proud of them throughout his life, often performing them in private and in public. Indeed, it was one such performance with Ricardo Viñes on 18 April 1916 that inspired Cocteau to collaborate with Satie on *Parade*, and it was (indirectly) through Debussy that Satie first met Viñes, his most important interpreter, at the première of Debussy's first two *Nocturnes* at the *Concerts Lamoureux* on 9 December 1900.

Satie's decision to improve his technical expertise by studying at the Schola Cantorum was entirely his own, and was made in the face of opposition from both Debussy and his future teacher, Albert Roussel. According to Cocteau, Debussy advised Satie to 'Take care. You are playing a dangerous game. At your age you cannot change your skin'. To which Satie replied: 'If I miss my goal, so much the worse for me. It will mean that I have nothing in me.'[37] But in the summer of 1905, Debussy's mind was preoccupied with his divorce from Lilly, his new life with Emma, and the birth of their daughter Chouchou (on 30 October), so his discussion was fortunately less positive than it otherwise might have been. However, there is a slightly mocking tone in Debussy's dedication of his first series of *Images* in January 1906 to 'my old Satie, the celebrated contrapuntist'[38] coming, as it did, only three months after the start of Satie's studies. But during his seven years of study with Roussel, d'Indy and others at the Schola (until November 1912), Satie showed the enhanced dedication of the mature student, coupled with a growing confidence in his abilities.

[36] 'Golschmann Remembers Erik Satie', *Musical America*, 22 (August 1972), 11. 'Poire' also means a child's 'spinning-top' and as the pieces evolved outwards from the centre by adding four introductory and concluding movements to the three central *Morceaux*, Satie may have considered this an apt analogy.

[37] '"Prenez garde", lui disait Debussy. "Vous jouez un jeu dangereux. A votre âge on ne change pas de peau". Et Satie répondait: "Si je rate, tant pis pour moi. C'est que je n'avais rien dans le ventre".' Cocteau, 'Fragments d'une conférence', 222.

[38] 'A mon vieux Satie, le célèbre contrapuntiste... janv. 1906'. Catalogue of the Satie Exhibition (ed. François Lesure) at the Bibliothèque Nationale de France (1966), item no. 62, p. 21.

Perhaps because Debussy avoided academic contrapuntal forms, he concentrated on evolving a new type of 'modern' fugue which he could use in his own compositions. Indeed, the *Aperçus* fugue, mentioned earlier, proved that by 1908 he could tackle more extended compositions and was far from having 'nothing in him', or from losing his individuality, as Debussy had feared. Despite his lack of external recognition, Satie seems to have grown ever more confident in his opinions and abilities as the century progressed, for his protégé Roland-Manuel says that, as early as 1910, Satie privately 'considered Debussy a musician of the past. Ravel illustrated the present, whilst the future was promised to Albert Roussel.'[39] Satie later came to down-grade his opinion of Ravel, and to substitute Stravinsky for Roussel, but his underlying opinion of Debussy remained constant. However much he must have admired the technical virtuosity of *Jeux* in 1913, he knew that vast orchestras, the sensual evocation of stage action, and the bourgeois concept of the diverting entertainment had had their day. And in this opinion he was backed by Diaghilev, who employed Satie and Stravinsky rather than Debussy for his future *Ballets Russes* commissions.

In reality, Debussy provided little beyond encouragement and occasional advice for Satie between 1897 and 1911, and it was only after Ravel had introduced Satie's early piano music (including the third *Gymnopédie*) to an enthusiastic audience at a concert of the *Société Musicale Indépendante* in the *Salle Gaveau* on 16 January 1911, that Debussy agreed to conduct his orchestrations of the *Gymnopédies* on 25 March. When Debussy expressed his surprise at the success of this concert, Satie was understandably annoyed. As he told Conrad on 11 April:

> One person who isn't pleased is the good Claude. It's really his own fault; if he had done sooner what Ravel – who makes no secret of the influence I had on him – has done, his position would be different... The success achieved by the *Gymnopédies* at the concert conducted by him at the *Cercle Musical* – a success which he did everything possible to turn into a failure – gave him an unpleasant surprise.

[39] 'Satie affectait de le considérer [Debussy] comme un musicien du passé, Ravel illustrant le présent, tandis que l'avenir était promis à Albert Roussel.' Roland-Manuel, 'Satie tel que je l'ai vu', *Revue Musicale*, 214 (June 1952), 9.

I'm not angry with him about it. He's the victim of his social climbing.[40]
Why won't he allow me a very small place in his shadow? I have no use for
the sun. His conduct has antagonised the 'Ravelites' and the 'Satieists', people
who have been keeping quiet in their place, but who are now yelling at each
other like polecats.[41]

Debussy's cool relations with Ravel also played a part in this, but there can
be no doubt that he disliked relinquishing the paternal upper hand as far as
Satie was concerned. Whilst Satie remained primarily a source of precur-
sive ideas, Debussy was more than willing to discuss them with him; but
when it came to doing something practical for his friend, or to realising that
he had the technical means to carry his ideas through successfully,
Debussy's side of the relationship is to be found wanting. Moreover, there
was an element of snobbery on Debussy's part too. He did not introduce the
eccentric Satie to wealthy patrons, or even to other close artistic friends like
Chausson, Louÿs and Mallarmé in the 1890s. In short, theirs was a relationship he preferred to keep private, and mostly within the confines of his own
family. If the truth were known, he was probably embarrassed by Satie's

[40] After Debussy's death, Satie made this view of his increasingly bourgeois
attitudes public in *L'Humanité* (11 October 1919), 2, shortly before he joined
the communist party (cited Satie, *Ecrits*, p. 50). 'Debussy', he complained, 'was
far more inconsistent in his political and social tastes than he was musically.
This artistic revolutionary was extremely bourgeois in his daily life. He disliked
the "eight–hour day" and other social customs. I can confirm this. Raising
salaries – other than his own, of course – was disagreeable to him. He had his
own fixed "opinions". A strange anomaly'. 'Debussy était loin d'avoir
politiquement, socialement, les mêmes aspérités de goûts que musicalement. Ce
révolutionnaire en Art était très bourgeois dans l'usage de la vie. Il n'aimait pas
les "journées de huit heures" ni autres modifications sociales. Je puis vous
l'affirmer. L'augmentation des salaires – sauf pour lui, bien entendu – ne lui était
pas très agréable. Il avait son "point de vue". Etrange anomalie'.

[41] 'Un qui n'est pas content, c'est ce bon Claude. C'est bien de sa faute; s'il avait
fait plus tôt ce que Ravel – qui ne cache pas l'influence que j'eus pour lui – a fait,
sa position ne serait plus la même... Le succès remporté par les *Gymnopédies* au
concert dirigé par lui au Cercle Musical – succès qu'il a tout fait pour changer en
veste – l'a désagréablement surpris.
Je ne lui en veux pas: il est victime de son arrivisme. Pourquoi ne veut-il pas
me laisser une toute petite place dans son ombre. Je n'ai que faire du soleil. Sa
conduite lui a mis à dos les "Ravelistes" et les "Satistes", gens qui se tiennent dans
leur coin, sans rien dire, mais qui gueulent maintenant comme des putois.' Erik
Satie to Conrad Satie, 11 April 1911. Translation from Volta, *Satie*, p. 147.

public persona as an unpredictable eccentric who was prepared to fight the critic Willy at a Chevillard concert in 1904, or publish libellous articles about respected public figures like Lugné-Poe and Alexandre Natanson. No doubt Debussy preferred to have Satie as a friend than an enemy and it must have been difficult to justify such a liaison to other friends like Louis Laloy, who became the victim of some of Satie's most abusive criticisms in the press after Debussy's death.

At the other extreme, René Peter calls Satie a 'parasite' and questions why Debussy 'suddenly became his benefactor',[42] as though there was some secret obligation on Debussy's part. But while this undoubtedly springs from jealousy on Peter's part that Satie's friendship with Debussy lasted much longer than his own, it remains true that Satie gave Debussy little more than ideas and moral support, and that at such busy times as the composition and orchestration of *Pelléas* his weekly visits must have been something of a burden for his more successful friend. Perhaps the true reason behind the longevity of their friendship does in fact lie in their joint interest in the occult, a world to which Satie may have introduced Debussy, rather than vice versa; but until we have anything beyond a string of coincidences to go on, this must remain an area for future exploration.

Despite his annoyance with Debussy's attitude to his success in 1911, Satie still retained a high regard for his music. After he had been to see the ill-fated *Le Martyre de Saint Sébastien,* he told Conrad on 29 May 1911 that 'M. Gabriele d'Annunzio gave us a very incomplete piece, poor man. A very select and numerous audience. Your brother was very hot. Very beautiful interpretation. Claude's music was very successful; it saved the situation.'[43] Given the current 'situation' between the two composers, and the fact that by no means all of *Le Martyre* is first-rate Debussy, this was a generous opinion. As always with Satie, it is a shame that he was so reluctant to enter into musical discussions of any length, and it is likely that he kept many of

---

[42] 'et puis n'était-il pas un peu, sinon à proprement parler son parasite, du moins son obligé . . . ne lui donnait-il pas, en conséquence, l'oubli passager de ses propres misères par le sentiment qu'avait Claude de devenir soudain un bienfaiteur?' Peter, *Claude Debussy*, p. 71.

[43] 'M. Gabriel[e] d'Annunzio nous donne une pièce bien incomplète, le pauvre homme. Public de choix. Nombreux. Ton frère avait très chaud. Très belle interprétation. La musique de Claude est très réussie; elle sauve la situation.' Letter from Archives FES.

his true thoughts about his august mentor to himself. In 1912, according to Roland-Manuel, Satie 'exasperated Debussy by promising him that his next publication would be a piece called *Sous la futaille* [The bottom of the barrel].[44] Nobody who loved music could dream of such a thing, in Debussy's opinion. But Satie did, as Bibliothèque Nationale de France (Music) MS 9632 shows, though he did change the title to *Avec camaraderie* before adding it as the fourth of his *Préludes flasques (pour un chien)*. But if Debussy was the 'camarade' in question in this lively dance, and did force a rare change of title on the reluctant Satie, the *Préludes flasques* were never published during Satie's lifetime and very little of the music was altered with the title.

In 1913 relations became closer again as Debussy sensed his own insecurity in the light of Stravinsky's ascendant star, and because he approached familiar Satie territory in his children's ballet *La boîte à joujoux*. Here, in September–October 1913 we find Debussy taking extracts from the popular classics, as Satie had done earlier in *Croquis et agaceries*, and using snippets from French popular songs, as Satie had done in his *Descriptions automatiques* that April, and in his *Embryons desséchés* two months later. Both composers used extracts from Gounod's *Faust* during September 1913, and it is hard to believe that they did not discuss their projects together, or that Satie's three sets of *Enfantines* that October did not spring from this joint interest in music for children. However, Satie's 'Chez le Marchand d'Or' (the first of his *Vieux sequins et vieilles cuirasses*) was completed by 9 September, whereas Debussy did not begin his second tableau of *La boîte* (with its references to Gounod's 'Soldiers' Chorus' one-third of the way through) until 6 September at the earliest. At the same time, Satie made numerous allusions to the composer he so admired in his 1913 piano pieces, as a sort of homage. Most of these are concentrated in 'Regrets des enfermés', the last of the *Chapitres tournés en tous sens*, as ex. 7.1, ex. 7.2, and ex. 7.3 show. Perhaps Satie regarded Debussy as an imprisoned man after his ostracising marriage to Emma Bardac, like Jonah and Jean-Henri Masers de Latude, whose stories he tells in this piece. It is based on the folk-song *Nous n'irons plus au bois*, which had similarly obsessed Debussy from

---

[44] 'il exaspérait Debussy en lui promettant la prochaine publication d'un morceau de genre: *Sous la futaille . . .*' Roland-Manuel, *Satie*, 10.

Example 7.1.

Example 7.1a. Debussy: *Images oubliées*, No. 3 bars 48–50 (1894)

Example 7.1b. Satie: 'Regrets des enfermés', systems 12–13 (5 September 1913)

his song 'La Belle au bois dormant' (1890), through the third of his 1894 *Images* and *Jardins sous la pluie* (1903) to *Rondes de printemps* in 1905–9. 'Regrets des enfermés' is dedicated to Mme Claude Debussy, perhaps ironically, though Satie's other piece dedicated to Chouchou Debussy[45] contains no such positive musical references.

There may well be a reminiscence (by melodic inversion) of Debussy's *Rêverie* (c. 1890) in 'Le bain de mer' from *Sports et divertissements* (1914), whose piano textures are also strikingly similar (ex. 7.4); and the ingenuous opening of the 'Idylle' Satie dedicated to Debussy in 1915 is by no means dissimilar to the start of the same piece, as ex. 7.5 shows. But Satie's main aim here was to divert his 'nervous' and hyper-sensitive friend, who felt the horrors of war so deeply, with an amusing pastoral creation. Undoubtedly, 'the sun ... with its beautiful golden rays' represents Debussy,

[45] 'Españaña', the third of the *Croquis et agaceries d'un gros bonhomme en bois*, which rather contains references to Chabrier.

173

Example 7.2.

Example 7.2a. Debussy: 'Nuages' bars 1–2 (1898–9)

Example 7.2b. Satie: 'Regrets des enfermés', system 10 (1913)

while Satie is the one whose 'heart is very small' and has 'shivers of fright'. In his sketch for the piece,[46] Satie added the words 'La Main sur la tête de Votre Âme', but he removed them from the published version, perhaps because he thought they were too personal and revealing.

But privately, Satie viewed Debussy's patriotism and lamented inability to help the national cause with suspicion. On 18 August 1915, five days before he completed his 'Idylle', he told Paul Dukas in an unusually violent outburst that 'Debussy bathes at the seaside in Dieppe . . . He understands nothing of the War. For me, this war is like a sort of Apocalypse, more idiotic than real.'[47] But, in this case, Satie misunderstood the true depths of Debussy's feelings. Debussy's creativity was reduced to a minimum by the worsening crises of 1914, and as early as 8 August he had told Durand that he was 'nothing more than a wretched atom hurled around by this terrible

---

[46] In the notebook (23 pages long), formerly in the collection of Jacques Guérin, sold at the Hôtel Drouot on 20 May 1992, Catalogue no. 112.

[47] 'Debussy se baigne du côté de Dieppe ... Il ne comprend rien à la guerre. Pour moi, cette guerre est une sorte de fin du Monde plus bête que la véritable'. Cited from a copy in the Archives FES.

Example 7.3.

Example 7.3a. Debussy: *Pour le piano*, No. 1: 'Prélude', end (1901)

Example 7.3b. Satie: 'Regrets des enfermés', end (1913)

cataclysm, and what I'm doing seems to me so miserably petty! It makes me envious of Satie and his real job of defending Paris as a corporal.'[48]

Debussy's frustration increased as he developed rectal cancer during the winter of 1915–16. Satie often visited him to try to cheer him up as his case became 'more and more serious'.[49] We find him playing 'backgammon with poor Debussy' all afternoon on 6 January 1916,[50] and telling Dukas after another such visit in March that 'our great friend seems rather better.

[48] 'Tout cela me compose une vie à la fois intensive et troublée, où je ne suis plus qu'un pauvre atome roulé par ce terrible cataclysme; ce que je fais me semble si misérablement petit! J'en arrive à envier Satie qui va s'occuper sérieusement de défendre Paris en qualité de caporal.' Letter from Debussy to Jacques Durand. In Debussy: *Correspondance* (1993), 343–4.† Satie was then serving in the Home Guard in Arcueil, and Debussy's only original work of 1914 was the little *Berceuse héroïque* written in November as a tribute to Albert I of Belgium, whose cause both he and Satie supported.

[49] 'Debussy est de plus en plus sérieux.' From a letter from Satie to Dukas, 22 November 1915. Archives FES.

[50] 'Après-midi – au jacquet avec ce pauvre Debussy'. According to a letter from Satie to Mme Fernand Dreyfus. Archives FES.

Example 7.4.

Example 7.4a. Debussy: *Rêverie*, bars 23–6 (*c.* 1890)

Example 7.4b. Satie: 'Le bain de mer', opening, (1914)

He is constantly in great suffering however. But let us hope! yes, hope!'[51] On 20 November, Satie told Cocteau how much he was troubled by Emma Debussy's letter about her husband's state of health, but by then Satie was working flat out on *Parade* and could spare less time to visit his ailing friend.

Early in 1917 Debussy rallied sufficiently to complete his last major work, the Violin Sonata. However much he disapproved of the direction Satie's career was taking, he still took an active interest in it, and it was probably his mockery of *Parade* that caused the break between them. For on 8 March Satie sent the following curt letter to Emma: 'Decidedly, it will be better if henceforth the "Precursor" [Satie] stays at home, far away. P.S. Painful teasing – and again and again, too! Yes. Quite unbearable anyhow'.[52] The *Ballets Russes* productions in the 1917 season that Debussy chose to review naturally did not include any mention of *Parade*, and thus Satie was deprived of the one public approval that really mattered to him. It is doubt-

---

[51] 'Notre grand ami semble aller mieux. Il souffre, pourtant, toujours beaucoup. Espérons! oui, espérons!' Cited from a copy in the Archives FES.

[52] 'Décidément, il est préférable que le "Précurseur" reste désormais chez lui au loin. P.S. Pénible taquinerie – et à répétition, encore! Oui. Très insupportable, en tout cas.' Translation from Volta, *Satie*, p. 148.

Example 7.5.

Example 7.5a. Debussy: *Rêverie* bars 1–6

Example 7.5b. Satie: 'Idylle' from *Avant-dernières pensées*, opening (1915)

ful if Debussy attended the première on 18 May, but he must have seen Satie's ballet on 25 May, for he wrote to Diaghilev to congratulate him on the success of *Las Meninas* (to music by Fauré) and *Petrushka*, and *Parade* was included in the same programme.[53] Satie's preoccupation with the libel case brought against him by Jean Poueigh after *Parade* meant that the rift with Debussy went unhealed until Debussy was on his deathbed. The fact that Satie, for the only time in his life, relented is a tribute to the strength of their friendship. As he told Henry Prunières on 3 April 1918:

> You know of Debussy's death, of course. I wrote to him – fortunately for me – a few days before his death. Knowing that he was doomed, alas, I didn't want to remain on bad terms with him.

> My poor friend! What a sad end. Now people will discover that he had enormous talent. But that's life![54]

On reading Satie's apology, Debussy simply muttered 'Sorry', though in the end each composer arrived at a better understanding of how the other had suffered, and in Satie's case his deeply felt and anguished song *Elégie* of 1920

---

[53] See Letter to Diaghilev, 2 May 1917. In Debussy, *Correspondance*, pp. 376 and 379.

[54] 'Vous savez la mort de Debussy, bien entendu. Je lui ai écrit – heureusement pour moi – quelques jours avant sa mort. Le sachant perdu, hélas! Je ne voulais pas rester fâché avec lui.

Ce pauvre ami! Quelle triste fin. Maintenant, on lui trouve un énorme talent. C'est la vie!' Translation from Volta, *Satie*, p. 150.

177

says it all. For once, he brought his inner emotions to the surface 'in remembrance of an admiring and tender friendship of thirty years' in a wide-ranging vocal line of almost exaggerated expressiveness as he set Lamartine's lines about the irrelevance of nature and material possessions after the loss of a single, cherished friend.

It might be uncharitably said that Debussy's passing had more influence on Satie's music than any event during his lifetime, and that its liberating effect allowed Satie to become a more serious composer in *Socrate* and the *Nocturnes*. But much of *Socrate* was composed while Debussy was still alive; so his death was really only part of a chain of events in which Satie's growing circle of younger friends had played a more significant role since 1911. In reality, their relationship was an attraction of opposite characters with the common goal of bringing French music into the twentieth century, and in very different ways each composer achieved his goal despite, as much as because of, the other. The vexed question of their reciprocal influence concerned ideas rather than techniques, and was essentially minimal as each composer followed his own path and put his own career first. Whilst Debussy found his way forward far earlier than Satie, the latter, during the war years, had the consolation of realising that his restrained orchestral forces, clear-cut sonorities, deliberate simplicity and a cabaret-derived ambience represented the voice of the future in French art – the '*Esprit nouveau*'. Their one common ground in these difficult years of change was their admiration for Stravinsky, who alone was able to reconcile Debussy's sophisticated orchestral wizardry with post-war aesthetics and neo-classicism. Being a realist, Satie saw that Debussy's death, however much he lamented it, had come at an opportune time both in terms of his career and their long relationship. As he wrote in 1922, from the heart:

> My poor friend! And to think that if he were still alive, we would today be the worst of enemies. Life – and the 'Debussyists' – would have taken it upon themselves to separate us, and to sow the seeds of hate between us. We were no longer on the same road; our horizons were continually shifting. So? . . .
>
> Our long friendship would have been ruined for evermore.[55]

[55] 'Pauvre ami! & dire que s'il avait vécu jusqu'à ce jour, nous serions, aujourd'hui, les pires ennemis. La vie – & les *"debussystes"* – se seraient chargés de nous séparer, de nous désunir haineusement: nous ne suivions plus la même route; notre horizon se déplaçait d'heure en heure. Alors? . . .
  Notre si longue intimité devait en être ébranlée pour toujours.' Satie, *Ecrits*, p. 68.

8 Semantic and structural issues in Debussy's Mallarmé songs

MARIE ROLF

No poetry occupied Debussy over a longer span of time than that of Stéphane Mallarmé. While the composer is most acclaimed for his realisation of Mallarmé's *L'Après-midi d'un faune* (1894), he also set four other Mallarmé poems as *mélodies*. In 1884, the year in which Debussy won the *Prix de Rome* as a student at the Paris Conservatoire, he composed 'Apparition'; twenty-nine years later, among the last songs Debussy wrote were settings of 'Soupir', 'Placet futile' and 'Eventail'. The sustained impact of Mallarmé's work on Debussy is extraordinary, and bears witness to the profound influence of the poet on the composer.

The aesthetic intersection between the two artists, especially as regards *L'Après-midi d'un faune*, has received a great deal of critical attention. In his orchestral score, Debussy responded to the semantic level of Mallarmé's *eclogue* without resorting specifically to the text;[1] through his music, he was able to convey the range and complexity of the Faune's emo-

---

[1] It is generally accepted that Debussy's score provided 'l'impression générale du poème', in the words of the composer himself (letter to Willy [Henry Gauthier-Villars] of 10 October 1895); see Debussy, *Correspondance 1884–1918*, ed. François Lesure (Paris, 1993), pp. 113–14. (In other sources in which this letter is cited, the date often appears as 10 October 1896, not 1895. The actual letter is dated 'Jeudi.10.oc./95' and the number 5 is smudged. In 1895, not 1896, 10 October fell on a Thursday.) Early programme notes for the *Prélude à l'après-midi d'un faune*, which Debussy apparently sanctioned, claimed that 'La musique de ce Prélude est une illustration très libre du beau poème de Mallarmé. Elle ne prétend nullement à une synthèse de celui-ci.' (See Léon Vallas, *Claude Debussy et son temps*, rev. edn. (Paris, 1958), p. 181.) Without denying this basic premise, Arthur B. Wenk, in his *Claude Debussy and the Poets* (Berkeley, 1976), pp. 148–70, goes so far as to trace a parallel structural relationship between Mallarmé's poem and Debussy's work, noting, among other things, that the poem's 110 alexandrines are matched by 110 bars in Debussy's composition.

tions in an appropriately abstract – or non-representational – yet immediate way. In setting the songs, however, Debussy was forced to deal more carefully with the syntactic structure of the poems as well as to interpret their imagery. In fact, the young Achille deliberately chose to compose texted works rather than purely instrumental music early in his career, much as the leaders of the second Viennese school would approach their early compositions, because he could rely on the poetic structure to dictate a musical form. Furthermore, the shorter length of the songs added to the fact that they involved only voice and piano (as opposed to full orchestra as in the case of the *Prélude à l' après-midi d' un faune*) allowed the composer to concentrate on issues of pitch, rhythm, and texture. Finally, the songs provided Debussy with an excellent training ground for refining his approach to prosody. This study will explore Debussy's musical response to Mallarmé's poetry by comparing his 1884 setting of 'Apparition' with that of 'Soupir' from the *Trois poèmes* of 1913.[2] It will focus on the composer's treatment of Mallarmé's syntax as well as his interpretation of the semantic content of the poems.

Mallarmé wrote 'Apparition' (probably 1863)[3] and 'Soupir' (1864) within a year of each other. Both poems are cast in two parts, and both are written in alexandrine verse and rhymed couplets. Although 'Apparition'

[2] Limitations of space preclude the possibility of discussing each of the *Trois poèmes*. I decided to focus on 'Soupir' because, of the three Mallarmé poems Debussy set in 1913, the poetic structure of 'Soupir' is most closely related to that of 'Apparition'. The sonnet form of 'Placet futile' and the five quatrains of 'Eventail', written by Mallarmé more than 20 years later than his other poems set by Debussy, offer less common ground for a semantic and structural comparison with 'Apparition'. Incidentally, both 'Placet futile' and 'Eventail' (i.e. Mallarmé's 'Autre Eventail') were revised by the poet much more substantially than was 'Soupir'. Further reasons for juxtaposing 'Soupir' with 'Apparition' are discussed in the following paragraph of this paper. Readers desiring critical commentary and analysis of all three of the *Trois poèmes de Mallarmé* may wish to consult David M. Hertz, *The Tuning of the Word: The Musico-Literary Poetics of the Symbolist Movement* (Carbondale and Edwardsville, 1987); and Carmen Sabourin, '*Trois Poèmes de Stéphane Mallarmé' de Claude Debussy: la relation texte-musique*, M.A. thesis (McGill University, 1981).

[3] Henri Mondor discusses the question of the date of 'Apparition', as well as its early publication, in his Stéphane Mallarmé, *Oeuvres complètes*, edited and annotated by Henri Mondor and G. Jean-Aubry (Paris, 1961), pp. 1412–14.

displays many Romantic characteristics, each poem is, in varying degrees, Symbolist, aspiring to Mallarmé's goal: 'évoquer dans une ombre exprès l'objet, par des mots allusifs, jamais directs, se réduisant à du silence égal...'[4]

Wallace Fowlie described Mallarmé's poetry as an

> art turning back on itself, art of self-reflection. Art of intense sobering silence. It was poetry of *absence* in which the clear outline of objects and their physical appearance were blurred and dimmed and decomposed so that the idea or meaning or symbolism of the object should assume the life of the poem. In being poetry of *silence*, it was not death-like, but life-capturing, life-deepening silence. The silence of dreams, perhaps.[5]

The *Trois poèmes de Mallarmé* in particular focus on reflective, silent, inner experiences, demanding from the reader an active interpretation of exterior objects or actions. Yet the poems are written in strict poetic forms, posing the double challenge to the would-be composer to reflect the suggestive qualities of the text as well as its more rigid structure, the latter task perhaps involving an illumination of the poem's often convoluted syntax.

This essay will first examine the poetic structure of 'Apparition' – its symbols and images; semantic content; rhyme scheme and rhythmic structure; formal design; poetic devices and the like – and then focus on Debussy's treatment of these elements in the context of both the Romantic and Symbolist features of the poem. A similar approach to 'Soupir' will facilitate a comparison of the two *mélodies*.[6]

It is easy to see why 'Apparition' was one of Mallarmé's most popular poems (see fig. 8.1). A curious fusion of Romantic and Symbolist qualities, it conveys a nostalgic reminiscence of the narrator's beloved, replete with such images as the moon, seraphim, viols, flowers, sobs, and a dream-like reverie. But, in typical Mallarmé fashion, these symbols are linked with unexpected elements. For example, anthropomorphism abounds: the moon grows sad; viols are dying; and perfume is melancholy. Other symbolic images, such as the emphasis on light and white, especially in the second half of this poem, link tangible objects with less tangible impres-

---

[4] Stéphane Mallarmé, article in *The National Observer* (28 January 1893).

[5] Wallace Fowlie, *Mallarmé* (London, 1953), p. 288.

[6] I am grateful to Peter Kaminsky, Steven Laitz, and Susan Youens for their comments on an early draft of this essay. They helped to focus the analyses – poetic and musical – that follow.

181

Figure 8.1. Text of 'Apparition' (translation by Marie Rolf)

Apparition

1 La lune s'attristait. Des séraphins en pleurs
2 Rêvant, l'archet aux doigts, dans le calme des fleurs
3 Vaporeuses, tiraient de mourantes violes
4 De blancs sanglots glissant sur l'azur des corolles.
5 – C'était le jour béni de ton premier baiser.
6 Ma songerie aimant à me martyriser
7 S'enivrait savamment du parfum de tristesse
8 Que même sans regret et sans déboire laisse
9 La cueillaison d'un Rêve au coeur qui l'a cueilli.
10 J'errais donc, l'oeil rivé sur le pavé vieilli
11 Quand avec du soleil aux cheveux, dans la rue
12 Et dans le soir, tu m'es en riant apparue
13 Et j'ai cru voir la fée au chapeau de clarté
14 Qui jadis sur mes beaux sommeils d'enfant gâté
15 Passait, laissant toujours de ses mains mal fermées
16 Neiger de blancs bouquets d'étoiles parfumées.

Apparition

1 The moon grew sad. Seraphim in tears,
2 Dreaming, holding their bows, in the calm of
3 Misted flowers, drew from their dying viols
4 White sobs sliding over blue corollas.
5 – It was the blessed day of your first kiss.
6 My reverie, fond of making me a martyr,
7 Knowingly grew intoxicated from the melancholy perfume
8 That, with neither regret nor disagreeable aftertaste,
9 The gathering of a Dream leaves in the heart which has gathered it.
10 So I wandered, my glance fixed on the worn pavestones,
11 When with the sun in your hair, in the street
12 And in the evening, you appeared, laughing, before me.
13 And I thought I saw the fairy with the halo of light
14 Who long ago in my lovely dreams of spoiled childhood
15 Passed by, still letting snow down from her half closed hands
16 White bouquets of perfumed stars.

sions; consider, for example, the lover 'avec du *soleil* aux cheveux' and the fairy 'au chapeau de *clarté*' who lets 'snow down white bouquets of perfumed stars' ('*neiger* de *blancs* bouquets d'*étoiles* parfumées').

As is often the case in his poems, Mallarmé blends reality with the ideal; in 'Apparition', the blond beloved merges with the image of the luminous fairy. In fact, Mallarmé's real-life inspiration for this poem was probably a mixture of individuals: his friend Henri Cazalis's beloved Ettie Yapp; his own fiancée Marie; and the memory of his dear sister Maria who had died about six years earlier.[7] In 'Apparition', Mallarmé merges the image of an actual beloved with the memory that 'the gathering of a Dream leaves in the heart which has gathered it' ('La cueillaison d'un Rêve au coeur qui l'a cueilli'). This deliberate confusion of the past with the present, the ideal with reality, lends a suspended, ethereal quality to the work, a quality that Debussy aptly portrays in his setting of the poem.

The poem consists of eight couplets dividing into two principal units: the first nine lines set the emotional backdrop of the poem, while the last seven lines focus on a specific memory of the poet's beloved in the sunlit street and in the evening. The first unit subdivides into two smaller sections: lines 1–5, and lines 6–9. Subsection 1 consists of two couplets leading to the statement in line 5, set apart visually from the rest of the poem by a hyphen: ' – C'était le jour béni de ton premier baiser.' This line sounds surprisingly abrupt in context, not only because it is short, compared with the previous sentence, but because of the emphasis on the plosive consonants of béni, ton, premier, and baiser following the mellifluous opening which features liquid consonants, especially the 'l': 'La lune…pleurs / l'archet…calme des fleurs / violes / De blancs sanglots glissant sur l'azur des corolles'. The plosive consonants underscore the physicality of the memory – a stark contrast to the celestial moon-world at the beginning of the poem. At line 5, the couplets begin to conflict with the semantic structure of the piece; in spite of the end-rhyme of lines 5–6,

<hr />

[7] Correspondance from Cazalis to Mallarmé, dated April and June 1863, indicates that both Ettie and Marie were in Mallarmé's thoughts when writing 'Apparition'. See Mondor and Jean-Aubry (ed.), Mallarmé: *Oeuvres complètes*, pp. 1412–13. In his *Introduction à la psychanalyse de Mallarmé* (Neuchâtel, 1963), pp. 77–8, Charles Mauron develops the psychological relationship between Ettie and Maria.

line 6 clearly begins a new thought. Similarly, line 9, which ends part one of the poem, rhymes with line 10, which begins part two. Only in the final two couplets of the poem do the rhyme scheme and the semantic structure become synchronous again.

Other irregularities in the verse include the frequent enjambement (first seen in lines 1–2 and 2–3, where the emphasis falls on the ethereal words 'rêvant' and 'vaporeuses') and the irregular placement of the caesura in the alexandrine lines.[8] Compare, for example, the classical placement of the caesura after the sixth syllable in line 1 – 'La lune s'attristait' – with the 4 + 8 syllable combination in line 3. Lines 11 and 12 provide an interesting contrast in their 9 + 3 and 4 + 8 syllabic divisions, respectively. The irregular alexandrine as well as the enjambement vary the interior rhythm of each line, creating a sense of fluidity throughout the entire poem.

The juxtaposition of various 'e'-vowels – '-uet', 'es', '-ait', and the like – found in lines 14–16 ('mes beaux sommeils d'enfant gâté / Passait, laissant toujours de ses mains mal fermées / Neiger de blanc bouquets d'étoiles parfumées'), and the alliteration, combined with the elongation of similar vowel sounds of line 9 ('La cueillaison d'un Rêve au coeur qui l'a cueilli') contribute to the sonorous aspect of the poem, often cited by critics for its 'musical' quality. Clearly, Mallarmé valued these passages, even at the expense of traditional grammatical constructs; for example, the verb 'laisse' at the end of line 8 precedes rather than follows its subject, 'la cueillaison d'un Rêve', in line 9.

Debussy was probably attracted to Mallarmé's 'Apparition', as indeed were other composers of the era,[9] by its pristine imagery. No doubt he also identified with the subject matter; in fact, 'Apparition' was composed for his own beloved at the time, Mme Marie-Blanche Vasnier, just as Mallarmé had penned his poem with his fiancée Marie, among others, in mind.

Debussy portrayed several of Mallarmé's images in his setting of

---

8 In 'Crise de vers' (Mallarmé, *Oeuvres complètes*, p. 362), Mallarmé argues for flexibility within the rigid constraints of the alexandrine: 'Les fidèles à l'alexandrin, notre hexamètre, desserrent intérieurement ce mécanisme rigide et puéril de sa mesure; l'oreille, affranchie d'un compteur factice, connaît une jouissance à discerner, seule, toutes les combinaisons possibles, entre eux, de douze timbres.'

9 See in particular the settings by Edmond Bailly (Paris, 1894) and André Rossignol (place unknown, c. 1893).

'Apparition'.[10] To cite only a few instances, the dreamy calm of the opening is depicted in the shimmering texture of the piano and by the scarcely moving melody of the voice. The 'white sobs' of the viols slide through a series of parallel dominant-seventh chords.[11] At the end of the song, the image of perfumed stars falling to the ground is exquisitely painted in the piano by the descending arpeggiated grace notes.

Debussy's musical imagery reaches a deeper semantic level than the surface elements just cited, however. For example, he responds not only to the calm of the opening lines but also to the poem's suspended quality: its synthesis of the ideal with the real; and its complex juxtaposition of poignant sadness with the rush of emotion in recalling the beloved's first kiss. As a result, he suspends our sense of tonality, delaying clarity until line 5, '– C'était le jour béni de ton premier baiser', where we hear a dominant–tonic progression in the key of G♭ major (ex. 8.1). It is significant that Mallarmé himself set off this line with a hyphen. The entire section preceding this moment is governed by a tenuous linear progression where neighbour notes, passing notes, and common notes provide the thread between successive harmonies (ex. 8.2). The conclusion of the second couplet on the g♯ half-diminished seventh in bar 12[12] acts as a tonal signifier; enharmonically, it is an altered ii^7 in G♭ major, smoothly leading to the V–I of 'C'était le jour béni', which, incidentally, is marked 'Fiévreuse' in the manuscript, a notation that never was incorporated into the printed edition.

A second semantic issue, involving a deeper reading of Mallarmé's poem, concerns Debussy's re-use of the musical material accompanying

---

[10] It is recommended that the reader obtain a score of 'Apparition', available as the last song of the *Quatre chansons de jeunesse* (Paris, Jobert, 1969).

[11] After the first two chords, the manuscript (in the Library of Congress) does not contain the same accidentals as those present in the printed edition. F♯^{7} – F^7 are followed by E^{M7} (No natural is notated before the d^2, either in the piano or in the vocal part, on beat 4; it could be argued that Debussy, in his haste, mistakenly omitted them.) and C^7 going to a d♯ diminished chord (not D major, as in the edition) in the manuscript. As a result, one still perceives descending seventh chords, though not all consistently M^{m7ths} (dominant sevenths) through the first six beats of the bar.

[12] The manuscript contains no natural for the d^1, resulting in a g♯^{m7} chord. Furthermore, the voice moves from f♯^{1} on beat 1 to f natural^1 on beat 7, suggesting an e♯ half-diminished seventh chord – functioning as a vii in G♭, which is subsumed by the D♭ dominant-seventh chord in bar 13.

Example 8.1. 'Apparition' bars 13–16

Example 8.2. 'Apparition': linear progression of bars 1–12 (lines 1–4 of poem)

Example 8.3.

Example 8.3a. 'Apparition' bars 13–16

Example 8.3b. 'Apparition' bars 41–4

the articulation of G♭ major. Its only reappearance occurs in bars 41–4, with the words, 'Et j'ai cru voir la fée au chapeau de clarté'. Debussy clearly equates the fairy with the beloved referred to in line 5, an association that Mallarmé suggests as well. It is noteworthy that Debussy juxtaposed the two passages musically even at the expense of the prosody: 'C'était le jour béni de ton premier baiser' follows the natural speech accent more closely than 'Et j'ai cru voir la fée au chapeau de clarté' (ex. 8.3).

186

Figure 8.2. Declamation and tonal structure of 'Apparition'

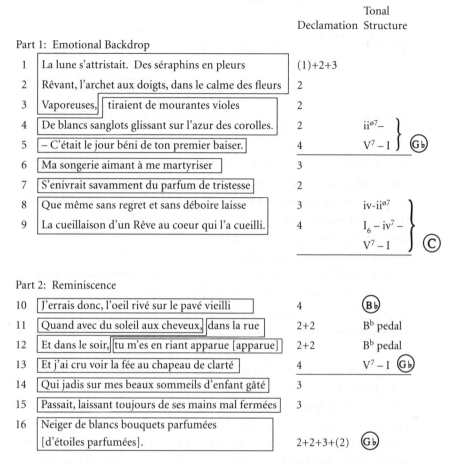

Debussy's respect for the structure of Mallarmé's poem is equally sensitive. The ends of couplets correspond to vocal articulations (breaths) at the ends of musical lines except in cases where enjambement or the irregular subdivisions of the alexandrine verse occur. Musical units are illustrated by the boxes in fig. 8.2; note that the musical and poetic units coincide for lines 5–7, 10, and 13–16. Similarly, Debussy respects all of Mallarmé's enjambements except at the beginning of line 15 with the word 'Passait'. At this point, Debussy begins a new vocal articulation, shifting from Gb major to F# minor, thus preparing the following D-major chord. By the end of line 15, on the word 'fermées', the passage has returned to the tonic of Gb. This momentary twist to the D sonority (enharmonic VI in Gb minor) provides

Example 8.4. 'Apparition' bars 22–26

an important association to the D chord in bar 9, whose passage was preparing for the song's initial arrival on G♭. The turn from a sharp-key to a flat-key carries semantic significance in that the latter seems to be associated with a Romantic concept of the beloved, while the sharp-key sets the suspended tone of the poem in a Symbolist sense.

The two large units of the poem correspond to cadences on C in bar 28 and on the tonic of G♭ in bar 57 (fig. 8.2). The subdivision of part 1 at line 5, in G♭ major, has already been discussed. Note that, up to the first arrival of G♭, the declamatory units have been quite irregular, corresponding to the enjambement and irregular alexandrine verse. The tonal arrival on G♭ is accompanied by a momentarily regular four-bar phrase which is followed by a quasi-transitional 3 + 2 + 3 bars (bars 17–24) for lines 6–8. The operative verb 'laisse' that ends line 8 leads directly into 'la cueillaison' of line 9 from both a linear point of view as well as for grammatical reasons (ex. 8.4). Four-bar units return to set up the C-major section at 'La cueillaison d'un Rêve au coeur qui l'a cueilli'[13] and another section immediately thereafter cadencing in B♭, corresponding to the end of line 10. Symmetrical four-bar phraseology continues throughout this passage, which includes the repetition of the word 'apparue' to accommodate the periodicity, and concludes with the G♭ return at 'Et j'ai cru voir la fée au chapeau de clarté'. The song ends as it began, with three- and two-bar units. Debussy's treatment of phrase structure thus parallels his tonal construct of the song; irregular phraseology predominates, except for passages that define tonal centres, as at lines 5 (G♭), 9 (C), 10 (B♭), and 13 (G♭)

---

13 In bar 25 of the manuscript, the piano's inner voice (in the thumb of the right hand) moves smoothly from g to a to b̲; for some inexplicable reason, the b was replaced by a crotchet rest in the printed edition.

in particular. Thus, tonal clarity is combined with four-bar phraseology at key structural points of the poem.

Several aspects of Debussy's setting of 'Apparition' are romantically conceived. The intensely dramatic treatment of lines 5 and 13 in terms of texture, tessitura, and dynamics, as well as the high C for Mme Vasnier on the repeat of the word 'apparue' in bar 39 (which is indicated as fortissimo in the manuscript), certainly stem from nineteenth-century tradition. Such outbursts are rare in mature Debussy; in fact, the only similar one from the songs that comes to mind is at the climax of 'Spleen' (bar 28), published in 1888 and without doubt also conceived for Mme Vasnier. The dramatic passages in 'Apparition' are heightened by a liberal dose of appoggiature and accented passing notes. Other clues in the score point to the fact that this song was set by Debussy early in his career. His treatment of prosody in 'Apparition' is not what it would become with his work on *Pelléas* and thereafter. Awkward moments, such as the passage already mentioned underlying line 13 (see ex. 8.3b) and even the opening 'Des séraphins en pleurs' (which could easily have been notated as ♩♩ ♪♪♩♩) mar the delivery of Mallarmé's text. Also, the repetition of 'apparue' and 'd'étoiles parfumées', as well as the melismatic treatment of 'apparue' in bars 38–40 and 'j'ai cru voir' in bar 41, is atypical of Debussy's mature vocal works.

In addition to these elements that allude to nineteenth-century formulae, Debussy imbues the song with forward-looking, Symbolist qualities. The melodic line that begins each section of 'Apparition' (line 1 in bar 2 and line 10 in bar 29) is understated in terms of dynamics, static motion, and tessitura. What comes to the fore as a result are the words themselves and the shifting colours of the vowels and consonants, as opposed to a memorable melody. The tonally ambiguous quality of the opening twelve bars, corresponding to the first four lines of text, delays the structural downbeat of the piece to bar 14 where G♭ major is established and where Mallarmé first reveals to us the true subject of his poem. This non-functional opening is echoed in the final twelve bars of the song; ex. 8.5 illustrates the parallels between these two passages. The tritone from E to B♭ is exposed in bars 1–7, with a secondary motion to D (via neighbour, passing, and common notes – see ex. 8.2), which in turn sets up the supertonic half-diminished seventh in G♭. Thus, a whole-tone palette is laid out by Debussy, although he quickly shifts into diatonic G♭ major. At the end of

Example 8.5.

Example 8.5a. 'Apparition' bars 1–14

Example 8.5b. 'Apparition' bars 47–59

the song, the harmony moves momentarily from G♭ to the referential sonority of D (bar 48) and then decorates the G♭ tonal centre with a whole-tone descent in the tenor voice (bars 54–9), outlining F♭ (enharmonically, E) to B♭ once again (as in bars 1–7), and then A♭ to G♭, completing the whole-tone collection. The quasi-symmetrical construct of the first and last twelve bars is striking, especially since in each case the text dwells on ethereal images – the sobbing seraphim, the fairy dropping bouquets of perfumed stars – rather than the concrete, Romantic, narrative of the poem. The fact that, for much of the song, tonality is implied rather than explicitly stated, may be considered Symbolist, bearing in mind Mallarmé's own words '*Nommer* un objet, c'est supprimer les trois quarts de la jouissance du poëme qui est faite de deviner peu à peu: le *suggérer*, voilà le rêve. C'est le parfait usage de ce mystère qui constitue le symbole: évoquer petit à petit un objet pour montrer un état d'âme, ou, inverse-ment, choisir un objet et en dégager un état d'âme, par une série de déchiffrements.'[14] Finally, Debussy's shifting between 9/8 and 3/4 in the song[15] continually juxtaposes subdivisions of 3 against 2, creating a

[14] Mallarmé, *Oeuvres complètes*, p. 869.
[15] The change in the piano part from 9/8 to 3/4, occurring in bar 13 of the printed edition, does not appear in the manuscript until bar 17 (at the beginning of the second page of the manuscript).

190

flexible rhythmic backdrop[16] for a poem that suggests multiple and complex associations in its use of Symbolist imagery.

The tritone E to B♭, heard in a whole-tone context at the beginning and end of Debussy's song, is reflected on a larger scale in the tonal centres he chooses for the main body of 'Apparition'. Passages of diatonic tonal progressions occur on G♭ (lines 5, 13, and 16) and C (line 9) – significantly, a tritone apart. The fact that the symmetrical tritone is used by Debussy in both non-functional and functional tonal contexts points to Symbolist as well as to Romantic leanings. Finally, Debussy's ultimate incorporation of ambiguous, whole-tone elements within a universe of G♭ tonic (see ex. 8.5b) reflects the poetic union of the ideal and the real posed by Mallarmé.

It is possible that Debussy attempted to set 'Apparition' a second time in 1913 when he composed his *Trois poèmes de Mallarmé*. A sketchbook with notes for 'Soupir' apparently contains sketches for a setting of 'Apparition' as well.[17] It seems unlikely that, while composing 'Soupir' around 1913, Debussy would simply copy out his early song of 1884, so we must conclude for now that these sketches might well represent an entirely new musical setting of 'Apparition'.[18] A second setting of 'Apparition', composed nearly thirty years after the first, would no doubt offer a fascinating glimpse into Debussy's compositional development, especially regarding

[16] The rhythmic treatment in the piano is quite similar to that of 'Recueillement' (1889), the fourth of the *Cinq poèmes de Baudelaire*, which pits 2 against 3, alternates 4/4 with 3/4 and 9/8, and ends with the quaver-crotchet iambic pattern at its 'Solennel' tempo marking.

[17] For a description of the sketchbook, see item 182 on pages 34–5 in Georges Andrieux (*expert*), *Catalogue du vente de livres précieux anciens, romantiques, modernes, manuscrits, documents et lettres autographes: collection Jules Huret* [1–154] *et collection Claude Debussy* [174–224], vente le 30 novembre 1933 . . . Les 1, 2, 4, 5, 6, 7, 8 décembre 1933 (place unknown, 1933).

[18] The text of 'Apparition' was certainly resonating in Debussy's thoughts on 9 December 1913, when he wrote to his wife Emma from Saint Petersburg, 'Ce soir, je vais manger du pain et du fromage, puis me coucherai . . . Ah! je les ai bien perdus *mes beaux sommeils d'enfant gâté!*' During October 1916, near the end of his life when the ill composer was resting at Arcachon, he wrote, this time to Robert Godet, 'Pour continuer, "*ma songerie aimant à se martyriser*", je ne me suis pas encore retrouvé. Cette horrible maladie a bouleversé mes plus belles facultés [*sic*], en particulier celle de trouver des façons inédites d'assembler les sons.' Both of these letters are cited in Margaret G. Cobb (ed.), *The Poetic Debussy: A Collection of His Song Texts and Selected Letters*, trans. Richard Miller, rev. 2nd edn. (Rochester, New York, 1994), pp. 236 and 250 respectively.

his musical vocabulary and his response to the Symbolist qualities of the text. Until this sketchbook is made available to scholars, however, this important question must remain unanswered.

Even though 'Soupir' (April 1864) was written only one year after 'Apparition', it presents complexities both as a poem and as a song that go far beyond the interpretative challenges posed by the earlier work (fig. 8.3). Rather than employing symbols to portray a nostalgic reminiscence, as in 'Apparition', Mallarmé uses them to suggest a transcendental state of being.[19] The poet sacrifices action in order to focus on inner sensations of the soul. Mallarmé himself described the poem as 'une rêverie automnale'.[20] In the first half of 'Soupir', the poet's soul strives increasingly upward – towards the brow, then the sky, just as the fountain sighs towards 'l'Azur'. For Mallarmé, the Azure represents the Ideal (note the capitalisation) which is never attainable – not unlike 'die blaue Blume' of the German Romantic tradition. This enigmatic symbol lies at the heart of 'Soupir'.

The sigh itself embodies two conflicting gestures – that of aspiration or excited anticipation as well as that of expiration, disappointment, or resignation. Although these emotions are intermingled throughout the poem, the first five lines reveal more of a sense of aspiring; the soul rises in expectation, just as an ebullient fountain sighs. The second half of the poem develops the autumnal images introduced in part 1, emphasising their melancholy, decaying qualities. As in 'Apparition', 'Soupir' represents Mallarmé's response to his sister Maria's death as much as – perhaps more than – his feelings toward his newly wed wife Marie. His reference to 'ô calme soeur', her 'oeil angélique', the Azure 'attendri d'Octobre pâle et pur', and 'l'eau morte' support this reading of the poem. Typically, Mallarmé blends images bearing multiple meanings, evoking the past and present of his own experience, and merging the unattainable ideal with reality.

Like 'Apparition', 'Soupir' is written in alexandrine verse, it consists of

---

[19] For Jean Royère, '"Apparition" est la nostalgie du temps, la vision du paradis en arrière, "Soupir", celle de l'espace; c'est le baiser suprême et suprêmement purifié'. Cited in Mallarmé, *Oeuvres complètes*, p. 1434.

[20] See Mallarmé, *Oeuvres complètes*, pp. 1433–4 for a full citation for this remark and for further references to the poems of others, for example to Baudelaire's 'Chant d'automne'.

Figure 8.3. Text of 'Soupir' (translation by Marie Rolf)

Soupir

1 Mon âme vers ton front où rêve, ô calme soeur,
2 Un automne jonché de taches de rousseur,
3 Et vers le ciel errant de ton oeil angélique
4 Monte, comme dans un jardin mélancolique,
5 Fidèle, un blanc jet d'eau soupire vers l'Azur!
6 – Vers l'Azur attendri d'Octobre pâle et pur
7 Qui mire aux grands bassins sa langueur infinie
8 Et laisse, sur l'eau morte où la fauve agonie
9 Des feuilles erre au vent et creuse un froid sillon,
10 Se traîner le soleil jaune d'un long rayon.

Sigh

1 My soul rises toward your brow where dreams, o calm sister,
2 An autumn strewn with freckles,
3 And toward the wandering sky of your angelic eye,
4 Just as in a melancholy garden,
5 Faithful, a white fountain sighs toward the Azure!
6 – Toward the softened October Azure, pale and pure,
7 Which mirrors in vast pools of water its infinite languor
8 And allows, on the dead water where the tawny agony
9 Of the leaves wanders in the wind and etches a cold trail,
10 The yellow sun to trail along in a long ray of light.

Figure 8.4. Arch form and mirror images in 'Soupir'

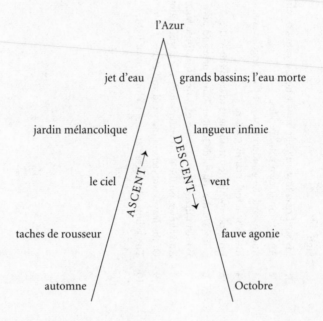

rhymed couplets (five in 'Soupir' as opposed to the eight of 'Apparition'), and it divides into two sections (equal in length in 'Soupir' as opposed to the asymmetrical 9 + 7 lines of 'Apparition'). Whereas 'Apparition' moved from the portrayal of an emotional backdrop in part 1 to a more concrete recollection of events in part 2, 'Soupir' opens with a more active gesture and then concludes with a passive elaboration of the same idea. In fact, the form of 'Soupir' is that of a sigh – an inhalation or upbeat followed by an exhalation or release of tension (fig. 8.4). In part 1, the subject, verb, and principal metaphor are unveiled; when Mallarmé's syntax is untwisted, we read 'Mon âme monte vers ton front et vers le ciel comme un jet d'eau soupire vers l'Azur'. Part 2 develops the metaphor of the Azure – 'vers l'Azur qui mire aux grand bassins sa langueur infinie et laisse se traîner un long rayon de soleil jaune'. Note that the entire poem consists of only one sentence, quite different from the grammatical construction of 'Apparition'.

The peak of the sigh pivots on the words 'vers l'Azur' in lines 5 and 6, set off by Mallarmé by a hyphen at the beginning of line 6 (similar to his treatment of line 5 of 'Apparition'). Images on either side of this pivot mirror each other: automne – Octobre, rousseur – fauve, jet d'eau – grands bassins and l'eau morte, mélancolique – langueur, to name a few (fig. 8.4). These images are treated, however, in a most unorthodox way. Mallarmé evokes an 'automne jonché de taches de rousseur', when we would expect the 'front' to be described as such. The 'ciel' rather than the 'oeil' is 'errant'. The 'agonie' rather than the 'feuilles' is 'fauve'. And the 'jet d'eau' is 'fidèle', but so is the 'âme'. The perceptive reader needs to assimilate and react to these anomalies; in a moment we shall see how much of Mallarmé's poem Debussy truly absorbed.

Both the irregular placement of the caesura in the alexandrine verse as well as the technique of enjambement occur in 'Soupir', as they did in 'Apparition'. The enjambement between lines 3–4, 4–5, and 7–8 works hand-in-hand with the irregular interior caesura of line 4 (2 + 10 syllables), line 5 (3 + 4 + 5 syllables), and line 8 (3 + 3 + 6 syllables). Just as the subject of line 1 elides to the verb of line 4, so the beginning of line 8 leads to the beginning of line 10 – 'et laisse . . . se traîner' – creating the effect of an enjambement over three lines and also setting up an irregular caesura after 'se traîner' in line 10.

Debussy's setting of 'Soupir'[21] reflects the two-part form of the sigh that is inherent in Mallarmé's poem. The song divides in half between bars 17 and 18, precisely between lines 5 and 6 of the poem. After the introduction in the piano, part 1 moves from an unaccompanied recitative to a section employing a triplet ostinato. Part 2 opens with the most lush textures of the piece and with a more animated tempo, then returns to a triplet ostinato, and ends in a slower tempo with the same iambic pulsating triplets that closed 'Apparition'. Debussy thus creates a musical arch in terms of texture, tempo, and rhythmic activity, reflecting the poetic shape of 'Soupir'.

The composer's parsing of the poem is shown in fig. 8.5. The issue of declamation has been eliminated from this example (unlike fig. 8.2) because the metres and tempos and even individual rhythms are shifting so

---

[21] The reader is encouraged to consult a score of 'Soupir', the first of Debussy's *Trois poèmes de Stéphane Mallarmé* (Paris, Durand, 1913).

MARIE ROLF

Figure 8.5. Debussy's parsing of 'Soupir'

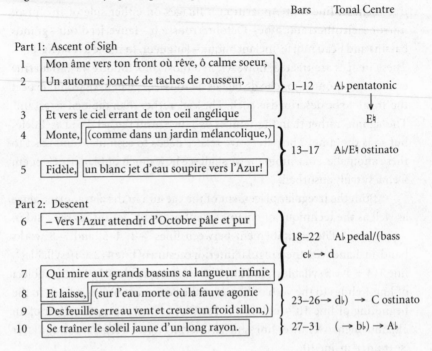

much more in this song that counting bars has far less meaning than it did in 'Apparition'. What becomes readily apparent to the listener is that Debussy is less concerned with such issues as the end rhyme or the internal caesuras of the alexandrine verse or even the painting of individual words of the poem (for example, the melody of 'Monte' descends!). Rather, he focuses on the issue of grammar and syntax, taking great pains to unravel Mallarmé's convoluted sentence.

Debussy separates the principal clause of Mallarmé's sentence from dependent clauses by tessitura as well as by differing note values. For example, the modifiers indicated within parentheses in fig. 8.5, in line 4 ('comme dans un jardin mélancolique') and lines 8–9 ('sur l'eau morte où la fauve agonie des feuilles erre au vent et creuse un froid sillon'), are delivered by the singer in a consistently low tessitura and are accompanied each time by the triplet ostinato in the piano. Even more remarkable is Debussy's

Example 8.6. 'Soupir': principal subject – verb in part 1

Example 8.7. 'Soupir': adjectival clause in part 2

Example 8.8. 'Soupir': symmetrical tonal construction

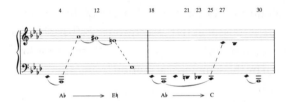

treatment of the principal subject-verb of the poem, shown in ex. 8.6. Not only are these words set apart by longer note values, but they also follow each other in a logical linear fashion, even over many bars! The crescendo on the operative verb 'monte' serves to link the 'âme' to 'fidèle'; significantly, it constitutes the first indication of dynamics in the vocal part since its opening entrance. From this analysis, it is clear that Debussy drew the semantic connection between Mallarmé's faithful 'jet d'eau' and the faithfulness of the poet's 'âme'. The adjectival clause modifying the Azure in part 2 of the poem is treated in a similar fashion to the grammatical model of part 1 (ex. 8.7); the melodic ascent from $g\flat^1$ to $b\flat^1$ on 'vers l'Azur' continues to c^2 on 'mire', then begins a descent on 'et laisse' to the final $g\flat^1$ on 'se traîner', which also incorporates the melodic peak on $d\flat^2$. As we have seen in fig. 8.5, in the process of being guided by the syntax, Debussy respects the enjambement of the poem at the beginning of lines 4, 5, and 8.

Debussy's treatment of tonality in 'Soupir' reflects not only the syntactic structure but also the semantic content of Mallarmé's poem (ex. 8.8).

Example 8.9. 'Soupir': symmetrical melodic construction

The opening melodic gesture moves from 'Mon âme' to 'Monte', centring on A♭ pentatonic and shifting to an implied area of E major, where the A♭ becomes a G♯.[22] The next section juxtaposes A♭ and E with the ostinato that runs through bar 17, completing the first half of the poem that rises toward the Azure. The second half of the poem divides into 5 + 4 + 5 bars, with the 5-bar units marking the clause 'qui mire sa langueur et laisse/se traîner le soleil jaune d'un long rayon'. Although the A♭ continues as a pedal throughout most of this half of the piece, the bass motion progresses from the E introduced in the first half through E♭ (bar 18), D (bar 21), D♭ (bar 23), to C (bar 25). In the last five bars, it subsequently passes through B♭ (bar 27) to A♭ (bar 30). Thus, the motion of A♭, or G♯, to E – down a major third – in the first half of the song is mirrored by the symmetrical motion from A♭ to C – up a major third – in the second half of the piece.

These major thirds on either side of the tonal centre of A♭ form an augmented triad – in fact, the same augmented triad sung on the key word 'fidèle' in bar 15 – and they mirror the symmetrical construct of Mallarmé's poem. Furthermore, the augmented triad of course accommodates a whole-tone scale, an element used for colouristic effect in this piece. Also symmetrical are the pitches of Debussy's melody (ex. 8.9), inverting exactly about A♭, as do the tonal centres of Debussy's song, perhaps reflecting Mallarmé's poetic mirror images (fig. 8.4).

The manner in which the tonal centre of A♭ is established has less to do with the poem's syntactic structure than it does with Debussy's response to the semantic issues posed by Mallarmé's work. Compared with 'Apparition', Mallarmé's 'Soupir' is far more abstract, less personal, and less specific. His words come closer to evoking a pure idea – that of the soul

---

[22] Theo Hirsbrunner, in his 'Zu Debussys und Ravels Mallarmé-Vertonungen', *Archiv für Musikwissenschaft*, 35/2 (1978), 81–103, notes the relationship between the sonorities heard in the piano under the words 'un automne jonché de taches de rousseur' and the opening two chords of 'Feuilles mortes'.

striving for oneness with the universe – rather than recalling any particular event, as in the reminiscence portion of 'Apparition'. The fountain is the principal metaphor in 'Soupir', yet the poem is not about a fountain; it has become a detached signifier, especially when compared with the moon, seraphim, *et al*, which set the stage for 'Apparition'.

What was Debussy's harmonic, musical analogue for this level of poetic abstraction? He chose to withdraw traditional tonal signifiers and to replace them with referential pitches that relate to each other but not in a functional way. In 'Soupir', the listener hears no tonal signifier such as the progression of the half-diminished seventh on ii–V^7–I in G♭ that so clearly bursts through the otherwise dreamy opening of 'Apparition'. Instead, A♭ is suggested as a tonal centre only by a pedal which takes on some importance over a period of time and in context with its linear surroundings. The movements to E and to C create secondary areas, symmetrical on either side of A♭, negating any functional, directional pull toward the tonic. Of course, the pentatonic and whole-tone scales used by Debussy in 'Soupir' reinforce this lack of tonal direction. The resulting aural effect is one of harmonic stasis – a perfect musical analogue to the inert state-of-being represented by the poem.[23]

It comes as no surprise that Debussy's 'Soupir' is fundamentally more attuned to Symbolist ideals than is his setting of 'Apparition'. The subtle, understated melody of 'Soupir', often sung unaccompanied and in a relatively low tessitura, ranging in dynamics from *pp* to *p*, is quintessential Debussy and highly reminiscent of *Pelléas et Mélisande*. Unlike 'Apparition', which is much more dramatically conceived, 'Soupir' offers the singer neither melismas nor repeated words for emphasis, nor even a memorable melody for the listener to hum after hearing the song. Rather than creating a melody that accommodates the harmonic basis of the song, as in the G♭ portion of 'Apparition', Debussy composed a vocal line that adhered closely to the syntactic and semantic structure of Mallarmé's 'Soupir' and then created an appropriately abstract harmonic – or, perhaps more accurately stated, linear – backdrop for the delivery of the text. The resultant melody is far more flexible in rhythm, involves more metric changes, and virtually

---

[23] 'Eventail' carries this concept of poetic and musical abstraction to the extreme, so finely attuned are Mallarmé's and Debussy's Symbolist aesthetic and technique.

abolishes any strong sense of a downbeat. Such rhythmic fluidity and sparseness of texture are features of many of the composer's later compositions, such as *Jeux*[24] or the Sonata for Cello and Piano. Finally, Debussy's more sophisticated, non-functional tonal basis for the song mirrors Mallarmé's increasingly abstract poetry whose tendency is towards evoking a pure idea, free of specific meanings and known signifiers, and the composer's symmetrical referential pitches – A♭, E, and C – reflect the symmetrical structure of Mallarmé's poem.

Just as Mallarmé's goal was to purify poetry, to refine it to an experience 'freely traced by the mind between what exists – our experience of the world, outer or inner – and what does not exist, passing through all the gradations of dream',[25] so did Debussy call for a new purity in music: 'Epurons notre musique. Appliquons nous à la décongestionner. Cherchons à obtenir une musique plus nue.'[26]

[24] In his article on '*Prelude to the Afternoon of a Faun* and *Jeux*: Debussy's Summer Rites', *19th Century Music*, 3/3 (1980), 225–38, Laurence D. Berman points to the linear conception of *Jeux* and discusses its greater rhythmic flexibility in comparison with the *Prélude à l'après-midi d'un faune*. One could easily continue the comparison: 'Soupir' is to 'Apparition' as *Jeux* is to the *Faune*.

[25] See Stéphane Mallarmé, *Poems*, trans. Roger Fry, commentary by Charles Mauron (New York, 1951), p. 39.

[26] Debussy, 'Concerts Colonne – Société des nouveaux concerts', *Revue de la S. I. M.* (1 November 1913). Reprinted Debussy, *Monsieur Croche et autres écrits*, ed. François Lesure, rev. edn. (Paris, 1987), p. 247.

9 'La jeunesse du Cid': a mislaid act in *Rodrigue et Chimène?*

RICHARD LANGHAM SMITH

It is by no means impossible that Debussy remained ignorant throughout his life of the true origins of Catulle Mendès's libretto based on *El Cid* that he accepted to set as his first opera, for one reason or another, and somehow or another, at some time during the earlier months of the year 1890.[1] Apparently unbeknown to him, the origins of the fabrication of this libretto dated back to the years of his early teens at which time he had hardly even decided upon the career of musician, let alone one who would turn his attentions to opera.[2]

It was the composer's close friend Robert Godet, both in well-known reminiscences published in the celebrated Debussy number of the *Revue Musicale* of 1926,[3] and in unpublished manuscript jottings,[4] who was the first to suspect that the libretto furnished to the composer was a 'white elephant' which had lain dormant in the drawers of its author for some years. Less well-known are the circumstances surrounding its early history in this respect which created a minor stir at the end of 1878 and during 1879. At this time Debussy, hardly interested in such wranglings, was just 17 years old.

---

[1] For reference to the opera itself, no score is yet available, though proofs already exist for the forthcoming volume in the *Oeuvres Complètes*. A CD of the version given at Lyon in 1992, orchestrated by Edison Denisov who also added additional material, with the libretto provided in the liner notes, was released in 1995 on ERATO 4509-98508-2. Both this and the programme for the Lyon performances in 1992 give a libretto but neither adequately distinguish between Mendès's original and material added by Georges Beck for the reconstruction.

[2] See R. Langham Smith, '*Rodrigue et Chimène*: genèse, histoire, problèmes d'édition', *Cahiers Debussy*, 12–13 (1988–9), 67 for an account of the various conflicting sources regarding Debussy's meeting with Mendès.

[3] Robert Godet, 'En marge de la marge', *Revue Musicale* (1 May 1926), 68–70.

[4] Kindly communicated to me by François Lesure.

201

The brouhaha was triggered by an announcement in the 'Nouvelles de partout' section of the penultimate issue of the 1878 *Journal de musique*:

> Monsieur Catulle Mendès 'is presently finishing off the libretto for a grand opera in 4 acts and 5 tableaux.
>
> Title: *Le Cid.*
>
> This work will not be an adaptation of Corneille's masterpiece, nor even of Guilhem de Castro's play, that the great Corneille followed fairly closely, as we know, and sometimes translated.' Monsieur C. Mendès has gone back to the original legends, to the *Romancero*, to *L'Historia del muy noble y valorosa caballero el Cid Ruy Diaz*, so that while keeping the poignant love-story of Rodrigue and Chimène as the basis of his work, he could add the strange and powerful local colour and all the unique atmosphere of Castilian and Moorish customs.
>
> What the tragedy [Corneille's] neglected and even shunned is triumphantly restored in our contemporary theatre.
>
> As for the composer, he cannot yet be named: let us only say that he is one of the shining lights among the present-day French school.[5]

Several points of interest emerge from this musical gossip-column whose quotation marks would seem to suggest that the information communicated originated from some sort of press release from Mendès himself. But the project was far from being fully negotiated and was in no way signed and

---

[5] 'M. C. Mendès "termine en ce moment un poëme de grand opéra en 4 actes et 5 tableaux. Titre: Le Cid. Cet ouvrage ne sera pas une adaptation du chef d'oeuvre cornélien, ni même du drame de Guilhem de Castro, que le grand Corneille a imité d'assez près, comme on sait, et quelquefois traduit". M. C. Mendès est remonté aux légendes primitives, au *Romancero*, à *l'Historia del muy noble y valorosa caballero el Cid Ruy Diaz*, de sorte que, tout en conservant comme fond de son oeuvre les poignantes amours de Chimène et de Rodrigue, il pourra y joindre une étrange et chaude couleur locale et toute la pittoresque singularité des vieilles moeurs castillanes et mauresques. Ce que la tragédie négligeait ou dédaignait est impérieusement réclamé par le théâtre moderne.

Quant au musicien, il n'est pas encore permis de le nommer, disons seulement qu'il est l'une des plus hautes gloires de l'école française.' Anon, 'Nouvelles de partout', *Journal de musique*, 3/134 (21 December 1878). I am indebted to François Lesure for first signalling to me the existence of this article which set me on the trail of the others cited in the present article. See his *Claude Debussy avant 'Pelléas' ou les années symbolistes* (Paris, 1992), pp. 95 ff. and *Claude Debussy* (Paris, 1995), pp. 111 ff.

sealed, regardless of whether the libretto was completed and a composer had been engaged. On the contrary, it would seem from subsequent progress reports (or the reverse) that no such willing composer had been found.

Regardless of this, Mendès's reference to the unusual literary roots of his venture is of some interest. He seemed to be proposing a more authentic and exotic *Cid* which would be less a series of epic escapades than a passionate love-story surrounded by copious local colour. Most interesting is the clear reference to the title of the piece, at this stage, as *Le Cid*.

In the following issue of the same *journal*, a subsequent note dispels back-stairs gossip, but does nothing to reveal the identity of the mystery composer:

> It has been wrongly announced that the music for *Le Cid*, the opera in 4 acts and 5 tableaux which M. Catulle Mendès is currently preparing, would be written by Monsieur Emile Pessard.
>
> The explanation of our esteemed colleague's confusion, is that M. Emile Pessard has already collaborated with M. Catulle Mendès, in *Le Capitaine Fracasse*, everyone remembering the charming music written on that occasion by this excellent musician.
>
> But as regards *Le Cid*, there has never been any question of M. Emile Pessard, and we should remember that at the present moment, *nobody* is authorised to name the composer – one of the most renowned of the French school – who will sing of the tragic love of Rodrigue and Chimène.[6]

Such promptness of response by this small and not very elegantly produced broadsheet seems to indicate that there was more to this story than at first met the eye: one senses that the mystery composer could not be named because there wasn't one! The affair was fuelled rather than quenched by an

---

[6] 'On a annoncé a tort que la musique du *Cid*, l'opéra en quatre actes et cinq tableaux, que prépare M. Catulle Mendès, serait écrite par M. Émile Pessard. Ce qui explique l'erreur de notre excellent confrère, c'est que M. Émile Pessard a déjà collaboré avec M. Catulle Mendès, dans le *Capitaine Fracasse*, et tout le monde se souvient de la charmante musique écrite a cette occasion par l'excellent musicien. Mais, en ce qui concerne le *Cid*, il n'a jamais été question de M. Émile Pessard, et nous rappelons que, jusqu'à l'heure actuelle, *personne* n'est autorisé à nommer le compositeur – un des plus illustres de l'école française – qui chantera les tragiques amours de Rodrigue et de Chimène.' *Journal de musique*, 135 (28 December 1878).

open letter to the newspapers and artistic journals by the rival librettist Louis Gallet. It appeared in *Le Figaro* and the *Revue du monde musical et dramatique* (and possibly elsewhere) on 4 January 1879. In this latter source it was printed as follows:

> M. Gallet, author of the libretto of *Le Roi de Lahore* and the faithful collaborator of M. Massenet, has just addressed the following letter to the newspapers:
>
> Paris, 30 December 1878
>
> Dear editor and colleague
>
> For some time, there has been somewhat persistent talk in theatrical circles of an opera *Le Cid*, for whom several authors have been named.
>
> I would be grateful if you would remind your readers, in order to establish my right of priority, that a libretto for *Le Cid* exists already, following the version of Guilhem de Castro, and of which I am the author, together with M. Edouard Blau.
>
> This libretto, read and approved by the Opéra since 1873, will be the first given in France by M. Massenet, at present finishing off his *Hérodiade*, specially written for the Italian stage.[7]

To what extent Mendès was aware of the Massenet–Gallet *Cid* is unclear. It is possible that he had recently discovered that his libretto overlapped in both title and content with this project, but it is equally possible that he considered the subject an open market, believing that his emphasis on the love aspect and his avoidance of both Corneille and Castro rendered his project able to co-exist. Perhaps he had made a

---

[7] 'M. Gallet, l'auteur du poëme du *Roi de Lahore* et le collaborateur fidèle de M. Massenet, vient d'adresser aux journaux la lettre suivante: Paris le 30 Décembre 1878 Monsieur et cher confrère/Depuis quelque temps, on parle avec une certaine persistance, dans le monde des théâtres, d'un opéra: *Le Cid*, pour lequel plusieurs auteurs sont nommés.

Je vous serais reconnaissant de rappeler à vos lecteurs, afin d'établir mon droit de priorité, qu'il existe déjà un poëme du *Cid*, suivant la version de Guilhem de Castro, et dont je suis l'auteur, en collaboration avec Edouard Blau.

Ce poëme, lu et agréé à l'Opéra depuis 1873, sera le premier ouvrage que donnera en France M. Massenet, qui termine en ce moment son *Hérodiade* écrite spécialement pour la scène italienne.' *Revue du monde musical et dramatique* (4 January 1879), 12.

faux-pas, and unaware of the advanced contractual and actual state of the Massenet opera, he had not only been pipped at the post, but had the added embarrassment of having chosen exactly the same title as his more successful rivals.

On the other hand, if he had considered the subject to be in the public domain, he was not alone. Several other composers emerged to have a similar work on the drawing-board, among them P.-J. (Jules) Barbier who had a version to be set by Victor Massé:

> I read in *Le Figaro* that M. Gallet is working on a *Cid*. In order not to seem to be taking his idea (after Corneille) I would be most obliged if you would mention that I have been working for ten years, with my friend Massé, on a *Cid* inspired by the work of Guilhem de Castro, which we hope to finish after *La nuit de Cléopâtre*. This said work would in no way encroach upon the rights of M. Gallet: *Le Cid* belongs to all the world.
>
> Sincerely etc.
> P.-J. Barbier[8]

The following issue of the *Journal de musique* had still more names to add to the list of composers working on operas with similar themes:

> We have announced that M. Catulle Mendès has just finished an opera entitled *Le Cid*, whose scenario draws on the one hand from Corneille, and on the others from the Spanish *Romancero*. Almost at once, a second *Cid*, written under the same conditions by M. Emile de la Rue, claimed rights of priority. Then M. Louis Gallet wrote that he also had a *Cid* in his portfolio, written in collaboration with M. Edouard Blau and set to music by M. Massenet. This libretto was read and approved by the Opéra since 1873. And that's not all: M. Jules Barbier also claims a *Cid* for whom Victor Massé is writing the music. And what about that of the sadly missed Bizet? What has become of that? Certainly we are going to see several *Cids* just as we have seen several *Hamlets*. In Italy in the last century, a libretto which pleased the

---

[8] 'Je lis dans *le Figaro* que M. Gallet s'occupe d'un *Cid*. Pour ne pas avoir l'air de lui prendre son idée (après Corneille) je vous serais bien obligé de mentionner que, depuis dix ans, nous travaillons, avec mon ami Massé, à un *Cid* inspiré de l'oeuvre de Guilhem de Castro, et que nous espérons bien le terminer après *la nuit de Cléopâtre*. Ceci soit dit sans vouloir empiéter en rien sur les droits de M. Gallet. Le *Cid* appartient à tout le monde. Agréez etc. P.-J. Barbier.' *Revue du monde musical et dramatique* (11 January 1879).

public would be set to music five or six times over, each composer enjoying the public acclaim one after the other.[9]

This issue's most important contribution to the debate was its identification of the unfinished *Don Rodrigue* of Bizet as the all-important factor in precipitating the race to mount a staged version of the *Cid* epic. Indeed, Bizet himself may justifiably be claimed as the motivating force behind the struggle for a staged *Cid* revealed by this sequence of articles, for following the international success of *Carmen* during the late 1870s, an opera based on *El Cid* must have seemed a winning formula for a box-office success.[10]

But this article is interesting from an another point of view, for the first time backtracking on Mendès's initial claim not to have drawn on Corneille and to have reverted to the original *Romanceros*. We are now informed that the opera will combine the two sources.

As far as the others were concerned, even this was not the end of the saga. In the following issue of the same journal a further name was added:

And now five!

We believe that in some library or another, says *l'Art Musical*, there is a fifth *Cid*, for we clearly recall that at the time of his death, the sadly missed and fine Aimé Maillard was working on a large-scale piece entitled *Le Cid Campéador*. What can have happened to it?

[9] 'Nous avons annoncé que M. Catulle Mendès venait de terminer un opéra intitulé le *Cid*, dont le scénario s'appuyait d'un côté sur le drame de Corneille et, de l'autre sur le romancero espagnol. Presque aussitôt, un deuxième *Cid*, écrit dans les mêmes conditions par M. Émile de la Rue, réclamait les droits de priorité. Puis M. Louis Gallet écrit qu'il a, lui aussi, en portefeuille un *Cid* écrit en collaboration avec M. Edouard Blau et mis en musique par M. Massenet. Ce poëme aurait été lu et agréé par le directeur depuis 1873. Ce n'est pas tout: M. Jules Barbier revendique aussi un *Cid* dont Victor Massé écrit la musique. Et celui du si regretté Bizet, que devient-il? Il est donc certain que nous allons voir plusieurs *Cid* comme nous avons vu naître plusieurs *Hamlet* etc. En Italie, au siècle dernier, un poëme qui plaisait au public était mis en musique cinq ou six fois de suite. Tous les compositeurs jouissant de la faveur publique y passaient l'un après l'autre.' *Journal de musique* (11 January 1879).

[10] Bizet's *Don Rodrigue*, actually composed simultaneously with *Carmen*, was thwarted by the fire at the Paris Opéra on 28 October 1873, and of course by the composer's death 2 years later. The opera exists in a manuscript score in the Bibliothèque Nationale de France (MS477, fonds du conservatoire). This was clearly enough for Bizet to give a rendition of the work *autour du piano*. (See the catalogue of the *Exposition Georges Bizet*, 1838–1875, Théâtre national de l'Opéra, Paris, Oct.–Nov. 1938).

These five *Cids* might have all been offered to the Opéra, but one fears that they will not all be performed. Some will no doubt be used for a parody in some small theatre, entitled 'Le Cid camping out'! [Le Cid Campédehors] There's always that possibility![11]

At last, in the summer of 1879, the composer of Mendès's *Cid* was revealed, although the previous failure to name any composer for the project had rather sidelined the interest of Mendès's project:

A new *Cid* is on the theatrical horizon, already crowded enough with *Cids*! Catulle Mendès's *Cid* has been accepted by M. Gevaert who will compose the music.[12]

For the time being this appears to have been the end of the grand parade, where all the aspirants for what Bizet termed the 'grand boutique' staked a claim for the *Cids* on their drawing-boards.[13]

[11] 'Et de cinq! Nous croyons qu'il doit y avoir dans quelque bibliothèque, dit *l'Art Musical*, un cinquième *Cid*, car nous rappelons parfaitement que, quand il est mort, le regretté et bon Aimé Maillard travaillait à un grand ouvrage intitulé le *Cid Campéador*. Où est passé celui-là?

Ces cinq *Cid* seront peut-être présentés à l'Opéra, mais il est à craindre qu'ils ne soient pas tous représentés! Quelques-uns serviront probablement de thèmes à quelque parodie de petit théâtre intitulée "Le Cid Campédehors". Ce sera toujours cela.' *Journal de musique* (18 January 1879).

[12] Un nouveau *Cid* à l'horizon théâtral, déjà chargé de *Cids* pourtant. Le *Cid* de Catulle Mendès a été agrée par M. Gevaert qui en composera la musique.' *Journal de musique* (26 June 1879). The composer in question was almost certainly the Belgian composer François-Auguste Gevaert who had some success in Paris with his operas which were mounted between 1850 and 1864. Since that period he had engaged in no operatic activity and this venture, if there was any truth in it, would have meant something of a comeback to the world of opera for a composer increasingly leaning towards musicology.

[13] 'J'ai fait cet été un *Cid* en cinq actes. C'est Faure qui m'a lancé dans cette affaire – je vais lui faire entendre un de ces jours. Si la chose lui plaît, il y aura espoir d'arriver à la grande boutique.' Bizet: letter to Paul Lacombe (n.d. [1874?]), quoted in Imbert, *Portraits et études* (Paris, 1894), p. 194. For extensive lists of operatic settings of *El Cid* see *The New Grove Dictionary of Opera* (London, 1992), entries on *Cid* and Corneille, Pierre; and the *Dictionary-Catalogue of Operas and Operettas*, compiled by John Towers (Morgantown, Virginia, 1910, repr. New York, 1967) under *Cid*, *Chimena*, and *Rodrigo*. This confirms considerable interest in the legend in Germany and Italy, but, apart from Massenet, little in France. Closest to Bizet's project were the operas *Der Cid*, by Peter Cornelius, premièred in Weimar in 1865 and an opera of the same name by the French composer Louis Théodore Gouvy, written for performance in Dresden in 1863 but never performed.

It was hardly surprising that Massenet and Louis Gallet won the race to the Opéra stage. Their *Le Cid* was first given at the Opéra in November 1885, and Gallet re-used some of the libretto originally written for Bizet's *Don Rodrigue*, although not the prominent beggar scene which is found in Bizet's unfinished manuscript. The success of the Massenet venture may at first sight seem to have rendered Mendès's version redundant, but closer examination of the respective aims of Bizet, Mendès and the Massenet/Gallet projects, reveal that the versions of the epic tale were angled very differently. Mendès's claim to an 'authentic' *Cid* went one stage further towards an original version than Bizet's unfulfilled aims in *Don Rodrigue* as reported by Gallet in the following memoir in which, incidentally, Bizet's enthusiasm for the beggar-scene was stressed:

> Finally, Georges Bizet himself finished his researches and put aside his hesitations, bringing me one morning a copy of the *Journal pour tous*, containing a translation of *La jeunesse du Cid*, of Guilhem de Castro.
>
> – 'Here is what I want to do', he said to me decidedly. 'It is not the *Cid* of Corneille, it is the original *Cid*, with its real Spanish colour. There is one particular scene, with a beggar, which is marvellous. Just think! Faure, I'm sure will be pleased with it. Le Cid the lover, the son, the Christian, the hero, the victor – what more could you want?[14]

For Bizet, Castro was authentic enough: Mendès went one better by claiming to go further back to the original epics. It is by no means impossible that in the later 1870s Mendès was well aware of the outline of the Gallet/Bizet libretto which may have been well-known among his circle of friends, and that he adjusted his own manifesto for his *Cid* accordingly. Certainly he must have been pleased to note that Massenet, and his librettists d'Ennery, Blau and Gallet explicitly announced on the *partition piano-chant* that their version was *d'après Guilhen de Castro et Corneille*,[15] and a further pos-

---

14 'Enfin, Georges Bizet lui-même mit fin à ces recherches et à ces hésitations en m'apportant un matin un vieux numéro du *Journal pour tous*, contenant une traduction de la *Jeunesse du Cid* de Guilhem de Castro.

  –Voilà ce que je veux faire, me déclarait-il très nettement. Ce n'est pas le *Cid* de Corneille, c'est le Cid original, avec sa couleur bien espagnole. Il y a là une scène: la scène du mendiant, qui est merveilleuse. Voyez cela. Faure, j'en suis sûr, sera content. Le Cid amoureux, filial, chrétien, héroïque, triomphant, que pourrait-il désirer de plus?' Louis Gallet, *Notes d'un librettiste* (Paris, 1891), p. 63.

15 Massenet, *Le Cid* (Paris, VS Hartmann n.d. [1885]), p. 1.

sibility is that because Gallet's version for Massenet did not make use of the beggar-scene, Mendès seized the opportunity to make extended use of this in his version, possibly re-working the libretto at some time after the première of Massenet's opera. All this, however, must remain in the realms of speculation until further pertinent documents, or a separate, dateable copy of the libretto comes to light. Certainly, the potential variants on the *Cid* epic must have helped convince Mendès that his advanced, if not completed, libretto might yet find a musical collaborator and reach the operatic stage. All that was required was to change the title to something other than Bizet's *Don Rodrigue* or Massenet's *Le Cid*: *Rodrigue et Chimène* would do nicely.

Whatever shortcomings may be found in what we know of Mendès's libretto, certainly considered by many a literary hack rather than a writer of merit, his sources are worth examination.[16] In his *Journal de musique* 'press release', Mendès had stressed two aspects of the story: firstly the 'poignant love-story' (*les poignantes amours de Chimène et de Rodrigue*), and secondly, the 'strange and warm local colour and all the picturesque singularity of the ancient Castilian and Moorish traditions' (*une étrange et chaude couleur locale et toute la pittoresque singularité des vieilles moeurs castillanes et mauresques*).

These features are certainly borne out by the libretto Debussy received and he responds to the first 'love' element with a rich tonal language whose roots may be seen in his early songs, and to the second with a

---

[16] Théophile Gautier's nickname 'crapule-tendresse' was the cruellest. Born in 1841, Mendès was nearly forty at the time he wrote *Rodrigue*, presuming the supposition that it dated from the time of press activity *c.* 1878–9. He had some success as a poet with allegiances to the Parnassians during the late 1860s, and before this had founded the *Revue Fantaisiste*. He was also known for his many enthusiastic writings on Wagner. George Moore wrote of the young Mendès 'Tout ce qu'il pense est faux.' Cocteau's vignette of the older Mendès was not the work of one man-of-letters respecting another: 'Il tenait du lion et du turbot. Son faciès aux joues, aux yeux et à la petite bouche en demi-lune de poisson, semblait être captif de quelque gelée qui le gardait à distance et mettait une épaisseur mystérieuse, transparente, tremblotante, entre lui et le reste du monde.' On the other hand Maupassant wrote in his favour: 'Poète aux intentions mystérieuses, frère d'Edgar Poe et de Marivaux, compliqué comme personne et dont la plume, soit qu'il fasse des vers, soit qu'il écrive en prose, est souple et changeante à l'infini.'

Example 9.1. *Rodrigue et Chimène*: act II, 2nd tableau

La plaine sur les bords du Duéro. Lointains déserts et arides, une chaine de montagnes dentelée à l'horizon. Au premier plan, à droite, sur un monticule, un bouquet d'arbres nains. Au second plan, à gauche, une haute croix de bois noir qui penche. Au lever du rideau, RODRIGUE, en armes, la visière baissée, se tient debout devant le monticule dont les branchages le dérobent à la vue des passants.

[The plain on the banks of the Duéro. Arid deserts as far as the eye can see, with a chain of rugged mountains on the horizon. Raised up, on the right on a hillock, a group of stunted trees. Further up, on the left, a tall black crooked wooden cross. The curtain rises on Rodrigue, in armour, his visor lowered, standing in front of the hillock whose branches hide him from the sight of passers-by.]

pseudo-oriental language obtained through a paring down of functional harmony to a minimum, and an extreme and somewhat experimental use of synthetic modes (ex. 9.1).

Paul Dukas, always astute in his perceptions, observed the former in his letter to d'Indy about *Rodrigue*: 'You will be surprised, I think, at the harmonic richness of certain scenes ... the episodes are exquisite and of a harmonic finesse that recalls his first songs',[17] while Gustave Charpentier's memoir of the composer working on *Rodrigue* would seem to pertain to the 'local colour' of the piece when he reported Debussy as remarking that 'the traditional side of the subject demands from me music which is not my own', adding that 'he said that more as if musing, rather than being discouraged'.[18]

[17] 'vous serez très surpris je crois de l'ampleur dramatique de certaines scènes: ... toutes les scènes épisodiques sont exquises et d'une finesse harmonique qui rappelle ses premières mélodies.' Paul Dukas to Vincent d'Indy, 1 October 1893, cited Georges Favre (ed.), *Correspondance de Paul Dukas* (Paris, 1971), p. 21.

[18] 'Le côté traditionaliste de ce sujet appelle des musiques qui ne sont pas les miennes. Il disait cela d'un ton plus rêveur que découragé.' Gustave Charpentier, 'Sa jeunesse et sa mort', *Chantecler* (24 March 1928), 1.

By far the most important discrepancy arising from the various columns about Mendès's *Cid* project is between Mendès's announcement that the work was to be in four acts and five tableaux, and Debussy's extant manuscript score which has only three acts. The two possibilities here would seem to be either that the libretto was compressed or remodelled into 3 acts before Debussy set it to music, or that Debussy's opera, quite clearly in 3 acts, lacks an act which he had, ready to set, in the now lost separate libretto.

The first possibility may be summarily dismissed. In the manuscripts which have so far come down to us three acts are clearly marked by name. The only mention of a 'tableau' is half way through the second act, where an orchestral interlude clearly heralds a scene change from the 'salle sombre et vaste dans le château de Bivar' to 'La plaine sur les bords du Duéro' where Rodrigue is to murder Gomez. Although act I is divided into 5 clear scenes, there can be no real changes of setting, for all five sections indicate a terrain near the 'château de Gormaz'. There is no orchestral music to facilitate a scene change in this act, except possibly at the end of the love duet before scene 3. But the subsequent stage directions for Iñez and Hernan indicate the continuing presence of the castle[19] and this moment in the opera would appear to be a transformation of the same scenery, largely by means of lighting, to mark the end of the lovers' nocturnal tryst and the breaking of dawn and entry of soldiers. Similarly act III cannot possibly be construed to have more than one tableau. No scene change in the missing pages in this act is possible, and continuous text leaves no other possible scope. It must therefore be concluded that Mendès announced an opera in 4 acts and 5 tableaux and Debussy composed an opera in 3 acts and 4 tableaux.

Before speculating on the possibility that the composer left his opera more unfinished than at first sight, possibly abandoning the work before having attempted the fourth act, the variants on the *Cid* epic, and in particular the sources used by Mendès, need further probing, as does Mendès's claim to have gone back further than Castro in his quest for a more authentic *Cid*. Study of the sources of the epic may provide addi-

---

[19] 'Iñez: (entrant vivement par la gauche et montrant à Chimène le Château de Gormaz)'.

tional support for the hypothesis that *Rodrigue et Chimène* is incomplete.[20]

The known sources of documentation and literature on the Cid, who is considered to have been an actual character, are as follows: the Latin chronicle *Gesta Roderici campidocti* (the *chronique latine*); the Spanish *Poema del Cid*, thought to date from the 15th century; the *Romances* or *Romanceros*; the *Crónica rimada* (*chronique rimée*); the *Crónica popular del Cid* of 1498; and the *Crónica particolar del Cid* of 1512. After this comes Guilhem de Castro's play *Las Mocedades del Cid* of 1621 on which Corneille's play of 1636 was based. One further source is Juan Bautista's play, modelled closely on Corneille, *El Honrador de su padre* of 1658.

As will be seen from the following list of French translations, literary interest in the legends was particularly strong in France during the second half of the nineteenth century, indeed this fact in itself must have been a catalyst for would-be librettists and collaborators. Translations into French, and even dual language editions of the various legends were abundant. They can be summarised as follows:

1. Translations of anonymous early versions of the legends cited above.
2. Versions of Guilhen [Guilhem] de Castro's *Las Mocedades del Cid* of 1621.
3. Abridged versions of, and commentaries on, Corneille's *Le Cid* of 1636 and of Diamante, a seventeenth-century Spanish author who modelled a version of the play on Corneille

---

[20] On the completeness of what has so far come down to us of *Rodrigue*, the publication of the critical score will reveal in detail exactly what Debussy wrote. To summarise: the opera is far more complete than early critics (e.g. Vallas) would have us believe. Acts I and III are both in short-score (particelle) while act II has been reduced to a piano-vocal score by Debussy. Act I is complete except for a few bars after the end of the text, but contains a long section where the choral parts are barely sketched. Act II is complete, but some crucial pages have been lost. Act III is complete, but again with sketchy sections and missing pages. There are many reworkings and different layers throughout, and it is clear that act II, although presumably copied from a now lost *particelle*, subsequently became a new working version. The 'completeness' of *Rodrigue* at issue in the present article is more to do with whether a final act was conceived by Mendès.

Among the first category the following may be cited as the most important French editions anterior to Mendès's work, which can almost certainly now be ascribed to 1878 or before:

a. [Diaz de Bivar], 'Romancero y historia del muy valereso cavallero Don Rodrigo de Bivar recopilado por Juan de Escobar: *l'Histoire en romances du très-valeureux chevalier Don Rodrigue de Bivar*', trans. Couchu [?], 2 vols. (Paris 1783).

It will be noticed that the Spanish title of this edition of the *Romanceros* is almost identical to the title of a source quoted by Mendès in his 'press release' of 1878 cited above (note 5). Several editions of the *Romanceros* or *Romances* (the two words were interchangeable in the Spanish titles) were also published in the original language during the nineteenth century, and the source cannot be considered in the least obscure. The *Romanceros* were, as he claimed, an important source for Mendès and are discussed in relation to a more recent and better annotated source below.

b. [Diaz de Bivar] 'Le Romancero du Cid', trans. Antony Réval, 2 vols., (Paris 1842).

c. [Diaz de Bivar], 'Poëme du Cid' Texte Espagnol accompagné d'une traduction française, de notes &c. par Damas Hinard (Paris, 1858).

As the most recent and best annotated edition, Hinard is a likely source for several details of Mendès's libretto. He presents a dual-language edition of the *Chronica rimada* (*Chronique rimée*) which deals with the Cid's early life, and of the *Poema del Cid* which deals with the latter exploits. It is from these sources that the name Gomez is used for Chimène's father, and several place names in his 'Notes géographiques' concur with Mendès's usage.

d. Hippolyte J. J. Lucas, '*La jeunesse du Cid*': Documents relatifs à *l'histoire du Cid* (Paris, 1860).

Lucas gave both anonymous early sources in résumé and a translation of Castro. He clearly explains that the rivalry causing the rift between Diègue and Gomez was caused by Gomez stealing sheep and the murder of a shepherd. In retaliation Diègue razes his 'faubourgs' to the ground and a 'hundred against hundred' battle is arranged to settle the matter. Rodrigue asks to fight, and though not yet thirteen years old, displays astonishing bravery by killing Gomez single-handed.

As the murder scene has been lost from the Debussy manuscript, and no separate copy of Mendès's libretto has come to light, it is impossible to know whether any details of Lucas were used. This source, however, does throw some light on Mendès's lines in act II where Gomez stresses Rodrigue's extreme youth:

DON GOMEZ: Enfant! calme ces jeunes fièvres!
On rit d'un chétif matador qui veut du sang
Ayant encore le lait de sa nourrice aux lèvres![21]

The last of these lines is almost directly lifted from Castro's 'Tu as encore sur les lèvres le lait de ta nourrice', as translated by Lucas.

> e. [Diaz de Bivar], 'La légende du Cid, comprenant Le poëme du Cid,
> les chroniques et les Romances', trans. Emmanuel de Saint-Albin,
> 2 vols. (Paris, 1866).

Saint-Albin's translation is one of the most scholarly and comprehensive editions of the period including all the anonymous sources cited above except for the 1512 *Crónica particolar*. It thus includes the *Romancero* cited by Mendès as a source he employed. Although, unlike the 'Poëme', this has the name Orgaz rather than Gomez for Chimène's father, several features of this translation of the *Romancero* suggest themselves as further models for Mendès, both in terms of details and of the style of language used. Indeed, the second Romance opens with a narrative which is strikingly close to Mendès's sequence of revenge:

> Diègue Laynez was tormented by the outrage perpetrated against his noble, rich and ancient clan . . . and he realised that he was not strong enough to avenge the insult.
>
> Unable to take revenge himself, on account of his age, and realising that the Count Orgaz, intoxicated with joy and renown, was able to walk free, with noone preventing him, Don Diègue could not sleep at night, nor eat meat, nor raise his eyes from the earth: he dared not leave his house, not even to talk with his friends, instead abstaining from speech altogether, fearful of offending them by the breath of his infamy.
>
> Thus, in order to lift the burden of this terrible dishonour from his heart, he tried a course of action which turned out to be fortuitous and summoned his sons. And without saying a word to them, he went from one to the other, shaking each one by their esteemed and tender hands. He did not turn to witchcraft, for sorcery of that nature did not exist in Spain. But with honour

---

[21] Libretto of Debussy, *Rodrigue et Chimène*: act II near end, immediately preceding Rodrigue's fatal duel with Gomez.

strengthening him, despite his years and his white hair; despite the blood congealing in his veins; and despite his dulled nerves and hardened arteries, he shook their hands so hard that they cried out:

'My lord, enough!' 'What is it you wish for! What is it you want? Leave us at once, or you will kill yourself!'

But when he got to Rodrigue, as if all hope of the outcome he had hoped for had faded, and just when nobody would even have dreamt that it could happen – now it was that with sparkling eyes, as if of a furious Hyrcanian tiger, in great anger and audacity, Rodrigue spoke to him, saying:

'Leave off, father, in this terrible hour, for if you were not my father, I would not be satisfied with words, but with mine own hand would I tear out your entrails, and my finger would bore into you like the point of a dagger or dirk.'

The old man, weeping for joy, said to him, 'Son of my own soul, your anger calms me, your indignation enchants me! Your railings, Rodrigue, show them in the cause of my honour which is forever lost if not recovered through victory.'

He recounted the cause of his outrage, and with his blessing gave Rodrigue the sword with which Rodrigue killed the Count, thus he began his exploits.[22]

---

[22] 'Diègue Laynez s'afflige sur l'outrage reçu par sa maison, noble, riche et ancienne . . . et il voit que les forces lui manquent pour la vengeance.

Inhabile à la prendre par lui-même à cause de ses vieux jours, et voyant que le comte d'Orgaz, ivre de joie et de renommée, se promène tranquille et libre sur la place sans que personne ne l'empêche, don Diègue ne peut plus dormir la nuit, ni goûter aux viandes, ni lever les yeux de terre: il n'ose sortir de sa maison, non plus de causer avec ses amis: pour eux, au contraire, il s'abstient de toute parole, crainte de les offenser par le souffle de son infamie.

Ainsi, comme à ces affreuses pensées de déshonneur son coeur se soulevait, pour tenter une expérience dont l'issue fut heureuse, il fit appeler ses fils. Et sans leur dit mot, il alla de l'un à l'autre, serrant leurs nobles et tendres mains. Il ne chercha point les raies de la chiromancie, car cette pratique du sorcier n'existait pas en Espagne. Mais l'honneur lui prêtant des forces malgré ses ans et sa tête blanche, malgré le sang figé de ses veines, malgré ses nerfs et ses artères glacés, de telle sorte les serra-t-il qu'ils s'écrièrent: "Seigneur assez! Que désirez-vous, ou que prétendez-vous? Lâchez-nous vite, car c'est vous tuer".

Mais quand il arriva à Rodrigue, comme l'espérance du résultat qu'il avait attendu était presque morte, – où l'on n'y pense pas quelquefois l'on rencontre, – voici que les yeux étincelants, tel qu'un tigre furieux d'Hyrcanie, avec grande colère et grande audace, Rodrigue lui a dit:

The summary is strikingly similar to Mendès's portrayal of Diègue's confrontation of his sons, both in outline and in lexical detail, as well as in its delight in repeated negatives. Diègue's fading 'forces' are common to both the Romance and Mendès, as are physical details such as the white hair and the blood congealing in his veins (Mendès: 'le sang figé de ses veines') as well as the stress on his lost honour (Mendès: 'mon honneur qui est perdu'). Also striking is the similarity of the reported speech in the two versions at the point where Diègue confronts Gomez:

Saint-Albin:

DIÈGUE: Seigneur assez! Que désirez-vous, ou que prétendez-vous? Lâchez-nous vite. . . .

Mendès:

DIÈGUE: Arretez-tous! Lâchez ces femmes! Arrière! Soldats sans honneur!

Similar details, such as the idiosyncratic mention of the finger used as a weapon, are sometimes transferred between the characters.

Saint-Albin:

RODRIGUE: 'mon doigt vous fouillerait comme la point du poignard. . . .'

Mendès:

DIÈGUE: O la fille qui pleure quand le doigt du vieillard l'effleure (act II, to Hernan)

A further moment of confluence between Mendès and Saint-Albin occurs when Rodrigue is given the sword of Mudarra[r] (a nomenclature shared

"Lâchez, père, en cette heure mauvaise, car si vous n'étiez point mon père, je ne prendrais point satisfaction en paroles, mais de cette même main je vous arracherais les entrailles, mon doigt vous fouillerait comme la pointe du poignard ou de la dague"
   Le vieillard pleurant de joie lui dit: "Fils de mon âme, ta colère m'apaise, ton indignation m'enchante. Tes transports, mon Rodrigue, montre-les dans la cause de mon honneur, qui est perdu, s'il n'est recouvré par la victoire."
   Il lui conta son outrage, et avec sa bénédiction lui remit l'épée avec laquelle Rodrigue donna la mort au comte, et commença ses exploits.' [Diaz de Bivar], 'La légende du Cid, comprenant Le poëme du Cid, les chroniques et les Romances', trans. Emmanuel de Saint-Albin, 2 vols. (Paris, 1866), Romance 2, vol. II, p. 6.

by both versions) given to him by Diègue to kill Gomez. In Saint-Albin's version this comes in a section of the third Romance entitled 'Le Cid se prépare à la vengeance paternelle'. In both cases Rodrigue addresses the sword in a kind of pre-battle benediction:

Saint-Albin:

RODRIGUE: Veuille croire, épée vaillante, que mon bras est le bras de Mudarra, et que le bras de Mudarra te brandit pour un sien outrage . . .[23]

Mendès:

RODRIGUE: Mais si tu sens trembler mon bras, Toi-même dans mon coeur, plonge-toi, bonne épée!

A feature turned to considerable operatic effect, though radically trans- formed, is the scene where Mendès has Diègue disguised as a beggar before he entreats his sons to avenge him in act II. This scene does not exist in this form in any sources, but several (including Saint-Albin's *Romances*) intro- duce an encounter with Saint Lazare as a beggar who prophesies Rodrigue's fate: 'Tu mourras d'une mort honorable sans jamais avoir été vaincu, mais toujours vainqueur.' But this is less a case of substantial difference than of Mendès opportunistically fusing two ideas: to put it bluntly, it is the modern professional (or hack) librettist truncating a verbose mediaeval epic to make a slick operatic libretto. Diègue and Lazare are thus fused to considerable dramatic effect.

In the scene, Mendès makes considerable use of the formula where repeated negatives are used: 'Diègue ne peut plus dormir la nuit, ni goûter aux viandes, ni lever les yeux de terre: il n'ose sortir de sa maison, non plus de causer avec ses amis.' This becomes transformed into a quasi-litanic denial by the as yet unveiled beggar:

LE MENDIANT (DIÈGUE): Je n'ai ni soif ni faim, je dois veiller sans trêves. La charité, seigneurs, la charité. [. . .]
Je ne voyage pas, j'ai de l'or et des terres. La charité, seigneurs, la charité.
HERNAN/BERMUDO: Que veux-tu donc, passant étrange?
HERNAN: Ni le pain, ni le vin?
BERMUDO: Ni la nuit dans la grange?
HERNAN: Ni le bel étalon tout de feu moucheté?
BERMUDO: Ni l'or ou l'argent que l'on compte?

---

[23] Ibid. p. 13.

Debussy responds to this with a third musical language more prophetic of *Pelléas* and together with the chess-scene which precedes it, it is one of the strongest elements in the opera. A chord-pair with no clear allegiance to any one key is repeated at the same pitch for Diègue's replies 'La charité, la charité', finally rising a fifth, underpinned by a clear F minor chord at the moment where Diègue reveals himself to his sons, announcing that the only alimony he wants is the head of Gomez (ex. 9.2).

Most interesting, and a distinguishing factor of the *Romanceros*, is that following Rodrigue's judgement at the court of King Ferdinand, Rodrigue and Chimène are married, despite Chimène's apparent inability to forgive Rodrigue. In Mendès's version, at least in what has come down to us of the libretto, Rodrigue simply rides away from the trial to fight the Christian cause, and the opera ends abruptly. Does this perhaps explain the discrepancy between Mendès's four acts and Debussy's three? Before further speculation on this, the two other categories of sources need to be examined.

The second category of possible sources, French versions of Castro, begins with Angliviel de la Beaumelle, 'Chefs d'oeuvre des théâtres étrangères: Espagnols'. *Le Cid* (Paris, 1823).

Beaumelle, a translation of Castro's 'Las Mocedades del Cid' of 1621, is a possible source for Mendès, although it is not out of the question that he read the work in the original language. Another possibility is that like Bizet and Gallet he came across the 'old copy' of the *Journal pour tous*, mentioned by Bizet as the source that gave him the idea for *Don Rodrigue*[24] or took the work from the Lucas book cited above. It begins at the death of le Comte d'Orgaz whose nomenclature Mendès does not follow (he becomes Gomez). But he follows Castro in the nomenclature of Rodrigue (here Rodrigue Diaz de Bivar); the two brothers Hernan and Bermudo; Chimène (here Chimène Gomez); Diègue (here Diègue Laynès) and King Ferdinand. All the other characters have different names.[25] After Beaumelle and Lucas, Castro's work had to wait until 1890 for a further French edition.[26]

---

[24] See note 14.

[25] Rodrigue himself is referred to in several ways. The original naming was Rodrigo Diaz de Bivar and his prowess in battle led to his nickname of the 'Cid campéador', 'sidi' in arabic meaning 'lord' and 'campéador' signifying a valiant warrior. El Cid lived *c.* 1043.

[26] Guillen de Castro, '*Première partie des Mocedadas de Cid de Don Guillen de Castro, publiée d'après l'édition princeps . . .*', trans. and ed. Ernest Mérimée (Toulouse, 1890).

Example 9.2. *Rodrigue et Chimène*: extract from the 'beggar scene' (act II). During the scene, the *mendiant's* phrase 'La charité, seigneurs, la charité' is repeated three times to the same pitches and harmonies, although the vocal score would seem to indicate an increasingly full orchestration as the climax of the scene approaches, when the beggar reveals himself as Don Diègue and announces that he has come for the 'head of the Count [Gomez]'.

In this and the following example bracketed accidentals are editorial.

219

Figure 9.2 (*cont.*)

From Mendès's point of view, the importance of Castro was that he placed the love of Rodrigue and Chimène before the revenge murder rather than after it, as did the anonymous sources, and in this aspect Corneille followed him. In addition, it was from Castro that Mendès took the idea of Rodrigue's two brothers Hernan and Bermudo, whose names are exactly copied. Seen against this background, Mendès's 'press-release' claiming no debt to Castro was entirely untrue.

The third possible source for Mendès's libretto was Corneille, although this was again denied in Mendès's first press announcement but later modified, if the decidedly secondary source is to be believed. Since Corneille himself used both the *Romanceros* and Castro as sources, to the extent of quoting sections in his *Avertissement* of 1648, it is sometimes difficult to assert definitive borrowings. However, certain features are clear. Firstly, on the whole, Mendès avoids proximity to Corneille to the extent of not copying rhymes. Indeed, he would have laid himself too open to plagiarism had he done so. Naturally, there is some considerable overlap of lexical fields in such matters as 'honour', whose attendant vocabulary could hardly be avoided. Chains of words such as 'coeur', 'courage', 'devoir', 'digne', 'gloire', 'glorieux', 'honneur', 'outrage', 'souillé', 'vaillant', 'venger', 'vertu' are repeated by both Corneille and Mendès. However this is hardly plagiarism, and relatively few passages can be said to overlap more than superficially, although there are clearly similarities of construction (repeated exclamations, rhetorical questions and so on.).

Two passages with a certain similarity may, however, be cited. Firstly Diègue's request that Rodrigue avenge the insult made by Gomez. In both cases Rodrigue's hesitancy and half-finished utterance of Gomez's name is used to convey the sudden realisation of his terrible dilemma:

Corneille:
DIÈGUE: C'est...
DON RODRIGUE: De grâce, achevez.
DIÈGUE: Le père de Chimène.
DON RODRIGUE: Le...
DIÈGUE: Ne réplique point, je connais ton amour;[27]

---

[27] Corneille, *Le Cid,* act I, scene 5.

Mendès:

DIÈGUE: Eh bien c'est . . .
    Je pressens ta peine, Rodrigue, hélas
RODRIGUE: Mais parle donc!
DIÈGUE: C'est Gomez de Gormaz, le père de Chimène.
RODRIGUE: Le père de . . .
DIÈGUE: N'achève pas![28]

Another parallel moment may be noted at the point where Chimène first encounters Rodrigue after the murder. Both Corneille and Mendès dwell upon the potential for the bloodstained murder weapon to reunite the blood of the two clans, and employ Chimène's confidante (Elvire in Corneille; Iñez in Mendès) as a foil.

Corneille:

CHIMÈNE: Elvire, où sommes-nous, et qu'est-ce que je vois?
    Rodrigue en ma maison! Rodrigue devant moi!
DON RODRIGUE: N'épargnez point mon sang: goûtez sans résistance
    La douceur de ma perte et de votre vengeance
CHIMÈNE: Hélas!
DON RODRIGUE: Écoute-moi.
CHIMÈNE: Je me meurs.
DON RODRIGUE: Un moment.
CHIMÈNE: Va, laisse-moi mourir.
DON RODRIGUE: Quatre mots seulement:
    Après, ne me réponds qu'avecque cette épée.
CHIMÈNE: Quoi! du sang de mon père encor toute trempée!
DON RODRIGUE: Ma Chimène . . .
CHIMÈNE: Ote-moi cet objet odieux,
    Qui reproche ton crime et ta vie à mes yeux.
DON RODRIGUE: Regarde-le plutôt pour exciter ta haine,
    Pour croître ta colère et pour hâter ma peine.
CHIMÈNE: Il est teint de mon sang. [29]

Mendès:

CHIMÈNE: Ciel! Rodrigue ici, devant moi!
RODRIGUE: Reste!

[28] *Rodrigue et Chimène*, act II.
[29] Corneille, *Le Cid*, act III, scene 4.

CHIMÈNE: Qu'as-tu fait meurtrier? Que veux-tu?

RODRIGUE: Le trépas . . .

CHIMÈNE: Va-t'en!

RODRIGUE: Écoute-moi!

CHIMÈNE: Dieu, cette main funeste . . .

RODRIGUE: Écoute!

CHIMÈNE: Je me meurs! . . .

RODRIGUE: Eh bien, quand ta maison à son tour est frappée,
    Venge ton père ainsi que j'ai vengé le mien,
    Et tue avec la même épée!

CHIMÈNE: Oh! toute rouge encore . . .

RODRIGUE: De ton sang, mon amour!
    Prends-le donc et sur la lame inhumaine
    Joins le sang de Rodrigue à celui de Chimène.
    Ne devaient-ils pas être unis un jour?[30]

If similarities may be detected in the above examples, these are amply balanced by considerable differences from Corneille's approach, and may lead to a final estimation of Mendès's relationship to his sources. He entirely eliminates several features of Corneille, notably the rivals in love of both Rodrigue and Chimène and the attendant intrigues these characters initiate, (Doña Urraque and Don Sanche respectively); as well as the minor foils to the opinions of the king (Don Arias and Don Alonse). In addition, Mendès retains Burgos as the setting of the action, rather than following Corneille in moving the play to the town of Seville.[31]

In the light of these studies, how much credibility can be given to Mendès's claim to authenticity? Certainly, in none of the sources is there any prolonged demonstration of the 'poignantes amours de Chimène et de Rodrigue', in the form of a love-scene, mentioned by Mendès in his 'press-

---

[30] *Rodrigue et Chimène*, act III.

[31] One further source may be cited, more to indicate the high level of interest in the *Cid* legend in the 1870s than to point to any particular influence. This was the French translation of the 17th century Spanish writer Juan Bautista Diamante's *El Honrador de su padre* published in 1873. The translation is a critical comparison of Diamante with Corneille, bringing similarities and differences to the fore. A. L. A. Fée, 'Études sur l'ancien théâtre espagnol: Les trois *Cid*' (Paris, 1873).

release'. In Castro the theme is introduced very near the beginning of the play but remarkably briefly:

DOÑA URRAQUE: Que te semble de Rodrigue, Chimène?
CHIMÈNE: Qu'il a bonne mine *(A part)*
Et que ses yeux causent à l'âme un tourment plein de charmes[32]

Little more than this is given by Castro, and Corneille similarly conveys the information about their love through the text rather than demonstratively through a love-scene, although in the list of characters Don Rodrigue is described as 'amant de Chimène'. The Massenet/Gallet project also goes no further than this. Mendès's extended love-scene is thus pure invention: an exploitation of the potential for a full-blown Romantic love-scene. Apart from the style of language (notably the corny rhymes) it is potentially an excellent operatic device, with its demands for changes in lighting and potential for the portrayal of space through distant voices, horn-calls and so on. Its inspiration clearly comes from the mediaeval *alba*, or dawn-scene. As the lovers' secret tryst can flourish only in the dark, watchmen (and in this case also Iñez) are employed to warn of impending dawn, the ultimate enemy of the lovers. The idea no doubt stemmed from the celebrated love-duet in act II of Wagner's *Tristan*, of which Mendès was a devoted and well-known worshipper.[33] Mendès's love-scene, which spreads over the first two scenes of act I, has nothing of the death-wish of Wagner's, nor, except at the end, is the language so ecstatic, but in form it shares the setting of a castle tower, as well as the beginning with the waving of a scarf in the gloom, to attract the attention of the lover. The English stage direction in *Tristan* reads:

---

[32] Hippolyte J. J. Lucas: *'La jeunesse du Cid': Documents relatifs à l'histoire du Cid* (Paris, 1860). In Beaumelle's version the passage reads:
    DOÑA URRAQUE: Que te semble de Rodrigue, Chimène?
    CHIMÈNE: Il est très bien *(A part)* Et ses regards causent à mon âme une peine délicieuse.

[33] Mendès was closely connected with Wagner from the 1860s until 1873, when he was deeply hurt by Wagner's parody of the French *Eine Kapitulation*. Judith Mendès, having reverted to the name Gautier (daughter of Théophile) had an affair with Wagner and worked on a translation of *Parsifal* until 1878, when relations between them suddenly came to a halt. See Elaine Brody, 'La famille Mendès: a literary link between Wagner and Debussy', *The Music Review*, 33 (1972), 177.

She waves with a scarf at first occasionally, then more regularly, at last with
passionate impatience more and more quickly. A gesture of delight shows that
she has espied her lover in the distance. She cranes higher and higher, the better
to survey the view, and then hurries back to the staircase from the topmost step,
from which she waves to him as he approaches.

TRISTAN: Isolde! Geliebte!
ISOLDE: Tristan! Geliebter!

Compare Mendès:

La fenêtre s'ouvre, Chimène toute blanche agite une écharpe dans la nuit
RODRIGUE: Vois Hernan la vitre s'enflamme
Une écharpe blanchit les brouillards frémissants
CHIMÈNE: Est-ce vous mon âme?
RODRIGUE: Est-ce vous mon âme?

The love-scene drew from Debussy the closest music he had ever written to
the famous music from Wagner's opera. And if *Tristan* comes to mind with
regard to the act I love-scene, the model for the following scene for 'Les filles
de Bivar' may well have been the flower-maidens from *Parsifal*. Lacking
from any of the sources is the chess-game, one of the most successful of
Mendès's inventions, where the chess-board seems to mirror the situation
of Rodrigue and Chimène in the eyes of his brothers. Chimène is symboli-
cally represented by the 'white queen' and Rodrigue by the knight, who
cannot move straight, but is constantly turning to the side. Study of the
sources reveals, in summary, that Mendès learnt from Corneille, incorporated ideas from Castro, and, true to his stated aims in 1878, based some of
his material on the anonymous Romances, in all these cases transforming
the material in time, detail, and nomenclature.

It remains to discuss the most crucial aspect, namely, the *dénoue-*
ment existing in all these versions. In essence this consists of the further
valiant exploits of the young Rodrigue against the heathen, and, most
importantly, his subsequent marriage to Chimène. This is clearly a high
point of all the sources whatever the differences, the most pregnant
action in that it crystallises the love–duty dilemma and effects the trans-
fer of power from Gomez's family to Diègue's. Most importantly, it
explores the necessity of the bridegroom murdering the father of his

bride to attain total power over her. Here, surely, is the crux of the story, the 'vieux moeurs castillanes et mauresques' which, as in Bizet's *Carmen*, presents a morality of 'otherness' to contrast with the Christian status quo.

A clear stress on the forthcoming wedding is woven into Mendès's libretto and Debussy responds to this both with specific themes (which have no chance to return) and with a passage introducing a bell-like idea at the first reference to the marriage in act I (ex. 9.3):

CHIMÈNE: Mais non, dites-moi "dame", et je dirai "seigneur'

        Jusqu'au jour des noces prochaines

RODRIGUE: Va! tu peux me nommer ton amour sans pécher

        Car la cloche d'or de nos épousailles

        Frémit déjà dans le clocher

Shortly before the end of act III Hernan throws a significant aside into the proceedings, just as Rodrigue is about to depart to fight for the Christian cause:

HERNAN: Reviens! Ta Chimène en son âme n'a pas rompu

        Les noeuds de votre doux lien.

Example 9.3. *Rodrigue et Chimène*: act I, 'wedding' motive, possibly indicating tuned bells.

In the final scene of act III, the unfulfilled promise of a future for the couple is clearly left open, rather than being exploited as a waste of the promise in the first act, where both fathers approved of the union. In particular, Chimène's failure to quell her feelings for Rodrigue, despite his murder of her father, are continually stressed, from the moment when she first sees Rodrigue, right through to his entreaties that she kill him:

CHIMÈNE: Criminelle à tes yeux, odieuse à moi-même,
    Malgré mon père mort qui gît, sanglant et blême,
    Malgré l'espoir évanoui
    Je l'aime, je l'aime, je l'aime!

And later:

CHIMÈNE: O chère voix, réveil plaintif des belles heures!
RODRIGUE: Eh quoi? ton bras m'épargne?
    Et tu pleures, tu pleures.
    Ah! si ton coeur brisé se laissait émouvoir!

All seems prepared for this theme to return in the final act, no doubt after more valiant deeds, and heart-searching from the two lovers. It is surely improbable that the marriage should have been omitted from Mendès's version and it may therefore be postulated that Mendès's libretto originally contained a further act, dealing with Rodrigue's subsequent acts of valour and the marriage to Chimène.[34] Is it possible that Debussy was in possession of this act, and either abandoned the opera before attempting to set it, or sketched or even completed parts of it which have now been destroyed or lost? As yet we cannot know, but we can speculate on the following grounds:

1. Mendès clearly described the opera as being in four acts and five tableaux whereas the single known source has three acts and four tableaux.

2. Nowhere in Debussy's score, nor in known correspondence nor in the few witnesses' testimonies is the opera described as being in three acts, nor is there any indication at the end of act III that the opera has been finished. Both Robert Godet, in the 1926 memoirs and Paul Dukas, in an admiring letter to d'Indy after having heard Debussy present extracts from *Rodrigue* at the piano, speak of two acts completed before abandonment, neither mention out of how many. In this context we should remember that the score which has come down to us is not one source, but an assemblage of two *particelles* and a vocal score. In short, it has no status as a finished score.

3. A crucial aspect of the *Cid* legend, whether or not the couple's love pre-dated the murder, is the marriage. To put it another way,

---

[34] No separate libretto is known to exist, nor have I been able to find any mention of the project in Mendès's manuscript letters in the Bibliothèque Nationale de France.

227

Rodrigue riding off, never to return, is hardly a satisfactory end to an opera centred on a 'poignant love affair'.

4. The exposition of the forthcoming marriage theme in Mendès's libretto remains unfulfilled, and musical themes used to portray this discussion are never recapitulated.

5. The end of act III does not close the key structure of the work. Its E major ending, which may seem an unsatisfactory and somewhat hurried end to the opera, is in fact a satisfactory third act ending to send Rodrigue off to further exploits, to be followed by a real end to the opera, and to the tonal structure.

Rodrigue et Chimène, it may be concluded, lacks an act. And if certain perceptive critics, after the Lyon première, found beautiful music but 'not an opera', this was perhaps why.

Index